Adobe Illustrator
CREATIVE TECHNIQUES

by Ellenn Behoriam
and Gary Poyssick

Hayden
Books

Adobe Illustrator Creative Techniques

Library of Congress Catalog Number: 94-73187

ISBN: 1-56830-133-2

97 96 95   4 3 2 1

Interpretation of the printing code: the rightmost double-digit number is the year of the book's printing; the rightmost single-digit number is the number of the book's printing. For example, a printing code of 95-1 shows that the first printing of the book occurred in 1995.

Dedication

To Mike Rose at Adobe Systems whose belief in the value of training and human resources and faith in us has been unswerving.

Credits

Publisher
David Rogelberg

Managing Editor
Patrick Gibbons

Acquisitions Editor
Oliver von Quadt

Development Editor
Marta Partington

**Copy and
Production Editor**
Meshell Dinn

Technical Reviewer
Michael J. Partington

Book Designer
Barbara Kordesh

Production Team
*Gary Adair, Dan Caparo, Brad Chinn,
Kim Cofer, Jennifer Eberhardt, Dave Eason,
Erika Millen, Karen Walsh, Robert Wolf*

Indexer
Michael Hughes

Foreword

Digital imaging, illustration, and creative tools have come a long way in the last ten years. Today, there are few communications environments where you can't find a personal computer being used to collect, create, modify, and manipulate design content destined for high-quality print vehicles.

There are many, many highly creative people pushing the envelope of technology. In a never-ending attempt to match their creative work to the constraints imposed by the prepress and production process, creators constantly seek new methods, techniques, and tricks that help them in their effort to achieve that vision.

This book is a collection of some of the finest digital artwork that has ever been produced in Adobe Illustrator. This award-winning material displays a lot of hard-earned knowledge, often gained in the wee hours of the night — about how the creators achieved the dazzling effects you'll find on the following pages. And dazzling they are.

Each of the books in the *Creative Techniques* series features the work of some of the world's leading creative talents. The name of each artist is featured on the pages where his/her work appears. Additionally, if you find any of the work in the book exciting, and in keeping with your own design needs, a brief profile of each artist (including information about how you might get in touch with them) can be found in the appendix.

We appreciate your purchasing *Creative Techniques*. We hope that you'll find the pages filled with excellent art, useful tips, and exciting possibilities.

Ellenn Behoriam and Gary Poyssick

February, 1995

Acknowledgments

There were many people involved in the creation of this book:

Ellenn Behoriam, president of Against The Clock, was responsible for the original idea, and managed the entire monstrous project for the last seven months. Collecting, gathering, moving, editing, reading, copying, shipping, and receiving literally thousands of individual files during the evaluation and acceptance process, she worked very hard to get this project to the publisher.

François Robert, who worked with us to develop many of the solutions you'll find in the book. With Kevin Dowler, François worked to match artwork to method, to determine the techniques used to achieve the effects, and dealt successfully with approximately 40 jillion layers, objects, type elements, custom colors, blends, masks, filters, formats, grids, rules, shadows, ghosts, and other Postscript® hobgoblins.

The hundreds of people with whom we come in contact on a yearly basis in our own courseware publishing and public relations efforts. They all contributed in some way to which tips, tricks, and solutions were included in the series. In the same breath, we should mention all the dedicated Newsgroup users on the World Wide Web, from which we collected dozens of FAQs about what was important, timely, and challenging in their daily use of Illustrator.

The people at Hayden Books, who worked tirelessly to make this project a reality: David Rogelberg, publisher of Hayden Books, who was ultimately responsible for providing us with the resources and latitude we needed.

Oliver von Quadt, acquisitions editor, for guiding us through the beginning stages of this project and encouraging us to produce the entire series; Meshell Dinn, production and copy editor, who worked day and night during the editing and composition process and without whose superb organizational skills, this project would never have come to fruition; our designer, Barbara Kordesh, whose interior and cover design skills tied together a wide range of disparate visuals; and Michael Partington, our technical editor, who actually tested and verified every technique in this book.

Our special thanks to Marta Partington, development editor, whose faith in the project from the beginning made the entire event happen. She molded the clay of our original idea to incorporate the talents of illustrators, artists, and designers from around the world. Thanks to her, this book truly redefines the meaning of the words "how to."

Most importantly, thanks to every one of the individual artists who contributed their beautiful work. We spent a lot of time working with illustrations, yet found ourselves continually amazed at the breadth of vision this work displayed. To each and every one of you — whether your work ultimately found its way to these pages or didn't — thanks from all of us.

To Our Readers

Dear Friend,

Thank you on behalf of everyone at Hayden Books for choosing *Creative Techniques* to enable you to learn more about the exciting world of Adobe Illustrator on the Macintosh. We know you'll enjoy the varied techniques and artwork in this book, while getting a true understanding of the conceptual nature of how Adobe Illustrator works on the Mac. If you like this book, be sure to look for other books in the *Creative Techniques* series, focusing on other design and layout applications.

What you think of this book is important to our ability to better serve you in the future. If you have any comments, no matter how great or small, we'd appreciate you taking the time to send us email or a note by snail mail. Of course, we'd love to hear your book ideas.

Sincerely yours,

David Rogelberg
Publisher, Hayden Books and Adobe Press

You can reach Hayden Books at the following:

Hayden Books
201 West 103rd Street
Indianapolis, IN 46290
(800) 428-5331 voice
(800) 448-3804 fax

Email addresses:

America Online: Hayden Bks
AppleLink: hayden.books
CompuServe: 76350,3014
Internet: hayden@hayden.com

Contents

Importing Photographs

Lithographic Issues

Managing Objects

Paths and Lines

Planning a Drawing

Preparing a Drawing for Export

Typography

Workflow Issues

Working with Copy

Working with Patterns

Planned Distortion

About the book

There are several components to each two page spread:

Artwork/Artist

The artwork is shown on the left side of the page. Since the samples provided by the individual designers naturally spanned a broad spectrum of sizes, shapes, and substrates, we had to standardize somewhat on the size of the image. Therefore, these images have been scaled up or down to fit the space allocated by our designers. The name of the artist responsible for the piece is shown under the artwork. An appendix provides more information about each individual.

Comments

The Comments section discusses global issues concerning the tip or technique found on that page.

Studio Usage

The Studio Usage section provides specific instances where a particular solution might be considered — in practical terms. This helps you to connect a particular technique to other projects you might be involved in at the time.

Related Topics

Each of the individual art files has been chosen to help you visualize the steps required to achieve a specific effect. In reality, though, each of the individual files has been constructed using dozens — even hundreds — of individual techniques used in concert with one another to achieve the desired end-result. This list provides a "pointer" to tips and solutions that either enhance or expand on the issues being discussed.

Steps

Wherever possible, each tip is broken into three or more specific steps that you can apply within Adobe Illustrator to achieve the effect in question. Some solutions are conceptual or theoretical in nature, and therefore provide information in steps to build and reinforce a specific idea. By looking closely at the artwork, and reading the steps (or, better yet, practicing them on your own projects), you will begin to see how the artists approached particular graphic problems, and how they solved them using Illustrator built-in functionality. Many times, they found methods not discussed in the program's manuals.

Bill Morse

Comments

Color theory is too complex a subject to tackle here, but having the ability to harmonize and change colors as needed is a great and powerful tool to have. This can be difficult in natural media, but in the electronic media making this kind of a change is quite easily accomplished.

Studio Usage

There are times when you need to make either a small change to an object, or a large change to the whole illustration. Using the Adjust Colors filter allows you to make these needed changes a lot faster than you could do otherwise.

Related Topics

1 | Select the Objects to Be Affected

First, select the objects that you need to change. The Adjust Colors filter only works on objects that are colored in CMYK (process colors). The filter will not work on objects that are painted with custom colors, patterns, or gradients. Also, type is not affected by this filter. If you want to change the type's color, either do it from the color palette or convert the type to outlines.

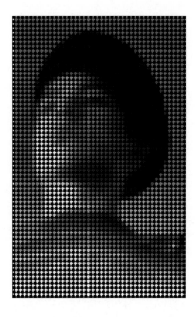

2 | Use the Adjust Colors Filter

Next, select the Adjust Colors filter. This filter is located on the Colors subpalette under the Filter menu. After this filter is selected, a dialog box appears, in which you can make the necessary adjustments. Remember that you cannot make positive and negative changes to colors in the same application.

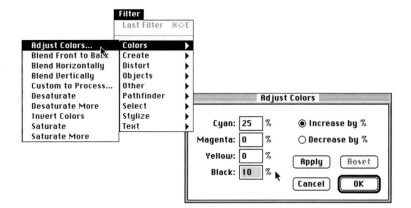

3 | Controlling the Palette

After you have set the color change that you need, you can either hit the OK button or the Apply button. If you hit the Apply button, the changes will take place, but the dialog box will not close. If you feel a need to make more changes, you can set up the dialog box with a new set of changes, or you can apply the same changes again. If you do not like what you've done, click the Reset button and start over. If you are happy with the changes, click OK and the dialog box will close.

Coloring Objects *Bitmapped Blends*

Kenneth Batelman

Comments

Adobe Photoshop is the most popular tool for blending colors; when a gradient is applied, there is no apparent stepping of colors. Illustrator, on the other hand, has steps appearing in every blend and gradient. Usually, this is not noticeable, but when it is, it's more appropriate to use Photoshop.

Studio Usage

It is often necessary to utilize a combination of tools when applying blends and gradients. Each project should be analyzed prior to beginning the illustration.

Related Topics

1 | Using Adobe Photoshop to Create the Blend

Create a new document in Adobe Photoshop that matches the area you're going to cover in your illustration. Make sure that the resolution (dpi) is set properly for your final output (generally twice the line screen of your final output, or 300 dpi for a 150-lpi screen). Create the blend artwork in Photoshop and save the file in EPS format. Illustrator prefers to work only with EPS images.

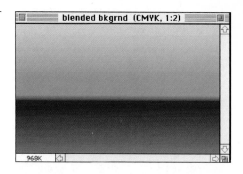

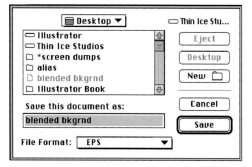

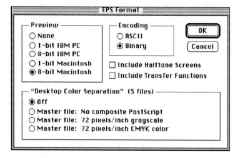

2 | Place the Blend in Illustrator

Place the blend into your illustration by using the Place Art command, located under the File menu. After the command is selected, an Open dialog box appears, allowing you to select the blend that you created in Photoshop. The blend appears in your illustration on the currently active layer. (A good tip: Put your blends on their own separate layer.) If you want to use a mask on your new blend, follow the procedure for masking shown elsewhere in this book.

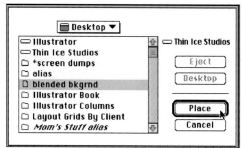

3 | Saving the Blend with Your Illustration

To save the blend with your illustration, choose the Save As command from the File menu. When the Save dialog box appears, click on the Include Placed Images check box. Save the illustration as normal, and the blend will be written into the Illustrator file. (Another tip: Don't throw away the original blend! In case the Illustrator file gets corrupted, you should save the illustration without the placed blends, too.)

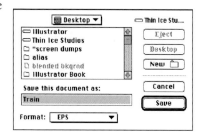

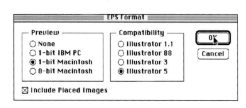

Coloring Objects *Blending Lines*

Roger Morgan

Comments

Lines or open paths can be used as well as shapes to create blends. A line speeds up working and printing times because less memory is used.

By adjusting the line weight, the resulting blends can be varied to create stripes, ranging from narrow line strokes to very smooth blends.

Studio Usage

In large files, single line blends are used to preserve file sizes and to speed up print times. Blends also can be used to build baselines for use in graphs, forms, or template grids. Blends that are used between lines work best with straight paths.

Closed paths should be used to create curved blends because overlapping of the open end points gives unpredictable results.

Related Topics

1 | Select the Lines

Make sure that the same number of anchor points on both lines are selected before you blend between lines. As a result, the lines blend smoothly with the correct anchor points blending to each other.

2 | Blending for Replicas

With the Blend tool, select the same anchor point position in both objects. For example, to create a set of evenly spaced strokes, enter the number of new lines required between the two selected lines in the number of blends area of the Blend dialog box.

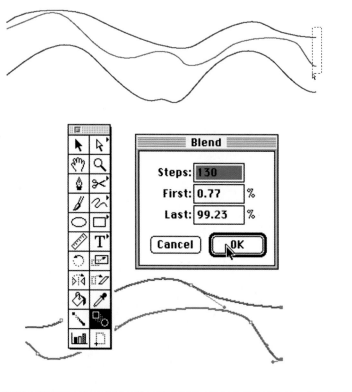

3 | Using Strokes to Create Blends

Select the same anchor point position in both objects with the Blend tool. After applying the Blend tool, a smooth blend should result. Zoom in and verify that no space exists between the blends; this will ensure that the stroke width is thick enough to give a smooth, solid blend. If you find space, delete the blend. Thicken the line stroke and repeat the blend until you achieve the desired line weight.

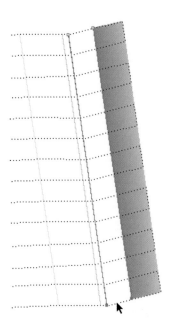

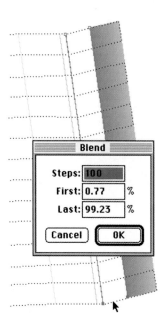

Scott MacNeill

Comments

Illustrator's Blend tool creates shapes by interpolating between two selected objects. The elements created by the blend function may be a series of morphs (steps) or a series of duplicate objects.

Studio Usage

Using blends in fills, you can create custom shading that resembles an airbrushed effect. The Blend tool creates evenly spaced duplicates of an object, such as fence posts. When used in animation, the Blend tool can make frames of morph changes between two objects. The blend steps can then be exported as frames into a video production program such as Adobe Premiere.

Related Topics

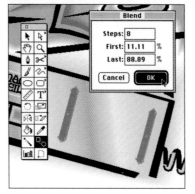

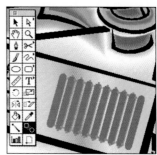

1 | Creating Blends for Replicas

When filling an area with duplicate objects, use two duplicates of the same object to calculate the blend. With the two objects selected, use the Blend tool at the same anchor point on each object. Enter the number of elements desired between the two originals in the Number of Steps box. The Blend tool fills the space between the original objects with evenly spaced replicas.

2 | Creating Blends for Fills

The automatic blends available on the Color palette do not always produce blends that match an object's shape. By drawing an object to match the desired blend, the blend will match the final object. The blend object can then be scaled and copied to create a second object that matches the blend in the final filled object.

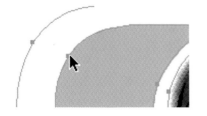

3 | Calculating Smooth Blends

The smoothness of blends depends on the resolution of the final output device and the line screen of the printed illustration. The Blend tool's suggested number of blends is based on a resolution of 256 levels of grey and the distance and color characteristics of the selected objects. It does not take into account the actual method of printing. Try this quick formula to determine the Number of Steps: take the Number of Greys available on the output device multiplied by the percent change in color. The Number of Greys is calculated by dividing the Output device resolution by the halftone screen's Lines per Inch squared.

4 | Smooth Blend Tips

The more similarities between the blended objects, the smoother the resulting blend will be. Blending between scaled versions of the same object also results in a very smooth blend. Choose anchor points that are either identical or in similar positions on the blended objects to ensure a smooth transition from one shape to the next. To further smooth a completed blend, export the file to Adobe Photoshop. Use Photoshop's Blur and Add Noise Filters and save the completed blend as an EPS file.

Coloring Objects *Blends as Backgrounds*

Chris Spollen

Comments

Blends can mimic the lighting characteristics of depth in a background. By adjusting a blend's color and intensities, a background acts as more than just a backdrop; it also adds to an illustration's depth. As light fades into the distance, color blends can fade in intensity—from a light shade to a darker shade.

Studio Usage

Background blends often are used only for the aesthetic effect of catching a reader's attention in simple advertisements and posters. When used to deepen an illustration's depth, a background blend becomes more than a background; it becomes an element of the illustration.

Related Topics

1 | A Simple Background Blend

With the background object selected, activate the Paint Style palette. After you select Fill, choose Gradient. You can use a supplied gradient fill, or you can create a custom gradient fill.

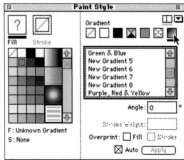

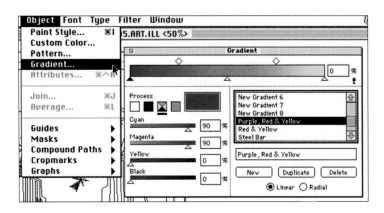

2 | Custom Gradients

To create a custom gradient, activate the Gradient palette under the Objects pull-down menu or double-click a gradient in the Paint Style palette. To create new blends on the Gradient palette, select New or Duplicate. The triangles below the gradient bar can be moved, added, and deleted to adjust color blends. The diamond(s) above the gradient bar adjusts the midpoint of the blend between two triangle colors. Select either Radial or Linear blend near the bottom of the Gradient dialog box. After the blend is made, enter the name in the title bar and close the Gradient palette to save the fill.

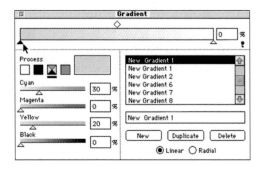

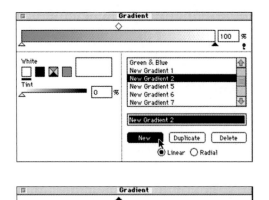

3 | Adjusting Fills

After a fill is applied, it can be manipulated further by adjusting its angle with the Angle box on the Paint Style palette or by using the Gradient tool. The Gradient tool sets the blend angle and determines where the blend begins and ends. The first click establishes where the blend's color starts, and the release of the mouse button determines where the blend's end color is reached. To set the required blend, the Gradient tool can be dragged across parts of an object or outside its border.

Bill Morse

Comments

No matter what the resolution of an imagesetting output device is, pixels are square. To "render" a perfectly straight diagonal line, an imagesetter or printer would have to be able to draw half, or even quarter, pixels (which they cannot do). Anti-aliasing is a programming "trick" that "softens" lines at points where such pixel-splitting is required. If a half-pixel is needed, then this pixel is created with a 50% tonal value. Have a quarter pixel? It gets replaced with a 25% tonal value pixel.

Studio Usage

If your artwork is comprised of high-contrast (black-and-white, for example) line art, anti-aliasing won't work. If you have very complex line art containing lots of overlapping and adjoining colors, anti-aliasing the illustration by importing it into Photoshop will accurately mix all the color pixels in the places that traps are required.

Related Topics

1 | Selecting the Right Artwork

The "Allegro Design" in the figure isn't suitable for anti-aliasing because it is just a simple black-and-white illustration. The "submerged" artwork figure, on the other hand, with lots of colors, details, objects, and blends, is perfect.

2 | Saving as an EPS File

To make this technique work, save the artwork as an EPS file (⌘-S). Usually, you should retain the original artwork. In this example, the Save As function is used to create an EPS copy of the original Illustrator file. If you don't save an illustration as an EPS file, Photoshop will fail to "see" the file and won't be able to open it.

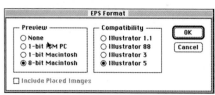

3 | Open and Rasterize in Photoshop

Using Photoshop, open (⌘-O) the EPS file that you created from the original artwork. You can control the resolution and size of the artwork. In the example, the resolution is set to create a 4" x 5" image at a 300 dpi resolution. This is sufficient to reproduce a 150 line screen in the final separation. You can pick the "color space" that your project requires (for example, you can convert CMYK Illustrator files to RGB video images). After you click OK, the program begins converting the EPS file to a raster (pixel) image. It takes some time, so consider executing this task *after* you've decided on the final size, placement, and so on. After rasterizing, place the rasterized artwork as you would any other scanned image.

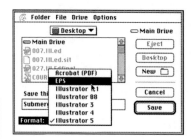

4 | The Effect on the Artwork

In this screen shot, the effects of rasterizing this image at 72 dpi are shown. This low-resolution visual clearly illustrates how pixels at the edge of each object "blend" together. The final result is a soft, high-resolution bitmapped image—similar to the result you'd get if you painted the original by hand and then scanned it into your system. The higher the resolution you select when first rasterizing the file, the finer the mixing of the "smoothing" colors.

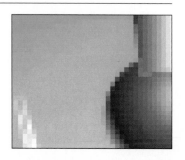

Coloring Objects *Converting Custom Colors to Process Colors*

Charles Akins

© 1994 Charles Akins / AkinStudio

Comments

Illustrator sees custom colors as preset CMYK mixes that can be applied as needed. The Custom to Process filter "spells" the custom color, converting it into its CMYK settings.

Studio Usage

Converting a custom color simplifies the printing process. The separation program doesn't have to look up the color each time it prints a separation. Most page layout programs will automatically import custom colors when you bring in an EPS file.

Related Topics

1 | Select the Object to Convert

First, select the object that you want to convert from a custom color to a process color. This filter does not work on gradients or patterns; it will work, however, on blends.

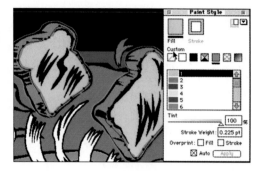

2 | Use the Custom to Process Filter

Then select the Custom to Process filter. The filter is located in the Colors submenu under the Filter menu. If it is not available in the Filter menu, find it in the "optional plug-ins folder" and copy it to the "plug-ins" folder. Both of the plug-in folders are in your Illustrator folder. Restart Illustrator and the Custom to Process filter will be installed. After you have selected the filter, a dialog box appears, asking if you want to convert tints (percentages) of the custom color(s) that you are converting. Usually, you will leave this box checked. After you click OK, the filter performs its work, and the results appear both onscreen and in the Paint Style palette.

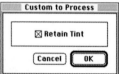

An image might contain more than one "tint" of a custom color. If you leave the Retain Tints box unchecked, only solid (colored) elements will be converted to their CMYK equivalents. This allows you to change only solids to CMYK and leave tints as spot colors.

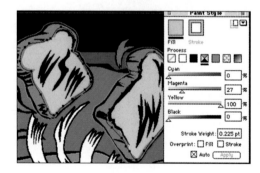

3 | Tips and Tricks

Some types of design projects rely heavily on spot colors—some examples include silkscreening and packaging. In the latter, almost all packages have CMYK values as well as two (or more) spot or "identity" colors. For some great ideas on the use of custom colors combined with CMYK, look closely at things like cereal boxes at the grocery store.

The use of spot colors in Illustrator certainly isn't limited to colors. Because designating a spot color results in an additional "plate" being generated in the shape of the object to which the color is assigned, these shapes can be used to carry colorants and coatings other than ink. Some examples include varnish plates (try gloss black varnish on flat black paper for a very subtle effect—many such color-on-color combinations work), thermographic inks (which "puff" when heated), and metallics. Other uses of custom colors may provide shapes for die cutting, foil stamping, or embossing.

Deborah Drummond

Comments

An outline saved in Illustrator's EPS export format can be read into Photoshop as an EPS file. When you use this type of EPS outline in a Photoshop file, you can create a mask to block out image areas and develop interesting fill effects.

Studio Usage

You can use Photoshop to crop photos into complicated shapes, but it's much easier to crop by creating a mask in Illustrator. Usually, when photographs are cropped inside a complex geometric shape, the shape is first created in Illustrator and then exported to Photoshop to be combined with the photo. Outdoor business signs and billboards combining photos and graphic shapes are often created this way.

Related Topics

1 | Creating the Mask Shape

Working from the specified design, use the Pen or Freehand tool to draw the intended shape. Fill the image with black and remove the stroke. Then save it as a regular Illustrator file for future reference or editing.

2 | Exporting to Photoshop

Select Save As from the File pull-down menu and save as an EPS file. In the EPS pop-up dialog box, select an appropriate onscreen preview (8-bit is preferable), and then select the appropriate Illustrator version. Keep in mind that selecting earlier Illustrator versions will lose newer version attributes that the earlier versions do not support.

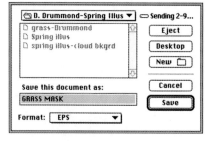

3 | Moving the Mask to Photoshop

Create a new channel for the mask in the destination file—call the channel "Mask." Open the file in Photoshop and copy it to the new "Mask" channel. After deselecting the mask, choose Invert under Map from the Image pull-down menu. Return to the composite image channel and choose Load Selection from the Select Menu.

4 | Applying the Mask

Select the image to be masked, copy it to the clipboard, and then return to the destination file. With the mask area still highlighted, choose Paste Into from the Edit pull-down menu. The image is now masked by the object created in Illustrator.

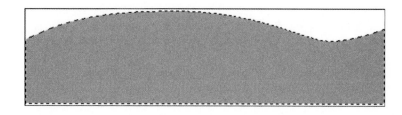

Ned Shaw

Comments

Blends are defined as smooth transitions between colors. A blend can be made up of one or more hues (such as blue to red or green to yellow), or shades (from 10% black to 90% black), or combinations of the two (10% cyan to 90% cyan and 12% magenta).

Studio Usage

Blends that are printed on high-resolution devices can cause major problems because fills often become "banded" or striped in Illustrator. You should experiment with the vendors that you intend to use. If you are familiar with Adobe Photoshop, consider doing blends in Photoshop and importing them as EPS files.

Related Topics

1 | Select and Group the Starting and Ending Steps

Select the starting and ending objects of your blend with the Selection tool (solid arrow). Then group the objects together (make sure that the objects are not part of another group). Grouping the objects at this point ensures that the completed blend will stay together when moved or manipulated on the document's page.

2 | Use the Blend Tool

Select the Blend tool from the Tool palette. Click a node point of one of the selected objects. After you select an object successfully, the cursor will change, adding a minus sign on the lower right. Then click the second object, choosing the node point that corresponds to the point selected on the first object.

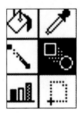

3 | Determining the Proper Number of Steps

After the second object is selected properly, a dialog box appears. This box contains a preset number of steps recommended by the program and the starting and ending percentages of the blend. These numbers can be changed, depending on the screen ruling (lpi). For a low screen ruling (under 85 lpi), set the number of blends to match the percentage change in the color (for example, a 20% change needs 20 steps). You may need more steps in the blend for larger areas, backgrounds, and so on.

For a high screen ruling (above 85 lpi), set the number of blends at two to three times the percentage change in color. This setting ensures that you'll have a smooth transition (nonbanding) of colors and clean reproduction of the artwork. You should never exceed 256 steps because most imagesetters cannot reproduce more than 256 shades of gray.

Javier Romero

Comments

If you need to make a mask for an image placed in Illustrator, it's simpler and more accurate to create that mask shape in the source program. By creating the mask shape in Photoshop, you can create a much better mask than by trying to draw it in Illustrator (a PICT preview is much tougher to work with!).

Studio Usage

Masks are used everywhere, from creating silhouettes to merely eliminating something that isn't needed in an illustration (other than deleting it). One of the greatest features in Photoshop is the ability to create a mask shape in Photoshop and modify it in Illustrator to include other objects.

Related Topics

1 | Create the Path in Photoshop

Open your image in Photoshop and choose the item that you want to mask. You can select it with any of the selection tools, or you can use the Pen tool (located on the Paths palette) to trace it. After you have made your choice with a selection tool, you will need to convert the selection to paths. This command is on the Paths palette.

2 | Saving and Exporting the Path

To save the path that you just created, use the Save Path command, also located on the Paths palette. A dialog box appears, allowing you to name the path (something descriptive is always helpful later). After you save the path, go to the File menu and scroll down to the Export submenu. Select the Paths to Illustrator option. A Save dialog box appears, allowing you to rename and save the path into the Illustrator document.

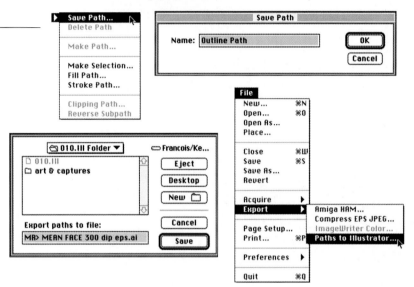

3 | Using the Path in Illustrator

Use the Open dialog box to open the Illustrator document that contains the saved path that you just created. In addition to the path, you will see a set of crop marks that will help you center the path on the placed Photoshop image. Release the crop marks so that you get a rectangle and copy the entire document. Paste the path into your illustration and place this path on its own layer. Then import the placed image and place it under the mask element. Modify the mask element as necessary, and use the Make Mask command (under the Object menu) to mask the placed image. Finally, group the image and the mask. You can now preview your results.

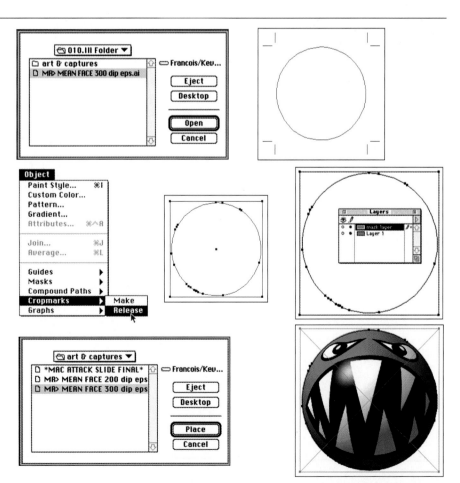

café eden

©david bamundo, 1994

David Bamundo

Comments

All objects have a defined fill, even if the fill is "none." The appearance of depth in an illustration cannot be achieved without color fills; depth is extremely important in most styles of illustration.

Studio Usage

Filling objects used to be a difficult menu chore in Illustrator. The new Paint Style palette and fill tools have made filling objects in an illustration much easier, faster, and more precise.

Related Topics

1 | Using the Paint Style Palette

To fill an object from the Paint Style palette, first select the object. Then open the Paint Style palette (⌘-I) and select the fill swatch. You can either select a color swatch from the left side of the palette or choose from the other fill options available: black and white, custom color, pattern, or gradient. After you select a pattern, custom color, or gradient, a box appears on the right, showing you more available options for the chosen fill. After making your choice, the selected object appears with the new fill.

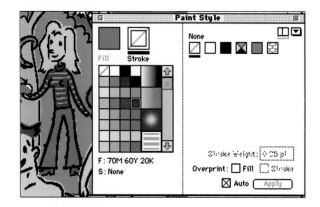

2 | Using the Eyedropper and Paint Bucket

The Eyedropper and Paint Bucket work best when the color that you need is already in the document. First, use the Eyedropper tool to select the color that you want from your illustration. Using the Paint Bucket tool, click on an object that you want to give that color. The object selected with the Bucket tool now appears with the new color. If you hold down the Option key while either the Paint Bucket or Eyedropper tool is selected, the opposite tool appears.

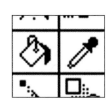

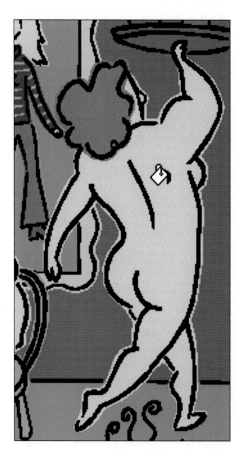

3 | What Can't Be Filled

Because type is considered a resource by the computer system, it must first be converted to outlines before it can be filled with patterns or gradients.

TP Design

Comments

Lines do more than define shapes; they also perform trapping and other tasks. You can greatly increase your control over an illustration by finding, selecting, and modifying all instances of a specific line weight.

Studio Usage

The select filters are great time-savers. In this instance, the Select Same Stroke Weight filter allows you to quickly and easily select all strokes with the same weight. This filter enables you to make global changes (such as thickening of lines) without a big hassle.

Related Topics

1 | Select an Object with a Line Weight That You Want to Modify

Select an object with a line weight that you want to modify. The object that you select must be a path; the Same Stroke Weight filter will not work on type unless the type is converted to outlines.

2 | Use the Same Stroke Weight Filter

Next, go to the Filter menu. Under the Select submenu, choose the Same Stroke Weight filter. All other paths with the same stroke weight will become selected.

3 | Modifying the Stroke Weight

To modify the stroke weight on the selected paths, open the Paint Style palette and select the Stroke Width field (on the lower right side of the palette). After you have selected your changes, press Return or close the palette. Your results will appear on the selected paths.

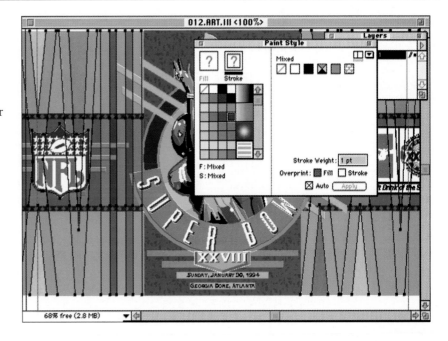

François Robert

Comments

When you invert a color, you change the color to its opposite, or complementary, color. The Invert Colors filter is designed to be very accurate and predictable.

Studio Usage

Inverting, or "flopping," colors is a very old design technique. It is used most often to accentuate differences in objects displayed in the illustration. The Invert Colors filter quickly tackles this daunting task, leaving you more time for other design decisions.

Related Topics

1 | Select the Objects to Invert

First, select the objects whose colors you want to invert. The Invert Colors filter will not work on custom colors, patterns, or gradients. If you need to invert a custom color, use the Custom to Process filter or choose a complementary custom color.

2 | Use the Invert Colors Filter

Next, select the Invert Colors filter located in the Colors submenu under the Filter menu. In grayscale mode, this filter will invert the amount of black in an object (25% black will invert to 75% black). In CMYK mode, the colors (but not the black) will invert (20% Cyan will change to 80% Cyan). After using this filter, the results will appear on the selected objects and on the Color palette.

Adjust Colors...	Colors ▶
Blend Front to Back	Create ▶
Blend Horizontally	Distort ▶
Blend Vertically	Objects ▶
Custom to Process...	Other ▶
Desaturate	Pathfinder ▶
Desaturate More	Select ▶
Invert Colors	Stylize ▶
Saturate	Text ▶

3 | Invert Colors Filter on CMYK

In CMYK mode, the Invert Colors filter works only on the cyan, yellow, and magenta portions of the color; black is not affected. To explain this further, if a color contains no black and becomes inverted, the new color will become, at best, a rich black (not exactly what you need!).

Coloring Objects *Managing Gradient Libraries*

Chris Spollen

Comments

Separate gradient libraries allow your working documents to be smaller because they don't have to carry unused gradients in their memory. This approach speeds up printing and saving, as well as the apparent speed of your computer.

Studio Usage

Gradient libraries make life easier; you don't have to go searching through dozens of different documents to find that one gradient that you used months ago. You simply store the gradient in your library.

Related Topics

1 | Creating a Gradient Library

To create a gradient library, you must first create a new document. In this new document, create a closed object—square, circle, star, etc. Open the Paint Style palette with the object selected. Click the gradient icon while the fill swatch is selected. Scroll through each gradient, making sure that the gradient(s) has actually been selected. After you have finished this process, save the document. Be sure to save in Illustrator 5 format! The program folder is a good place to save your gradient library. You will find a gradient folder with several libraries already in place in the program folder.

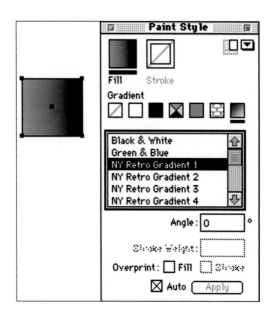

2 | Adding to a Gradient Library

To add a gradient to an existing library, open both the document containing the gradient and the gradient library. Next, follow the procedure described in Step 1. Save the library.

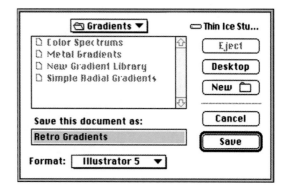

3 | Deleting a Gradient from an Existing Library

Open the library and select the Gradient palette to delete a gradient from an existing library. In the selection box on the right, select the gradient(s) that you want to delete and press Delete. After you have deleted the gradient, save the library.

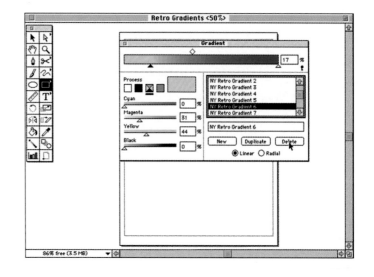

Deborah Drummond

Comments

Color is an artist's stock in trade; without color, art would be very flat and boring. The color palette in Illustrator allows you to color objects and make color changes easily and intuitively.

Studio Usage

The color palette is extremely flexible; using this tool wisely can help speed up the color art creation and any color modifications. When using Illustrator 5.5's color palette controls with the Select filters, you can make global color changes far more quickly than was possible in previous versions of Illustrator.

Related Topics

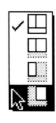
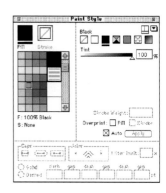

1 | Controlling the Size

The Color palette has three views that can appear together or singly. These views are controlled via a pop-up menu on the right-hand side of the palette. The left side is a swatch palette, from which you can apply colors to objects directly. The right side is for selecting colors, custom colors, patterns, and gradients. You can also create colors in CMYK by using the slider bars that appear when you select the CMYK box. Below these bars is the stroke attributes area, where you can set line attributes and create dashed lines, if needed.

2 | Adding Colors to the Palette

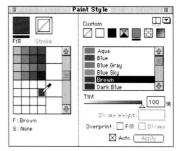

To add the current color, pattern, or gradient appearing in the swatch at the top, simply drag the color to an open box on the swatch. The color is loaded and saved with the document. You can also save a document that is loaded with sets of colors, such as a custom color set like the Pantone® series.

3 | Removing Colors from the Palette

To remove colors from the Paint Style palette, hold down the Command key and click or drag on the swatches you want to remove. The swatches will disappear, and you can load new colors as needed.

4 | Adding Custom Colors, Patterns, and Gradients

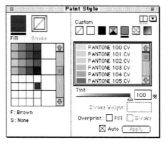

To add custom colors, gradients, and patterns to the right side of the palette, go to the Import Styles command under the File menu. An Open dialog box appears, allowing you to select any Illustrator file you want. When you open the selected file (import the styles), the new colors appear in the box below the color model boxes from the Illustrator file you selected.

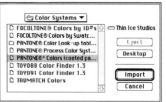

5 | Tips & Tricks

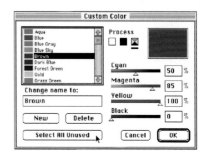

When your illustration is finished, go to the Custom Color and Patterns commands (under the Objects menu) and eliminate all unused patterns and custom colors. This saves memory and speeds up print times.

If you want to use the same fill and stroke colors, simply color one of the swatches of the Paint palette to the color you need. Then click on that swatch and drag it over to the swatch that you want to color. The swatch will turn to that particular color.

Bill Frampton

Comments

Mixing colors in overlapping objects allows for more realistic art by creating a feeling of depth, opacity, and transparency that could not be generated otherwise.

Studio Usage

The Mixing filters help you visualize how colors will interact with each other. The Mix Soft filter can create pastel colors much easier than mixing the two overlapping colors and lightening their intersection.

Related Topics

1 | Select the Objects to Overlap

Select the objects that you want to overlap. You must select two objects. The objects cannot be colored with custom colors, patterns, or gradients, and the objects must overlap. Type needs to be converted to outlines because the filters work only with objects that have outline paths.

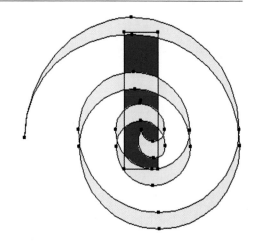

2 | Use the Mix Hard Filter

To create the effect of overprinting, use the Mix Hard filter located on the Pathfinder submenu in the Filter menu. The effect created is that of an overprint; the filter takes the overlap of the two objects, places a divide to create the overlap path, and combines the two colors to create the overprint's fill color.

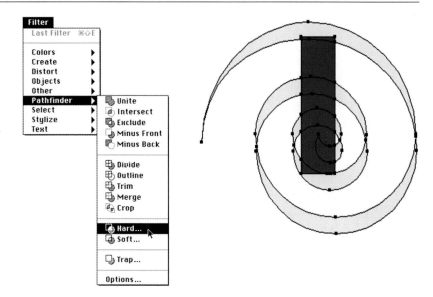

3 | Use the Mix Soft Filter

To create the effect of transparency, use the Mix Soft filter. Select the Mix Soft filter from the Pathfinder submenu under the Filter menu. After the filter is selected, set the amount of transparency for the overlap in the Mixing rate area of the dialog box that appears. A value of 1 will produce the most transparent effect, while 100 will produce almost no transparency. Once you have made your choice, click OK. The results will appear onscreen.

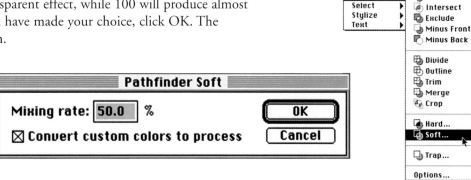

Coloring Objects *Saturation*

Charles Akins

Comments

The saturation filters are great for creating a "pastel color" effect in your artwork, as well as boosting or cutting the color content in any illustration.

Studio Usage

Control over color intensity is a requirement in any studio. These filters are designed to work with any object that is selected in your illustration.

Related Topics

1 Select the Objects to Modify

Use the saturation filters to select the objects that you
need to modify. These objects must be in either CMYK
or grayscale modes; these filters will not work on custom
colors, patterns, or gradients. If you need to use these filters on custom colors, use the Custom to Process filter
first to convert your custom colors to CMYK colors.

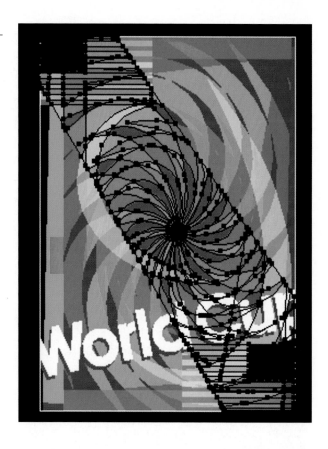

2 Use the Saturation Filters

Next, select one of the Saturation filters, located in the
Colors submenu under the Filter menu. Each of the
four filters work a little differently: the Saturate filter
will boost the color content of an object by about 10%;
the Desaturate filter will cut the color by about 10%;
the Saturate More and Desaturate More filters will
boost and cut, respectively, your colors by about 25%.
Once selected, the filter does its work, and the results
appear onscreen. To reapply the same filter, either
reselect the filter or use (Ò-Shift-E).

TP Design

Comments

Changes in color can balance an illustration, make the coloring more harmonious, and accommodate a client's particular needs.

Studio Usage

Imagine that your client walks in and asks you to change one particular color used throughout his illustration. Using the Select filters, you can change that one color in the illustration quickly to satisfy your client (not to mention, saving your own sanity).

Related Topics

1 | Select the Color to Change

First, select an object containing the color that you want to change throughout the illustration. Any object colored with a fill or stroke will work fine.

2 | Use the Select Filters

Use the Same Fill filter located in the Select submenu, under the Filter menu, to select all fills that have the same color. To select all strokes of the same color, use the Same Stroke Color filter (in the same menu). Use the Same Paint Style filter (also in the same menu) to select all objects with the same fill and stroke.

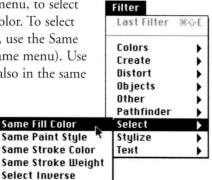

3 | Change the Color

With the objects selected, use this filter to open the Paint Style palette and change the paint attribute(s) as desired. After making the changes, close the Paint Style palette. Your changes will appear in the illustration.

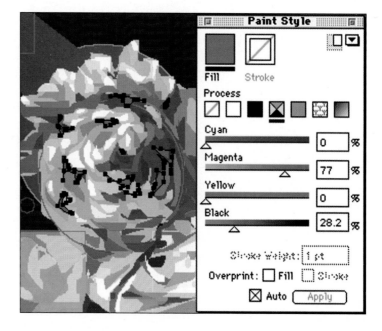

Coloring Objects *Using Blends for Complex Forms*

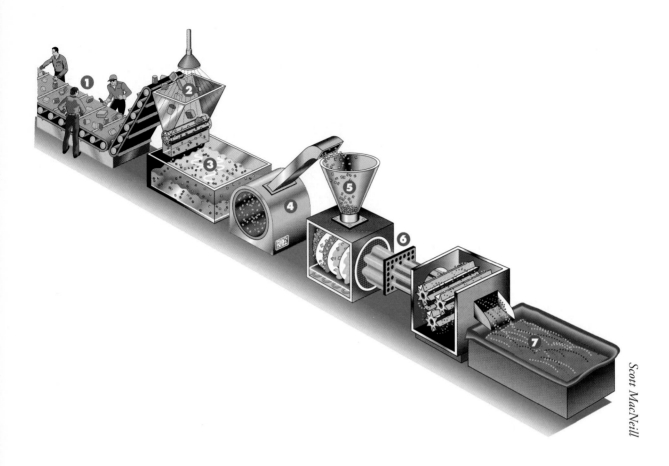

Scott MacNeill

Comments

Applying blends rather than solid fills can make an object appear more realistic. A blend is a fill that is composed of gradual color changes. Blends help to create the illusion of colors and depth in a three-dimensional environment.

Studio Usage

When trying to create a realistic illustration, a blend is a powerful tool in the artist's hand. Blends create smooth changes in color intensities that can mimic the original lighting, shadow, texture, and perspective of a photograph. Blends used to define lighting and texture are commonly seen in magazine illustrations and news graphics.

Related Topics

1 | Setting the Light Source

Decide where the light source in the drawing is before you apply blends. The relationship of the light source and the blends is shown where the blend and the highlight color are set in the object. The highlight position should be common in all elements, in order to reproduce uniform lighting as seen in the real world. When creating the highlight blend, blend between the object color and white. To achieve the best results, repeat the blend on both sides of the highlight.

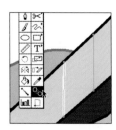
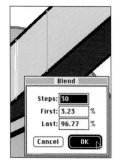

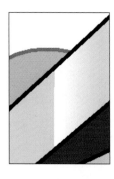
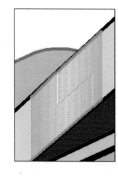

2 | Creating Depth

The shadow color will blend to its highlight color. To create a shadow, color the blend lines appropriately for highlight and shadow, based on the light source position. Then use the Blend tool on the selected elements. Colors can be repeated for consistency by adding the highlight and shadow colors to the Color palette.

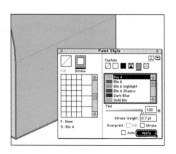
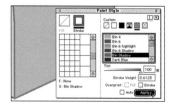

3 | Surface Textures and Blends

By adding blends, the reflective texture of an object appears more realistic. By adding the color of adjacent shapes, the blend appears to have been created by the adjacent object.

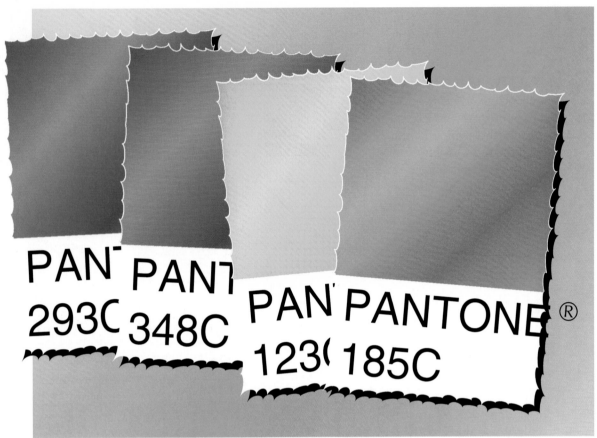

François Robert

Comments

Pantone® is a widely accepted method of defining colors to ensure consistent results over a broad range of different presses.

Studio Usage

If you've ever worked in a professional color environment, you are probably familiar with Pantone®. The ability to use Pantone Matching System (PMS) colors in a drawing is important to today's digital artist. When selecting Pantone® colors, always double-check and compare the colors with a Pantone® chip book. You may be using another color management system with a reliable monitor, but remember that the printed colors *never* lie.

Related Topics

1 Placing Pantone Colors in the Paint Palette

To add Pantone® colors to the Paint palette, choose the Import Styles command from the File menu. An Open File dialog box will take you to the Pantone® Colors document. This document is located in the Color Systems folder inside the Adobe Illustrator program folder. Once you have reached this location, select the Pantone® Colors document and click OK. The Pantone® colors will appear when you select the custom colors icon on the Paint Style palette.

2 Using Pantone Colors

To use the Pantone® colors, select the object that you want painted and open the Paint Style palette (⌘-I). In the Paint Style palette, select either a fill or stroke swatch. Click the custom color icon (the green box on the right, under the fill and stroke swatches). When selected, a box with all available Pantone® colors will appear below the color options.

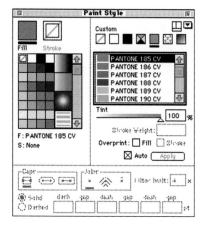

3 Defining the Pantone System

The Pantone® system used in Illustrator is the 747 series, which uses three-and four-digit numbers to represent colors. Just type the number of the Pantone® color that you want to use. The color will then appear. If you don't know which color you want, scroll through the colors until you find the color that you need or refer to a Pantone® color in their chip book. Press the Return key or close the Paint Style palette to see your choices appear.

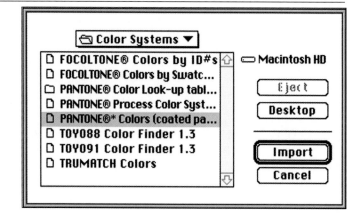

Charles Akins

Comments

Two types of colors can be printed on paper: spot color, which is made from a solid ink color (green, pink, lemon yellow, and so on), and composite color, which is made from a combination of process inks (usually cyan, magenta, yellow, and black).

Studio Usage

Not every job is a four-color process. You may find yourself working in two- or three- or four-color spot color work. If possible, always work in real (spot) color because it aids creativity and production in many ways. You also should eliminate unused colors before output.

Related Topics

1 | Creating a Spot Color

To create a spot color, select the Custom Color command from the Object menu. The dialog box that appears allows you to create a new color from scratch, or you can modify a Pantone®, Trumatch™, or Toyo™ color set. The color model used to create new custom colors is CMYK, which allows you to separate the colors accurately when printing.

2 | Using Spot Colors

To use a spot color, select the object to be colored. Then select the Paint Style palette (⌘-I). In the Paint Style palette, choose the Fill or Stroke swatch and select the custom color icon (the green box to the right). A box containing custom colors appears; scroll to the color that you want, or type the name (or number) of the desired color. After you choose a color, close the Paint Style palette. If the auto apply box is not checked, press Return to apply the color. Your color(s) will appear onscreen and will be saved with the illustration.

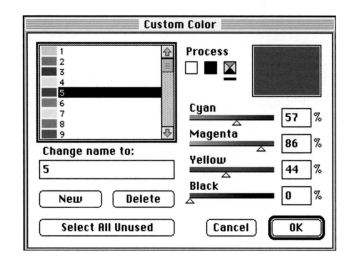

3 | Deleting Spot Colors

If you need to delete a spot color from an illustration, call up the Custom Color dialog box under the Object menu. Select the desired color and hit the Delete button. All objects painted with that color will become 100% processed black.

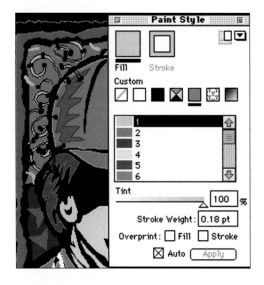

Javier Romero

Comments

Creating the illusion of three-dimensional drawings on paper is no simple task. Paper offers only two dimensions—height and width—leaving depth to illusion. The third dimension in drawing, painting, and photography is created with angle, color, and perspective. Illustrator offers control over these three photographic qualities to create the illusion of depth. The complexity required of the three-dimensional object determines which tool or combination of tools is used to create the illusion of depth.

Studio Usage

Two-dimensional computer art may have been sufficient when computer-based illustration began, but with today's powerful computer applications there is a demand for three-dimensional illustration. Basic three-dimensional drawings, such as those commonly seen in magazine and newspaper graphics, can be achieved with Illustrator. Animation sequences for advertising, computer games, and film sequences also can be created in Illustrator. Using Adobe Dimensions (or other three-dimensional rendering programs), combined with Illustrator files, you can create incredibly life-like, three-dimensional illustrations.

Related Topics

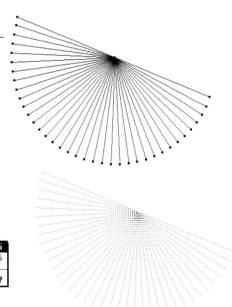

1 | Perspective

A primary rule in creating depth is defining a "vanishing" point. Use custom guides to determine a horizon and a vanishing point so that a template for depth can be created. Take a look at the example. After the vanishing point and horizon were defined by lines drawn with the Pen tool, the paths were selected and converted to guidelines. The angled guidelines define the angle to be used when drawing the depth dimension.

Object

Paint Style...	⌘I
Custom Color...	
Pattern...	
Gradient...	
Attributes...	⌘⌃A
Join...	⌘J
Average...	⌘L
Guides ▶	Make ⌘5
Masks ▶	Release ⌘6
Compound Paths ▶	✓Lock ⌘7
Cropmarks ▶	
Graphs ▶	

2 | Height, Width, and Depth

When you are drawing elements, the width and height dimensions should be drawn at right angles. The depth can be added at the angle determined to be the vanishing point. In isometric drawing, the common depth angle is always 30° and no vanishing point is used.

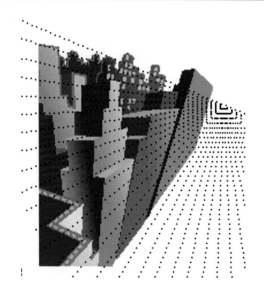

3 | Lighting

Lighting is an important part of three-dimensional drawing. The key is "one light source." When drawing, use a single light source and keep its angle and intensity constant throughout the illustration. Imagine a lamp above and to the left of the art board. More than one shadow angle can ruin an illustration. Keep in mind that color characteristics in the shadow areas should be adjusted to match the lighting. Three-dimensional drawing can be achieved by using the Colors option in the Filter pull-down menu and then selecting the Saturate or Saturate More filter. In addition, you can use color blends in fills to suggest a three-dimensional drawing.

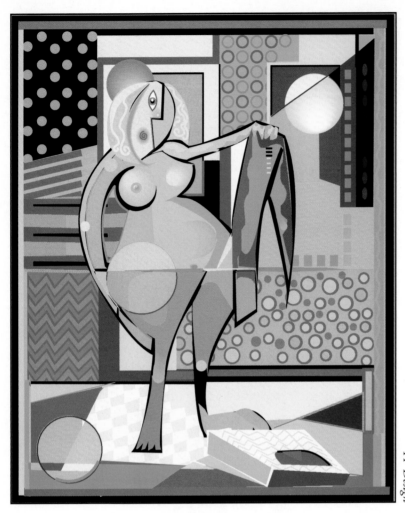

TP Design

Comments

The need to add or delete anchor points depends on how the current object is created. When using the Freehand tool, too many anchor points often result; anchor points in the freehand curve must then be deleted with the Pen tool. The Add Anchor Point and Delete Anchor Point tools reduce this to a simple task. Using the Delete Anchor Point tool, you can remove anchor points without breaking a closed object's path (which results when you use the Delete key to remove unwanted anchor points in a closed path). The Add Anchor Point tool adds curve or straight line anchor points, depending on the type of path selected.

Studio Usage

The more you use the Freehand and Pen tools, the more you will use the Add and Delete Anchor Point tools. Line segments often are manipulated after completion or when placed into Illustrator from other applications. As a result, artwork cleanup is becoming more frequent. Usually, anchor points are removed from imported illustrations to simplify editing, but that is not always the case. Some silk screen cutters and map plotters work best when curved paths are defined by many anchor points between straight lines instead of a curve between two anchor points. The opposite is true for PostScript® printing.

Related Topics

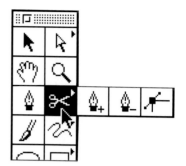

1 | Determining the Required Anchor Point Changes

You should assess each object individually to identify the necessary anchor point changes. These changes depend on the design of the final product and the printing process. This sample uses traditional printing. The goal here was to reduce the number of anchor points without losing the line accuracy in the map.

2 | Deleting Points

Select the Delete Anchor Point tool by holding down the mouse button on the Anchor Point Manipulation section of the toolbox. Click an anchor point to delete it. The line segment redraws itself from the adjacent anchor points.

3 | Adding Points

Anchor points can be added to an object by switching to the Add Anchor Point tool. After points are added to a curved path, curve control handles are added to the new anchor point. Adding points to a straight path adds an anchor point with no curve handles. Curve handles can be added to the point by dragging control handles while adding the point, or they can be added later with the Convert Direction Point tool.

4 | Adjusting New Anchor Points

Newly added anchor points should be examined at a magnified view and at the printed size view to determine whether they need further positioning to achieve the desired effect.

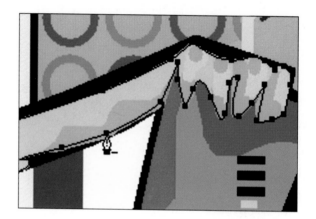

Tim Dove

Comments

The Create filters use complicated macros to build shapes that match the characteristics entered in each filter's pop-up dialog box. Before these filters existed, building these shapes involved drawing circles and using rotated lines—an odious task similar to creating shapes in calculus classes with a compass and a straight-edge.

Studio Usage

The geometric elements—star, polygon, and spiral—are commonly used in traditional and modern design. These shape filters are used by advertising artists to create splash boxes and by sign makers to create bold borders. Because the objects can be colored and manipulated like any other element, they can be customized to meet your needs.

Related Topics

1 │ Selecting the Star Filter

Activate the Star filter located in the Create submenu under the Filter pull-down menu. In the dialog box, enter the characteristics to create the desired star shape and fill in the number of points required. The 1st Radius sets the distance from the star's center to the outside tips. The 2nd radius determines how deep the star's points cut into its body, because it sets the distance from the star's center to the inside tips.

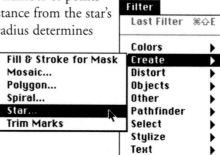

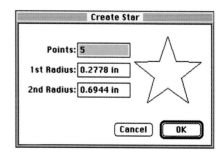

2 │ Selecting the Polygon Filter

The Polygon filter builds symmetrical polygons with equal sides that are the same distance from the polygon's center. Select the Polygon filter from the Create submenu under the Filter pull-down menu. A dialog box appears, allowing you to set the desired number of sides and the size of the element's radius.

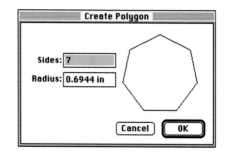

3 │ Selecting the Spiral Filter

Select the Spiral filter from the Create submenu under the Filter pull-down menu. The most specific of the filters, the Spiral filter also is one of the most effective. The spiral's turns can be directed clockwise or counterclockwise. After you choose the filter, a dialog box appears, allowing you to specify the number of winds, the radius, and the spiral direction.

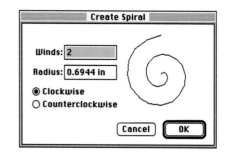

4 │ Manipulating the Objects

The created geometric shapes can be further manipulated to match the needs of the illustration. In the example, the objects were given a dotted line treatment, scaled, sheared, and rotated as needed.

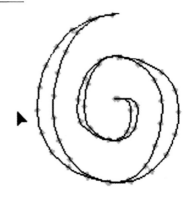

Chris Spollen

Money Magazine-75 Ways

Comments

The Average command positions two or more anchor points in relation to each other based on the axes selected in the dialog box. The dialog box displays three axis options: Horizontal, Vertical, and Both.

Studio Usage

Anchor point averaging is used in the studio during the cleanup of drawn or scanned artwork. The options you select depend on the results you need. After cutting a closed path with the Scissors Tool, the end points of the path often are combined with another path's point by using the Average command.

Related Topics

1 | Averaging along the Vertical Axis

A ray effect was needed in the sample. The desired 3D effect was achieved by selecting all of the bottom anchor points and applying the Average command (⌘-L) with the Vertical Only option.

2 | Averaging along the Horizontal Axis

Averaging points on a horizontal axis is similar to the vertical axis process. The only difference is that the Horizontal Only option is selected instead of the Vertical Only option. Again, make sure to select only the points that need to be averaged. Selecting all the points will create, at best, a lumpy pancake.

3 | Averaging along Both Axes

Points that need to be averaged together (to join paths, for example) should be averaged using the Both Axes option, the default setting in the Average dialog box. First, select the points that you need to average and choose the Average command. Be sure to choose only the points that need averaging; if you choose all the points in an object and then average, your result may look like a mad spider or a ball of string. Select the Both Axes option in the dialog box and click OK. The result will appear onscreen.

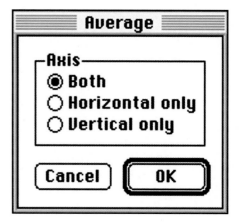

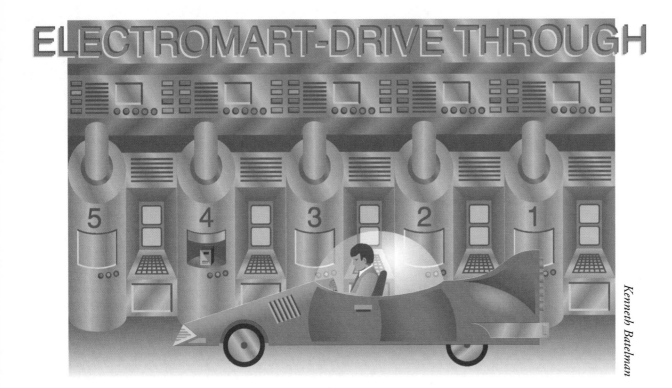

Kenneth Batelman

Comments

By using a combination of guides and basic principles of geometry, you can create realistic items more easily. Most objects include the basic geometric shapes—ellipse, regular and irregular polygons—all of which are quickly created in Illustrator. Realistic objects can be made by combining the Oval and Polygon tools with basic geometry. By visualizing an object geometrically, the required tools can be selected and appropriate guides can be placed before starting the drawing.

Studio Usage

You probably use basic geometry more than you consciously think about it when creating realistic objects. For example, basic geometry is used to create the degree of shadow from a light source or the degrees of intersections to divide a circle into parts. Much of the geometrical drawing is done by the program, but the planning and efficient use of existing tools can become a valued skill in creating professional quality graphics.

Related Topics

1 | Calculating the Guides

In the sample, a gear is going to be drawn. The gear requires 12 units to delineate the 12 teeth; therefore, the 360° of a circle must be divided into 12 units (360° / 12 = 30°). A circle (used to base the gear radius on) is drawn and converted into a guide. Elements created with the Oval and Polygon tools can be converted to act as guides.

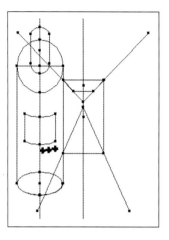

2 | Applying the Guides

After the appropriate calculations are completed, the guides can be set. Guides are used to represent the locations for the gear teeth. Center points drawn by the Polygon and Oval tools become very important when setting the step; they repeat because the center point marks the radius point's axis. Copies of a path drawn from the radius to the outside of the circle are rotated in 30° intervals around the circle to mark the shape and position of each tooth. All lines are selected and converted to guides in the Make Guides pull-down menu.

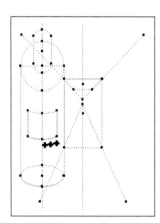

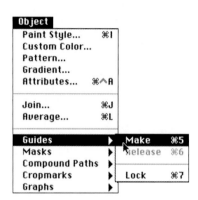

3 | Drawing the Object

After the guides are in place, the drawing becomes the easy part of the job. With locations and planning already done, the task of drawing is much simpler. After the geometric elements are completed, coloring and transformations can be added to the object as needed.

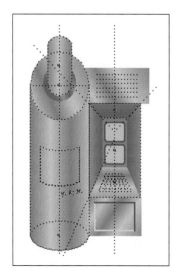

Darryl Brown

Comments

The Blend tool creates intermediate steps between two selected objects, enables mass-duplication of selected objects, and produces a shading technique that is not otherwise possible in Illustrator.

Studio Usage

By blending objects, you can create letters that fade back into the distance, a shadow that falls into a certain space, and shading that cannot be done with any other tool. Careful use of blending can create objects that appear almost photographic.

Related Topics

1 | Select Objects for Blending

First, select two objects that you want to blend. These objects must be paths, both open or both closed (you cannot mix the two types). The paths are not required to have the same number of anchor points. If you want to blend type, it must be converted to outlines before blending. Be sure that the objects are colored correctly before blending them. It's much easier to do the right blend the first time!

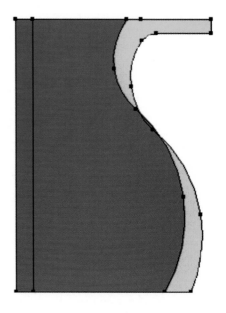

2 | Use the Blend Tool

Select the Blend tool in the Tool palette. Select the first object, and the tool will add a minus sign on the lower right. Select the second object, and a dialog box will appear. You can specify the number of steps for the blend in this box. Click OK, and the results will appear onscreen.

3 | Tips and Tricks

Remember to set the number of steps high enough for reproduction purposes; rough color banding may occur if not enough steps are used in a blend. If you are unsure about the number needed, use the default number that appears in the Blend Tool dialog box.

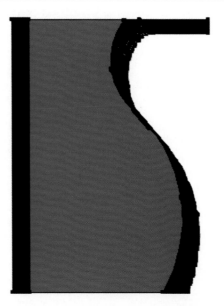

Scott MacNeill

Comments

When it comes to making blends, blended lines can be better tools than blended, filled shapes because fewer nodes are used to control the shapes of lines. Blended lines also allow for much greater flexibility than blended fills because lines can be drawn smaller and be sized to fit in detailed areas of an illustration more easily.

Studio Usage

Blending rules is great for odd shapes, such as complex drop shadows or highlights that show complex surface texture on an object. Use blended lines anywhere in an illustration where detailed texture needs be flexible and controllable.

Related Topics

1 | Select the Lines to be Blended

First, select the lines that you need to blend. These lines should contain only strokes and should not belong to any group. (Make a copy of the line if it belongs to a group.) The lines do not need to contain the same number of anchor points; Illustrator will add points as needed. After these lines are selected, group them together. This will allow you to select (at any time) the blend with its end lines.

2 | Use the Blend Tool

Select the Blend tool from the Tool palette. Then click the end point of the first selected line. Click any point if the line is a closed shape. Once selected, a minus sign is added to the Blend tool cursor. Click the end point of the second line or the corresponding point on the second closed shape. A dialog box appears, allowing you to enter the number of steps that you need. Click OK.

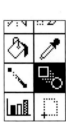

3 | Tips and Tricks

Remember to make your strokes thick enough to fill the gaps between the lines. If you need to make thicker lines, select the Blend tool and open the Paint Style palette. Change the line weight in the box near the bottom and close the Paint Style palette. If banding occurs, you can redo the blend with more steps.

Creating Objects *Complex Masks*

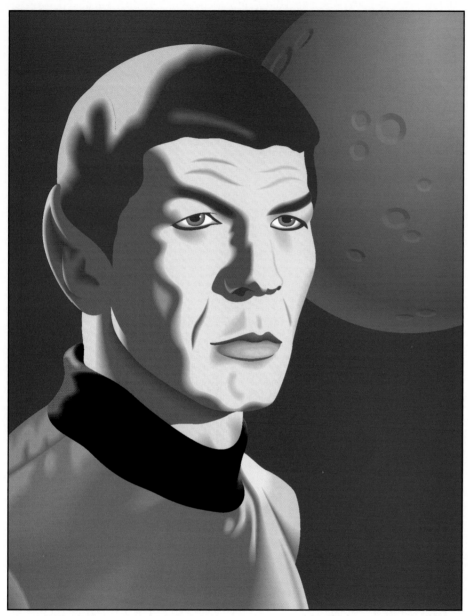

Kenneth Batelman

Comments

Working with multiple masks on the same set of objects can be tricky. The trick is to choose the elements for the mask and compound all of them, so that Illustrator treats the compound as one object.

Studio Usage

A complex mask is extremely useful; type used as a mask is, by definition, a complex mask. The ability to put holes in a mask can greatly simplify an illustration, helping to eliminate duplicates of the same object with different masks applied to them.

Related Topics

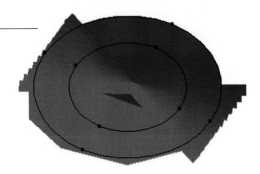

1 | Select the Mask Elements

Select the elements that you want to make into a mask. Make sure that all type is converted to outlines, and that no grouping or compounding occurs within the selected objects.

2 | Compound the Objects

With the mask objects still selected, compound the elements (⌘-8). To check the compound, you may preview the selection (⌘-Option-Y) to confirm that the compounding was done correctly. If there is a problem with one of the mask elements, select it with the hollow tool and bring up its attributes box (⌘-Control-A). Turn on or off the Reverse path direction check box as needed. Click OK, and the element in question should now pop out, like a donut hole.

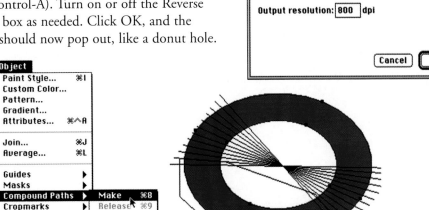

3 | Applying the Mask

When you are certain that the mask element is correctly compounded, select both the mask and the objects to be affected by it (make sure that the mask is on top of the objects). Use the Make Mask command (located in the Object menu). Because of the compounding, the complex mask element will behave more like a traditional cut rubylith rather than a plain, simple cropped object.

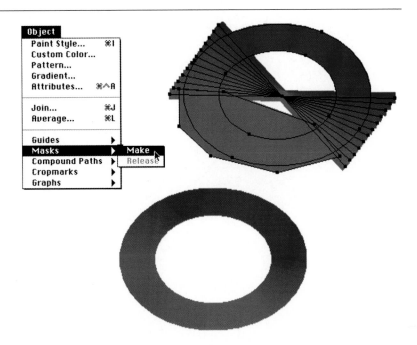

Bill Frampton

Comments

A compound works like a cookie cutter. When two selected items are compounded, it "cuts" the shape of the topmost object out of the background element.

Studio Usage

A good illustration of compounds is the letter "O." The center (counter) of the typeface needs to show whatever is behind it. If you simply draw a black circle and then place a white circle on top of it, it would look funny if you screened the background. The "hole" would remain white.

Related Topics

1 | **Select the Paths to Compound**

First, you need to select the paths to compound. You can use any of the selection tools or the Select All command (⌘-Shift-A) to compound everything visible.

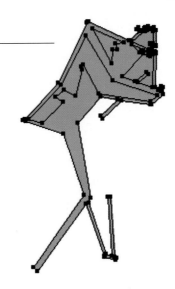

2 | **Compound the Paths**

Select the Compound Paths command from the Object menu (⌘-8). The path should "knock out" as if it were a donut with a hole in the middle.

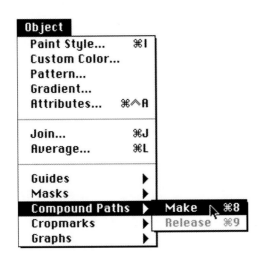

Object	
Paint Style...	⌘I
Custom Color...	
Pattern...	
Gradient...	
Attributes...	⌘⌥A
Join...	⌘J
Average...	⌘L
Guides	▶
Masks	▶
Compound Paths	▶
Cropmarks	▶
Graphs	▶

Make ⌘8
Release ⌘9

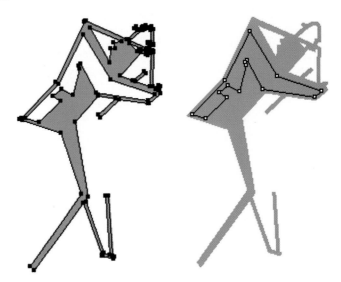

3 | **Troubleshooting Compounds**

A compound may not always work properly. Most of the time, you will get a dialog box warning you of the problem. If this is the case, select the part that is not previewing correctly. Then open the Attributes dialog box under the Object menu (⌘-Shift-A). Turn on (or off) the Reverse path direction check box to test the look of the compounds again. Click OK and preview the illustration. Repeat as needed for all compounds in your illustration.

Attributes

Note:

☐ Show center point   ☒ Reverse path direction

Output resolution: 800 dpi

Cancel   OK

Creating Objects *Creating Automatic Objects*

Kenneth Batelman

Comments

Illustrator is basically an oversouped-up geometry program; creating rectangles and ovals automatically is a natural function in almost every illustration done in the program.

Studio Usage

At first glance, drawing circles and squares may not seem like a big deal, but try to draw them freehand. Suddenly, you see why these tools were created!

Related Topics

1 | The Rectangle Tool

First, select the Rectangle tool from the Tool palette. Click-and-drag the mouse on a diagonal *away* from the point where you started. You should see an outline showing the size and shape of your rectangle. Once you are satisfied with its size and shape, release the mouse button, and your rectangle is created. If you need rounded corners on your rectangle, you can select the type of corner that appears on the pop-up menu beside the rectangle.

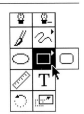

2 | The Oval Tool

The Oval tool works in much the same way. Select the tool, and then click-and-drag the mouse. While you are clicking and dragging the mouse, the Oval tool creates an imaginary rectangle that your oval falls into. Once again, when you are satisfied with the size and shape of your oval, release the mouse button, and the oval is created.

3 | Creating Perfect Squares and Circles

To create a perfect square or circle, hold down the Shift key while dragging out the shape. Using the Shift key constrains the object into creating a perfect square or circle.

4 | Drawing From the Center Point

To draw a circle or square from the center point, hold down the Option key before you click-and-drag with the mouse. You also can press and hold the Shift key to make perfect squares and circles from a center point.

5 | Using the Dialog Box

To use the dialog boxes, select the tool and hold down the Option key while clicking the mouse (do not drag the mouse). The dialog box appears, allowing you to enter the size of the rectangle or oval. After the sizes are entered, click OK and a new object will be created to match the sizes entered.

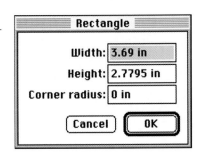

François Robert

Comments

A mask is an outline of an object that is used when two or more items are either merged together or placed on top of one another (layered). A mask can have a stroke (outline) or a fill. Masks often allow you to achieve effects that you couldn't create with other tools.

Studio Usage

If you are developing custom drawings, you will have to create masks often. You should use a fill for a mask when you have type inside of a screened area and want to mask (hide) a portion of the type while maintaining the background screen. Then set the fill of the mask equal to the background color.

Related Topics

1 | Select the Mask Only!

Use the Direct Selection tool (top right column in the Tool palette) to select the mask. Make sure that only the mask is selected because the filter won't work if non-mask objects are selected!

2 | Color the Mask

Open the Color Attributes palette (⌘-I). Notice that when you open it, the colors are blank. Color the mask as you need and close the palette.

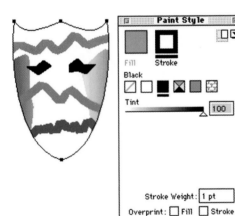

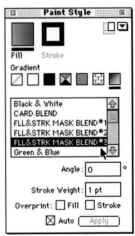

3 | Apply the Fill & Stroke for Mask Filter

Apply the Fill & Stroke for Mask filter located under the Create submenu in the Filter menu. Preview the results. If you are satisfied with the results, you're finished. If not, go back two Undos (it will take you back to Step #1) and start over.

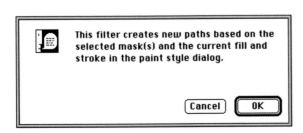

Creating Objects *Creating Symmetrical Objects with the Reflection Tool*

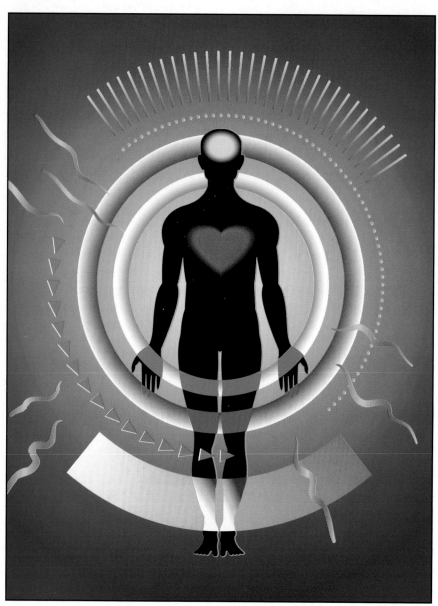

Bill Morse

Comments

When drawing symmetrical objects—objects that can be split along an axis to form identical halves—there is no reason to draw more than half of the object. The completed half of the object can be mirrored and copied into position with the Reflect tool. The symmetry will be exact because the second side is a copy of the original path.

Studio Usage

The Reflect tool (also known as the Mirror tool) is commonly used to create copies of objects. Rather than cluttering the Artboard with many guide lines to ensure symmetry, the Reflect tool is used to create the second side of symmetrical objects. The tool also works extremely well in creating shadows of completed objects.

Related Topics

1 Setting the Axis

Create a guide to mark the object's axis of symmetry. Based on the axis, create the first half of the object with the appropriate tool.

2 Using the Mirror Tool

If the rotation is around the vertical or horizontal axis, use the Reflect tool dialog box. Select the axis rotation point, depress the mouse button, and then click on the appropriate button—Vertical or Horizontal axis. If the axis of rotation is tilted, select your object to mirror and then click along an axis guide line with the Reflect tool: first, on the end point above the object to be copied; second, while holding the Option key, click below the object on the other end of the guide line.

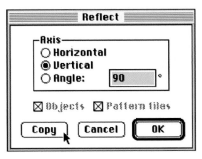

3 Creating a Single Object

Select one of the overlapping point pairs resulting from the symmetrical copy and use the Average command followed by the Join command to join the two paths into one. Any required transformations can then be added to the object.

Tim Dove

Comments

When an element is moved, a copy is created in the new position. Holding down the Option key redraws a duplicate element in the new position and leaves the original in position. When you use Option-drag, it copies grouped elements or single paths depending on what is selected for the operation. If the element contains a patterned fill, element movement is affected by the General Preferences: Snap to Point, Constrain Angle, and Transform Patterned tiles.

Studio Usage

Option-dragging is an easy way to create multiple objects in many different situations. This key-and-mouse combination simplifies the creation of repetitive elements in an illustration. Option-drag, in conjunction with the Repeat Transformation function, creates pages of evenly spaced elements (such as logo sheets, people in a crowd, or lines on forms) very easily.

Related Topics

1 | Selecting the Element

How the element is selected affects the result. Depress the Option key with the mouse button to move and copy the selected elements. Depress the Option key *after* pressing the mouse button to move and copy only the single element from a multiple selection. When elements are moved or copied with the Option key combination, a hollow selection arrow appears below the solid selection arrow.

2 | Dragging into Position

If you drag the selection to the new location and release the mouse button before releasing the Option Key, a copy is placed and the original is left unchanged. Hold down the Shift key to constrain the movement horizontally or vertically. Guidelines may also be pre-set to aid in movement. In this example, the copy was then rotated and joined to the original object to create the "dog eats dog" artwork.

3 | Repeating the Movement

After you copy-and-move and before you perform any other actions, use the Repeat Transformation function under the Arrange pull-down menu to repeat the operation. You can apply Repeat Transformation as many times as you need; it is limited only by machine RAM.

François Robert

Comments

Deep down inside, Illustrator is a geometry program. As such, it knows about the existing shapes of the objects that you create. Illustrator can easily apply a series of movements and distortions based on parameters that you set.

Studio Usage

A measured amount of distortion often can achieve results that aren't possible without an incredible amount of calculation, pencil grids, inking, and redrawing.

Related Topics

Perspective Grids   95

1 Select the Objects to Distort

First, select the objects that you want to distort. All type must first be converted to outlines because the filter does not recognize type as objects.

2 Choose the Free Distort Filter

Choose the Free Distort filter located under the Distort submenu in the Filters menu. A dialog box displays the object as a wireframe with anchor points at the corners of a bounding box. You can turn off the check box marked "Show Me" underneath the object if you don't need the preview.

Create	▶	
Distort	▶	Free Distort...
Objects	▶	Roughen...
Other	▶	Scribble...

3 Distorting the Objects

To distort the object, grab one of the anchor points on the bounding box with the Selection tool (it's already selected for you) and move the anchor point to another position. The wireframe preview automatically updates and shows the distortion effect. If you want to start over, click the Reset button. The bounding box will return to its original position. When OK is clicked, the selected distortion is applied to the selected object(s) in the illustration.

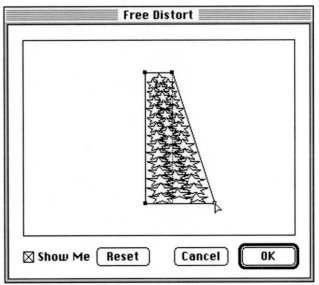

TP Design

Comments

Illustrator's Pathfinder filters divide objects into separate paths based on the objects' intersections. The intersections create new elements for coloring and color separation purposes.

To form these new elements, Pathfinder filters create new paths without overlapping elements. To use the Pathfinder filters in version 5.5, the computer must have a math co-processor.

Studio Usage

Paths often are divided and split when building files that include manual trap and spread information for color separation. Pathfinder filters are much easier and faster to use than the Scissors tool and Join command. The filters operate similarly to the Compound Path command, which creates a single solid element based on overlapping portions of combined elements. Pathfinder filters greatly reduce the task of preparing art files (for example, vinyl lettering and screen masks for sign shops and silkscreen shops).

Related Topics

1 | Deciding What Needs to be Divided

The complexity of the division and the desired effect determines whether to divide paths manually (with the Scissors tool and Join command) or with the Pathfinder filters. In a complicated instance it is best to try the appropriate Pathfinder filter first. In the sample, knocking out and recoloring the company name using state map silhouettes as a background achieves the desired effect.

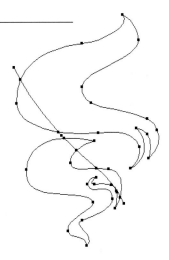

2 | The Outline Filter

The Outline filter divides the selected element paths into individual paths at every overlapping intersection. The filter leaves only stroke information because fill information is not used on paths.

3 | The Divide Filter

The Divide filter divides the overlapping elements into closed paths based on overlapping elements. The fills remain as they were before the filter was applied. When dividing a fill with lines, make sure that the lines are not painted with a fill or stroke; this guarantees that only the filled object is divided and not the stroke width of the line, too.

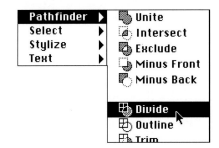

4 | The Crop Filter

The Crop filter works like the Mask command; only elements inside the uppermost closed path are visible after the filter is applied. The difference between cropping and masking is that the Crop filter deletes elements outside of the mask while the Mask command hides the elements outside of the mask.

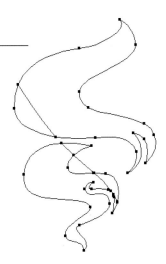

Creating Objects *Drawing Freehand*

Charles Akins

Comments

The ability to create smooth, perfect lines is not the goal of every design project. The Freehand tool allows you to draw freeform objects as though you were using pencil and paper, although the result is a rough approximation, rather than a precise rendition of the line. The Freehand tool creates a path based on the movement of a mouse or digital pen. The accuracy between the created path and the drawn path depends on the speed and direction of the drawing tool movement. The Freehand tolerance, set in the General Preferences dialog box, controls how closely the created line matches the drawn line. The default setting is two; the higher the setting, the fewer the number of anchor points.

Studio Usage

The precise lines and objects easily created with the computer are not the best way to illustrate all ideas. For example, the Freehand tool works without the draftsman quality so often associated with the computer. The Freehand tool adds the right feel to create a hand-drawn look for letters and shapes, and it works well for creative book illustrations and cartooning. The tool also works well for tracing small template areas that the Auto-Trace tool may miss.

Related Topics

1 | Selecting and Using the Freehand Tool

If the tool is not visible on the tool box, click and drag the Auto-Trace tool to switch to the Freehand tool. Clicking and dragging the drawing tool draws a path as a dotted line, which Illustrator uses to create its path. Releasing the mouse button ends the freehand path, and the dotted line changes into a solid one.

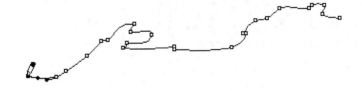

2 | Extending an Existing Path

To extend an existing path using the Freehand tool, position the tool over the path's end point. When the tool's pencil eraser icon turns black, depress the mouse button and continue drawing the line as required.

3 | Erasing Part of a Path Being Drawn

Without releasing the mouse button (while using the Drawing tool), depress the Command key and drag over the dotted line to where the line is to be redrawn. While selecting the portion of line to be edited, the pencil icon changes to an eraser. Anchor points can be erased with the Delete key and moved as required with the selection tools.

Creating Objects *Soft Drop Shadows*

Kenneth Batchman

Comments

Drop shadows are useful for giving depth to an illustration. A designer often tries to achieve a sense of roundness that is unattainable with a simple flat drawing.

Studio Usage

Soft drop shadows are normally the domain of Photoshop users; however, they can also be applied within Illustrator by using the Blend tool. This technique is useful for giving depth by adding shadows to elements in an illustration.

Related Topics

1 | Create the Outline of the Shadow

First, draw the outside of the shadow using the Pen or Freehand tool. When defining the shape of the shadow, keep in mind which direction the light is coming from. Color this outside line the same as the background; you can add some black (5-15%) to help define where the shadow ends, if you need a hard edge to your shadow.

2 | Create the Dark Section of the Shadow

Next, draw the section of the shadow that will appear the darkest in your illustration—color this with the same color as your background. Then add a fair amount of black (often 30-50% more) to this shape.

3 | Previewing and Grouping the Shapes

With both shadow shapes drawn, preview the shapes (⌘-Option-Y) to make sure that the dark section is on top of the outline of the shadow. After this is confirmed, group the shapes (⌘-G.)

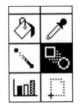

4 | Using the Blend Tool

Finally, select the Blend tool from the tool palette. With the shapes selected, click on one of the objects. Then select a corresponding point on the other object. Once completed, a dialog box will appear. You can enter the number of blending steps needed. Click OK in the Blend dialog box, and the shadow blends will be drawn. If the shadow looks OK, save the illustration; if not, delete the blends, recolor, or reshape the shadows as needed.

Ned Shaw

Comments

Selecting, moving, and editing related elements becomes much easier when they are in a single group. To select and move a number of objects with a single mouse click, the objects must be grouped first. Combining multiple objects into one unit is called grouping.

Studio Usage

Illustrations rarely have single elements. Grouping related elements makes editing the illustration much easier. Grouping should be used in almost every illustration for convenience and organization.

Related Topics

The Hollow Tool   44

Using Layers   75

1 | Selecting the Group

Select the objects that you want to group. Depending on the complexity of the illustration, you can select objects by clicking and dragging a marquee around the objects. You also can click the individual objects while depressing the Shift key to select them. Another trick is to temporarily lock or hide elements that you want to exclude from a specific group.

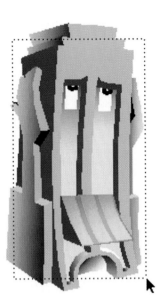

2 | Creating the Group

Select Group (⌘-G) from the pull-down Arrange menu. The selected objects are now grouped. Clicking a single object in the group will now select the entire group.

Arrange	View	Object
Repeat Transform		⌘D
Move...		⌘⇧M
Bring To Front		⌘=
Send To Back		⌘-
Group		**⌘G**
Ungroup		⌘U

3 | Moving a Group

Moving the group is similar to moving single objects, except now all the objects move as one. The Direct Selection tool can move or edit single objects of the group without ungrouping. To ungroup a group of objects, select Ungroup from the pull-down Arrange menu. You can use the hollow arrow tool to adjust elements within a group without having to ungroup them.

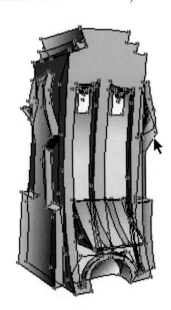

Arrange	View	Object
Repeat Transform		⌘D
Move...		⌘⇧M
Bring To Front		⌘=
Send To Back		⌘-
Group		⌘G
Ungroup		**⌘U**

David Bamundo

Comments

The concepts "perfect" and "curves" are not often used together in art studios. But when precision drawing is required, the ability to create smooth perfect curves is highly esteemed. Planning and practice are the best ways to become adept at using the Pen tool. You can use Illustrator's maze and curve templates as good practice drills to become familiar with the Pen tool.

Studio Usage

The ability to draw perfect curves is a valuable skill in numerous studio tasks. The Pen tool is used in nearly every function requiring custom illustration; a graphic artist cannot work efficiently and competitively without mastering this tool. The Pen tool is commonly used to trace templates. Matching template curves quickly and accurately is important when redrawing scanned artwork.

Related Topics

1 | Planning Ahead

When beginning a curved path, always remember to drag the curve information for the following curve. Think of the curves as bumps that are calculated from the length and direction that the control point handle is moved; drag the Pen tool in the direction of the required curve. You can also use guides and grids to align anchor points and control point handles to reproduce curves.

2 | Use the One-Third Rule

The one-third rule is used by many illustrators. Drag the control point handle one-third of the length of the line length that the curve requires. With practice, the one-third rule is applied without consciously thinking about the angles and distance dragged. Another rule to remember in planning curves is the fewer the control points, the better. More anchor points can be added later after the path is drawn.

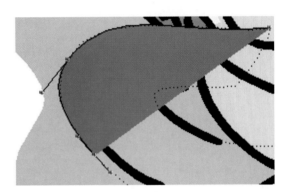

3 | Editing While Drawing

Often a curved line drawn by the Pen tool will change direction from the previously drawn curve. To change the curve direction, depress the Option key. Select the active anchor point and drag a new control point handle in the direction required for the curve. Holding the Shift key down while dragging control point handles will constrain the curve information in 45° increments. Even though the curves will be more accurate with these steps, curves should still be reviewed after drawing. If needed, edit them with the Add or Delete Anchor Point tools.

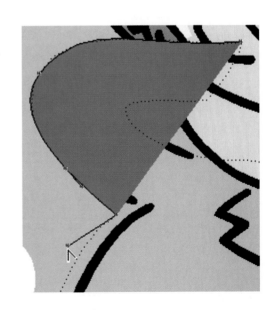

Money Magazine-Global Finance

Chris Spollen

Comments

Reflecting, also called "flopping," is a standard design tool used to add symmetry to a design or to point out a lack of symmetry in an illustration.

Studio Usage

The Reflecting tool is used to create these mirror effects, either by clicking and dragging, or by using the Reflect dialog box, which enables you to control the angle of the reflection.

Related Topics

1 | Select the Object to Reflect

First, select the object that you want to be reflected. The Reflection tool works on any object—paths, type, or placed images.

2 | Choose the Reflection Tool

Choose the Reflection tool in the Tool palette. Click anywhere on the illustration to establish an axis for the reflection. Next, either click a second time to position the reflection, or click and drag the object to the position where you want the reflected object to appear. After placing the object in the desired position, release the mouse button. The object is now reflected. To make a reflected copy of the original object, hold down the Option key while clicking a second time with the Reflection tool.

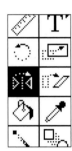

3 | Using the Reflect Dialog Box

To open the Reflect dialog box, click once on the object that you want to be reflected, while holding down the Option key. A dialog box appears, allowing you to choose the angle of reflection, as well as horizontal and vertical axes. After you have made your choices, select either the OK button or the Copy button (if you need a copy of the selected object). The object will appear reflected. You can then reflect the right dollar sign to its exact position.

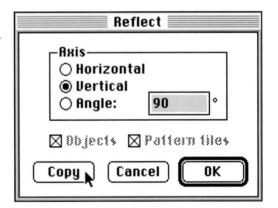

Creating Objects *Simplified Map Making*

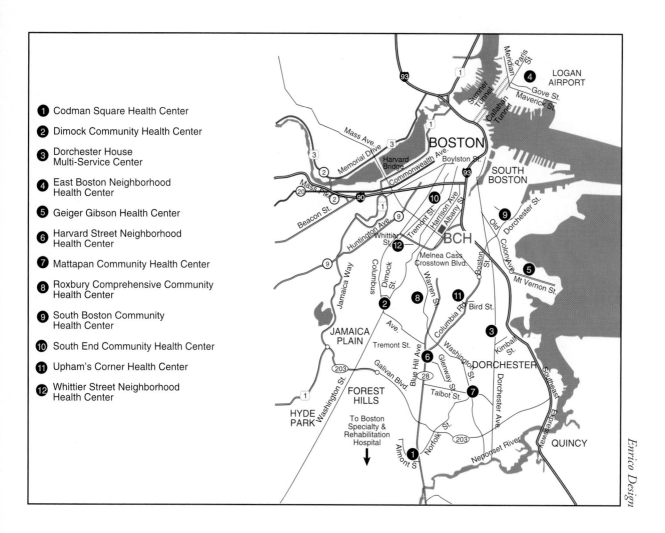

1. Codman Square Health Center
2. Dimock Community Health Center
3. Dorchester House Multi-Service Center
4. East Boston Neighborhood Health Center
5. Geiger Gibson Health Center
6. Harvard Street Neighborhood Health Center
7. Mattapan Community Health Center
8. Roxbury Comprehensive Community Health Center
9. South Boston Community Health Center
10. South End Community Health Center
11. Upham's Corner Health Center
12. Whittier Street Neighborhood Health Center

Enrico Design

Comments

Maps, by their very nature, are multilevel, multilayered artistic creations. The capabilities within Illustrator allow maximum productivity while maintaining the flexibility to make needed changes.

Studio Usage

Making maps is far easier when you make use of layering. Using separate layers for type, roads, landmarks, and symbols can speed things up considerably when it comes time to modify the drawing. Custom views work great with maps, allowing you to zoom into a specific location.

Related Topics

1 | Setting up Guides

Depending on your source material, you may be able to scan a primitive, hand-drawn map, or you can set up ruler guides to help align the elements of your map.

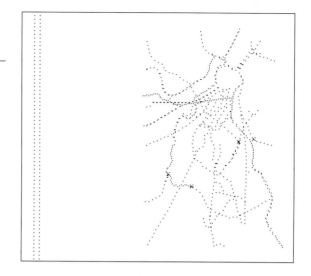

2 | Using Layers

You can use layers to help organize your work, such as separate layers for street names, major and minor roads, guides, and so on. Using the Layers palette, you can view how much work has been done for each type of element in your map making.

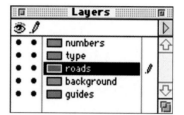

3 | Using Custom Views

Use the Custom Views setting to easily hop around to various parts of the map in progress. This can save you the tedious task of scrolling and zooming between heavily worked areas.

4 | Using the Selection Filters

The Selection filters can help select various common items within your map, such as all roads colored red, icons colored blue, all the road name type styles, and so on. When you need to change things on a global scale, this filter helps immensely.

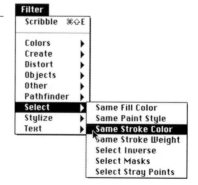

5 | Using Symbol Fonts and Libraries

To save time, you may keep a library of commonly used symbols (road signs, special numbers, etc.), or you can use dingbats or symbol fonts such as Zapf Dingbats or Carta. You might also find specialized fonts specifically created for map making; try contacting font companies for these.

Creating Objects *The Brush Tool*

David Bamundo

Comments

The Brush tool allows you to draw shapes that automatically become closed paths when you "lift" the tool by letting go of the mouse. The Brush tool can be adjusted to meet your needs. With adjustments to the width, style, and thickness controls in the Brush Preference dialog box, you can imitate most brush and ink pen strokes. Because the created object contains a fill, you can fill the brush stroke with custom blends that simulate the changing paint opacities of natural brush strokes.

Studio Usage

The Brush tool is commonly used to imitate the brushed letters of calligraphers. With proper adjustment of the Calligraphic angle in the Brush Preference dialog box, the tool does a very good job of simulating calligraphy. This tool also can imitate the ink pen tips used by sign painters and cartoonists.

Related Topics

1 | Adjusting the Stroke

Double-clicking the Brush tool activates the Brush Preferences dialog box. Use the options to customize the stroke. When using a pressure sensitive stylus and pad, select the Variable Width option. The unit is the maximum stroke thickness when the pressure stylus is pressed on the digitizing pad.

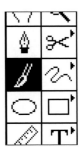

2 | Applying the Stroke

Position the tool where the stroke is to begin. Select the Brush tool and drag the path. After the tool is released, the stroke ends (unlike the Freehand tool, the path cannot be extended by reselecting). Anchor points are created along the stroke after the Brush tool is released. You do not have control of the anchor points of the Brush tool because the Freehand Tolerance General Preferences setting does not affect it.

3 | Customizing the Stroke

You can adjust the stroke to meet your needs by changing the calligraphic angle, end caps, and corner points in the Brush Preference dialog box. The angle of the Calligraphic tool represents the pen tip angle based on 0 degrees as the horizon line across the page.

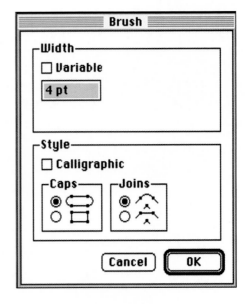

Creating Objects *The Hollow Tool*

TP Design

Comments

Selection tools usually are very general in their effect, but the Hollow Selection tool and Direct Selection tool break the hierarchy of the selected element. They enable you to select individual anchor points (buried deep in groupings and layers) without undoing layers or groupings of elements. After a selection is made, more points can be added to the object by holding down the Shift key while clicking on the element. By holding the Option key while selecting, the hierarchical groupings can be added to—from the completed path to groupings—until the entire group is selected.

Studio Usage

The Direct Selection tool is often used to redraw previously completed work. It allows changes without undoing complicated groupings and the cumbersome task of re-layering elements in Illustrator. The tool can be used for various levels of action, from changing small details by moving single points or path segments to selecting large groups in a portion of a complicated illustration. The Direct Selection tool is often used to adjust Pen tool anchor points and import clip art drawings.

Related Topics

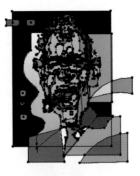

1 | Direct Selection over the Selection Tool

The Selection tool selects all parts of an element, or group of elements, which makes ungrouping necessary to work on individual parts of a multi-element illustration. With the Direct Selection tool, individual anchor points and paths can be selected for changes without ungrouping or re-layering. Selections can be made by direct selection or by clicking and dragging a marquee to select larger parts of elements. Changing the view to Artwork mode may help in selecting and adjusting control points that are not accessible in the Preview mode.

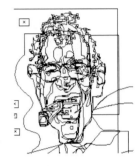

To select an entire element, click inside the element—on its fill. Click the edge of the element to select an object's path. Do not click on an anchor point because not all the anchor points will be selected. To activate the element, click on its path only.

2 | Adding to the Selection

Holding down the Shift key and selecting with the Direct tool on the desired points will add points to the selection. To deselect points, hold the Shift key and click the unwanted anchor points. To add to the selection according to element groupings, use the Option key while selecting. The first click selects the individual point; the second click selects the entire path of the first point. Subsequent clicks will select the group containing the path, adding to the next group's level with each click.

3 | Moving with the Direct Selection Tool

A selection can be moved by dragging. Holding the Shift key down will constrain the object to a vertical or horizontal movement. The angle of constraint (which by default is set to vertical, diagonal, and horizontal) can be changed by adjusting the values in the General Preferences dialog box (for example you can "shift" the entire drawing "universe" if you need to). If you hold down the Option key while dragging, you can create clones of the original object along the lines of constraint.

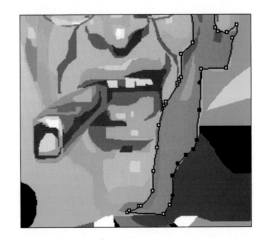

Creating Objects *The Pen Tool*

Charles Akins

Comments

The Pen tool creates smooth curve lines with few anchor points. Using the PostScript® language and mathematical formula, the Pen tool creates smooth adjustable curves between two anchor points. The ability to draw smooth Bézier curves on the computer brought computer drawing programs out of the science labs and into the art studios.

Studio Usage

As with any instrument, mastery of the Pen tool takes time and practice. After you become familiar with the tool, you can use it to create illustrations rivaling those done with traditional art tools. Very few computer-based illustrations are done without the use of a Pen tool and Bézier curves. Some bitmap-based paint programs include a Pen tool layer where PostScript line information can be added to illustrations. The Pen tool enables you to draw complicated lines with far fewer anchor points than the Freehand tool requires. Fewer anchor points improve the ability to edit the curve, print it, and store it as a smaller file.

Related Topics

1 | Drawing Straight Lines

Click the Pen tool on the starting point and release. Move the Pen tool into position for the second anchor point and repeat until the line is completed. By holding down the Shift key, you can constrain the anchor points to right angles in 45° increments. Click the original anchor point to close the path and to create a closed element. To create an open line path, hold down the Command key and click away from the line segment or change the tool.

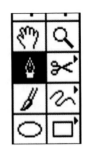 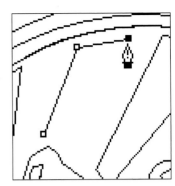

2 | Drawing Curved Lines

Click the mouse in position for the first anchor point. Before releasing, drag the mouse in the direction of the desired curve (dragging about one-third of the desired curve height works well). Then click the mouse where the second anchor point is required and drag in the direction of the next curve. In some instances, changing the direction of a curve cannot be done without distorting the previous curve; concentrate on getting the previous curve correct and releasing the mouse button.

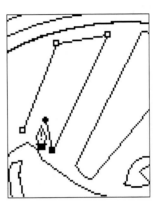 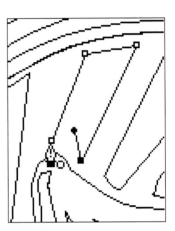

To set the direction for the next curve without affecting the previous curve, deselect the Option button and click and drag a new control handle in the appropriate direction. No matter how familiar you are with the Pen tool, you should review the finished path for smoothness. Use the curve control handles and move the anchor points to adjust the curves as required.

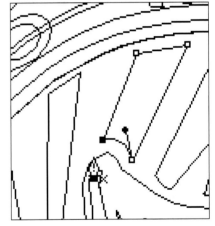

3 | Efficient Use of the Curve Tool

You should strive to use as few anchor points as possible. They can be added later with the Add Anchor Point tool. The fewer the anchor points, the smaller the file size, which simplifies all aspects of working with the file. Printing complicated line paths can cause printing delays and problems at service bureaus, resulting in larger service bureau bills.

4 | Color Attributes

Open paths always fill from one open end point to another open end point; this can result in good or bad effects. Open line segments usually have no fill attribute, unless a special effect is desired. Closed paths fill with the same results as do other closed elements by using solid, blended, or patterned fills.

Julie Pace

Comments

The Freehand tool reacts to the movements and speed of the Drawing tool. The slower the drawing tool is moved, the more precise the created path will be. All adjustments made to the tolerance and tool speed should be based on the desired style of the finished illustration. Adjusting the Freehand tolerance controls before starting a freehand drawing can make the drawn path either rougher or smoother than the path dragged by the Drawing tool.

Studio Usage

By adjusting the Freehand tool's characteristics, it can be customized for personal working habits and job requirements. The customized tool is used in studios for creating cartoons, manual tracing of templates, and creating masks for Photoshop.

Related Topics

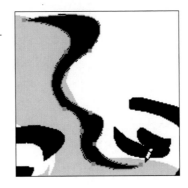

1 | Planning the Drawing

Coordinating screen magnification and final drawing size can simplify what might otherwise be a complicated drawing process. Art board magnification is relative to mouse movement. A half-inch mouse pad movement at two different screen magnifications creates two different length paths. A smooth path can be ruined by dragging off the mouse pad or running out of drawing board space. By adjusting the art board magnification to the planned illustration, you can greatly ease production.

2 | Accuracy

Adjusting the Freehand tolerance in the General Preferences dialog box can greatly increase, or reduce, the number of anchor points in the element. The default setting is two; the higher the setting, the fewer the number of anchor points. When adjusting the tolerance, keep in mind that the more anchor points, the larger the file, making it slower to work with and slower to print.

3 | Drawing Straight Lines

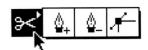

Drawing straight lines is made easier by placing guide lines where straight lines are required before beginning. The Freehand tool also can add to, and combine with, previously drawn Pen tool paths. To draw a straight path without changing tools, depress the Command key to change to the Erase tool. Instead of dragging backward over a drawn path to erase the line, drag forward with the Command key and release it when you reach the end of the straight line that you want drawn.

4 | Cleanup

After a drawing is finished, take time for cleanup—adjust the anchor points with the selection of the Add or Delete Anchor Point tools.

Creating Objects *Using Multiple Windows*

Bill Frampton

Comments

With several views and magnifications of the same illustration available at a glance, you can quickly distinguish relationships of elements and see how changes made to them look at different magnifications. Although many windows are available, there is only one source file. Regardless of which window is used when saving, work is saved to the original file.

In earlier versions of Illustrator, all work had to be done in Artwork view. The view was then switched to Preview mode for onscreen proofing. At that time, multiple windows were one way of previewing work as it was being drawn. With Illustrator 5.5, drawing can be done in the Preview view.

Studio Usage

The New Window command from the Window menu is still used today to preview work, but in more varied ways. In complicated illustrations, it is faster to work in Artwork view and to have a second window for viewing the Preview view. The window in the Preview mode also can be used to view different magnifications of the illustration. While a detailed view is being worked on in the Artwork mode, a Preview can be watched in a second window. It's also useful to work in Artwork view when working with elements close together in patterns, blends, and solids because the colors do not interfere with object selection.

Related Topics

1 | Creating a Second Window

With the current window active, select New Window under the Window pull-down menu. The new window is identical to the original window's size and view. Changes to the view in individual windows do not affect any other window. Only the changes made to the illustration are updated in all the other windows.

2 | Moving the New Window

Using the gray title bar, click and drag the new window into position. Resize the window appropriately so that both windows are visible.

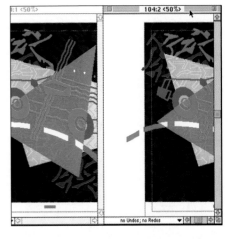

3 | Working in Alternate Windows

All changes done in any of the file windows will be updated in the other windows. In the example, the work is done in an Artwork view window to ease the object selection process; working in the Preview mode may be difficult if you need to select objects that are hidden by color fills. Notice how elements otherwise hidden by color fills are accessible in the Artwork mode.

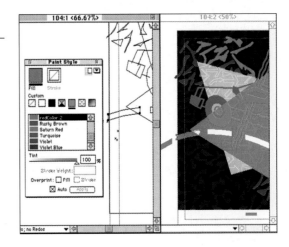

4 | More Windows

You are not limited to working with two windows. Application, RAM, and monitor size are the only limits to the number of windows that you can use. In the example, the working window is the Artwork view; the second window is used to preview color work; and the third window is used to view the changes in relation to the completed picture.

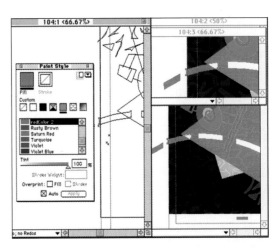

Creating Objects *Using Temporary Guides*

Chris Spollen

Comments

Guides do not have to be permanently placed on a document page. Guides can be moved, copied, cut, converted, and deleted as required.

Studio Usage

Temporary guides aid in drawing repeated elements and can be created by converting an object or path. Illustrations that contain custom fonts, architectural elements, and drafting elements use temporary guides.

Related Topics

1 | Recognizing Repeating Shapes

Before beginning a project, assess which work- and time-saving tools can be used in the drawing and determine the processes required to complete the drawing. This is the stage where repeating elements are recognized and guides and temporary guides are created and set.

2 | Placing Guides and Drawing

Before you begin to draw, place the ruler guides, working guides, and temporary guides. Convert to guides (⌘-5). Remember to use the ruler guides and zero point to position permanent and temporary guides. Make sure that the guides are Locked (⌘-7) under the Guides options in the Object pull-down menu.

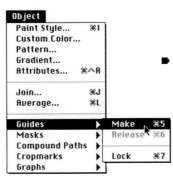

3 | Moving Temporary Guides

To move a temporary guide, activate the Selection tool and depress the Control key followed by the Shift key. You can now move guides by selecting and dragging with the mouse. If you hold down the Option key, the guide is duplicated in the new position. This method enables only one guide to be moved at a time. Select Lock (⌘-7 under the Guides options in the Object pull-down menu) toggles between locked and unlocked guides. Unlocked guides can be moved as ordinary objects.

4 | Releasing and Erasing Guides

Guides may be removed after the illustration is completed. Temporary and working guides can be hidden under the View pull-down menu: Hide Guides to remove; Show Guides to view. To permanently remove guides, first unlock the guides (⌘-7). Then select Release Guides (⌘-6) under the Object pull-down menu and delete the guides after they are converted to paths.

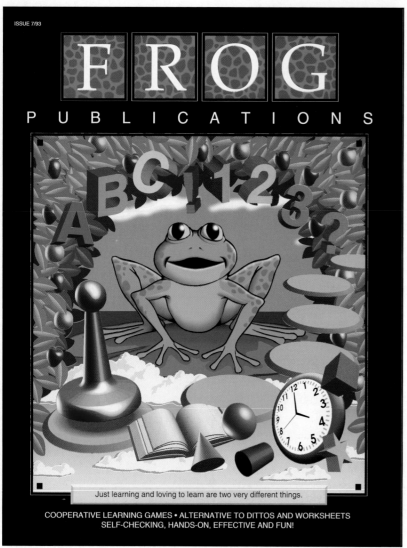

ISSUE 7/93

FROG
P U B L I C A T I O N S

Just learning and loving to learn are two very different things.

COOPERATIVE LEARNING GAMES • ALTERNATIVE TO DITTOS AND WORKSHEETS
SELF-CHECKING, HANDS-ON, EFFECTIVE AND FUN!

Frog Publications

Comments

Dimensions is a useful "3-D" program from Adobe. Dimensions creates simple three-dimensional renderings by calculating changing perspective and angles from one- or two-dimensional objects created in Illustrator. Dimensions also enhances lighting and surface characteristics to your specifications.

Because drawings created with Dimensions use the same stroke and fill techniques as Illustrator, Dimensions' files can be enhanced and further manipulated in Illustrator.

Studio Usage

Raised letters, embossing techniques, logos, and other artwork often benefit from the illusion of depth. Picture a long street lined with tall buildings; you can see many shapes that could be simulated using this solution—the signs, buildings, overhangs, even the flag poles.

Related Topics

1 | Art for Extruding

When creating art for Dimensions, careful planning can smooth the art's conversion to three-dimensional art. For Illustrator files that use text, the width and height are already established and require the third dimension of extrusion to add depth; a major concern is avoiding intersecting loops in the two-dimensional Illustrator text. Elements with compound paths and other sharp angles will work, but the results are unexpected. In some cases of intersecting paths, it is best to convert the objects separately and combine them after rendering.

2 | Art for Revolving

It is easier to create a symmetrical object in Dimensions by using a guideline to mark the pivot point for a curved stroke. Convert the vertical pivot line into a guide (⌘-5) and then draw the curved stroke using the guideline as a reference. Revolving an object in Dimensions is more consistent if the curved stroke is drawn to the right of the center guideline. The stroke's anchor points can be further edited in Dimensions, if necessary.

3 | Coloring

The element's paint characteristics can be selected in Illustrator before exporting to Dimensions, but paint characteristics can be altered again later in Dimensions. You should avoid pattern fills, bitmap fills, and gradient fills when working with Dimensions. The color should not be left as black because Dimensions builds its shading blends by adding blacks. If a black-shaded object is the goal, color it gray before rendering.

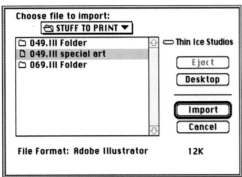

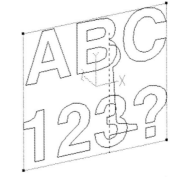

4 | Transferring the Image from Illustrator to Dimensions

There are two ways that you can move an object (or group of objects) from Illustrator to Dimensions. The first way is by using the clipboard; simply copy (or cut) and paste the desired object from one to another. The second approach is by saving the illustrator file in EPS format; you make it accessible to Dimensions from the standard File/Open dialog box. You also can "save as EPS" for exporting to programs like Photoshop—where you can truly "fine-tune" the look and feel of the object.

Ned Shaw

Comments

Controlling the size of your Illustrator files has a great effect on the performance of your system. Planning your design and format carefully can lead to faster previews and smaller files that print much faster.

Studio Usage

To place your illustrations in another program and keep all the defined color elements accurate, you need to save in EPS format. Why make the file bigger than it needs to be? The lower the EPS preview's bit depth, the smaller the final file will be.

Related Topics

1 Determine Your Final Destination

First, determine where you are going to use your Illustrator document. If the illustration is going to be used in another program, you will need to save it in EPS or Acrobat PDF format. If the illustration is going to someone who doesn't have Illustrator, or it is going cross-platform (PC or UNIX), the PDF format is best. Otherwise, save the document in Illustrator format.

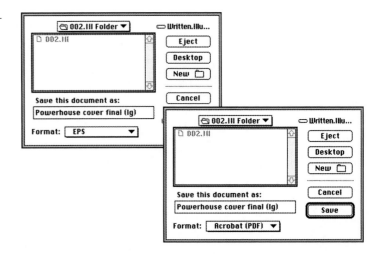

2 Illustrator Formats

If you are going to print the illustration directly from the program, there is no need to save the document in EPS format; instead, save the document in Illustrator 5 format. This format is the smallest, by far. No EPS code is generated, and gradients stay in their native format. Saving a document in older Illustrator formats is helpful only when you need to export the document into Photoshop 2.5, or when you are sending the illustration to someone who has an older version of Illustrator—beware of gradients getting oversimplified, in this case.

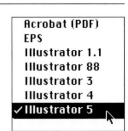

3 EPS Formats

If you need to separate the illustration using Adobe Separator, you can save the document in EPS format with no preview; you will get a bounding box instead of a preview. Using 1-bit preview is best if you are placing the illustration in a page-layout program; this will allow you to see, crop, and size the illustration, while allowing fairly quick screen redraws and keeping the file size down somewhat. Selecting 8-bit preview is recommended only when you must see the preview in color in your page-layout program; an 8-bit preview can sometimes exceed the file size of the whole illustration!

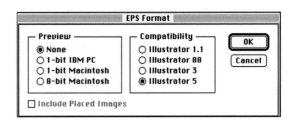

Do not save your EPS illustration any larger than it will appear in the final piece; larger illustrations require larger previews, which require larger files.

Make sure that the Include Placed Images check box is off when saving in EPS format; this will reduce your file size immensely if there are any placed images.

4 Acrobat PDF Format

When crossing platforms or when special fonts and placed images are required for the file to print properly, saving your document in Acrobat PDF format is your best bet. The PDF format also has built-in compression, which can help decrease the file size by as much as 50%.

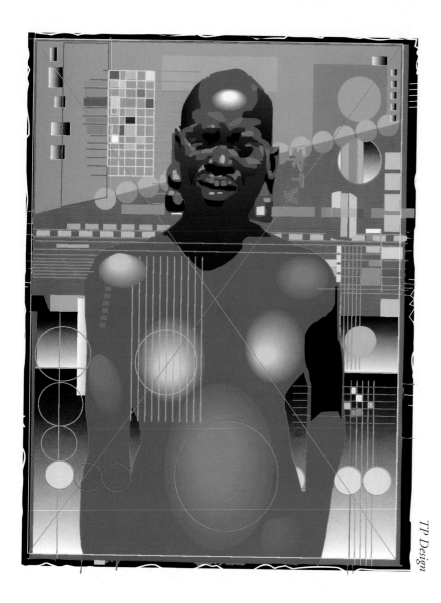

TP Design

Comments

You may find that you cannot achieve your complete creative vision by using only one program. You often need to create an element in one program and place it into a design being executed in another application. While Illustrator can serve as an excellent page layout program, achieving photographic effects can best be done in a program like Photoshop and subsequently imported as an EPS image.

Studio Usage

Encapsulated Postscript is a file format available in most applications, either as a Save As option or as a Print File to Disk option within a program's Print dialog box. The file format is extremely "portable" and can be read by almost any application with the capability to "import" or "place" files created in drawing or painting programs. You can even use EPS as a method of moving files from one platform to another—for example, from a Macintosh to a Windows system.

Related Topics

1 | Save the Placed Image in EPS Format

From within the creator application, save (or print) your file to an EPS disk file. If the program provides an "include preview" option, use it. This option generates a low-resolution "screen image" that will facilitate speedy display when the file has been import-ed into Illustrator.

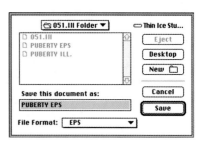

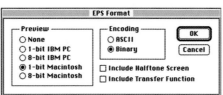

2 | Importing EPS Files

To import an EPS file into your illustration, select the Place Art command under the File menu. An Open dialog box appears, allowing you to select the EPS file that you want to import. Click OK and your file will appear.

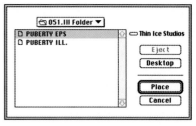

3 | Manipulating EPS Files

You can manipulate the placed images in your file like any other objects; remember that resizing a Photoshop or other bitmap-type image may result in a loss of quality. Initially, you should create a bitmap image at the size and resolution needed for the final illustration.

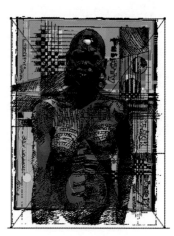

4 | Saving the Illustration

If Illustrator is the final destination for your placed images, save your Illustrator document in Illustrator format. If you are going to use Adobe Separator, save the file in EPS format with no preview option (this will help save memory, and you really don't need the preview for the separation process). If you need to place the file in a page-layout program, you may want to consider using Adobe Acrobat as the preferred format.

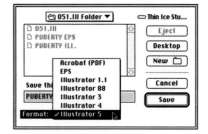

5 | Photoshop Trick

If you need to edit a placed Photoshop image while in Illustrator, Option-double-click on the image; this will open the placed image in Photoshop, where you can edit it as needed. When you're done with your edits, the links between files will be updated automatically.

LIVE AT THE
CAFE BOHEMIA

Mike Dowdy

Comments

Many bitmap-type images, such as those generated in Adobe Photoshop, can reach gigantic proportions (upwards of 100 megabytes). By using OPI (Open Prepress Interface) to create low-resolution versions of the same file, you can manipulate these smaller images and avoid memory, space, and speed problems and still apply cropping and scaling as needed.

Studio Usage

The quality of most OPI files is good enough for a client to proof the material. The original large file images can replace the smaller ones later in the prepress process. You can rotate and crop, but not retouch these for position only (FPOs).

Related Topics

1 | True OPI Files

A true OPI usually is generated at a prepress company or service bureau where high-resolution scans, color correction, and so on, are applied to the scanned image. At that time, a low-resolution version is generated, with links to the high-resolution version. You can use these "low-res" files from the service bureau to lay out your Illustrator document. When you send the final file back to the service bureau, the prepress program that created the low-res versions of your scans will automatically print your file with the "high-res" versions.

2 | Using DCS as an OPI Creator

If you prefer to modify your own scans, create your own Photoshop art from scratch, or simply don't have the budget to use true OPI, you can use the Desktop Color Separations (DCS) option in Photoshop. A DCS file consists of a master, low-res file that you can place in Illustrator, plus four hi-res files (one for each of the four process colors). First, you must save the Photoshop file in EPS format. When the second Save dialog box appears, a section devoted to DCS will appear, where you can choose the appropriate options, such as the resolution of the master file. Usually, you shouldn't need a resolution higher than your screen resolution, but if you do, you can change it in the Master Resolution field. You can then place the master image into Illustrator. Remember to include the four "high-res" files and the master "low-res" file when you send the file to be printed.

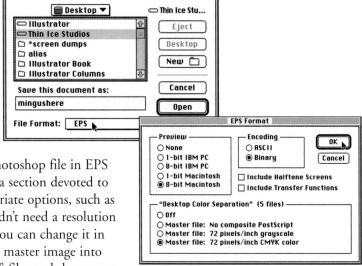

3 | Creating Your Own OPI Files

Generally, creating your own OPI files is done as a last resort, or if DCS is not available. You can create a "low-res" file by first making a copy of the "high-res" file and resampling the file down to screen resolution (or whatever is needed). Save this file in EPS format and place it into Illustrator. When it is time to send the file to the service bureau, instruct them to swap the "low-res" version in the illustration for the "high-res" version on a separate disk (they may charge you extra for this service). Check the output proof to make sure that the "high-res" version was used.

François Robert

Comments

A mask is an electronic "outline" that surrounds the visible portion of an image and cuts out (sort of like a cookie cutter) the shape from the background.

Studio Usage

You need masks in almost any complex drawing. In this example, they are used to knock out the background so that the leaf prints properly. You can also use masks to create a silhouette and drop it into a shaded or screened background.

Related Topics

1 | Select the Objects

First, select the objects that you want to mask, including the object that you want to use for the mask. Make sure that the mask object is the topmost object because the program will turn that object into the mask.

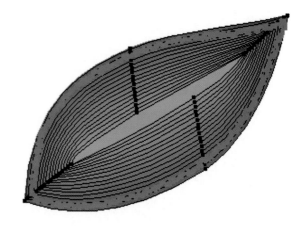

2 | Use the Mask Command

Go to the Objects menu in the Masks submenu and choose Make. The topmost object will lose its paint attributes and become the mask, while the objects underneath will be masked.

3 | Tips and Tricks

To remove an object from a mask, select the object and cut (⌘-X). Then paste the object in front of (or behind) the masked group. To add an object to the mask, cut the object and paste it in front of (or behind) an object within the masked group. To create a complex mask (more than one object working as a mask), compound the mask object before you use the Mask command.

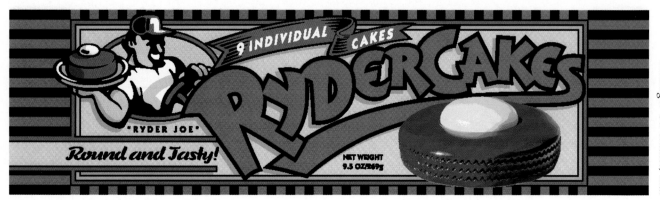

Midnight Oil Studios, Ltd.

Comments

It is possible to place an image into one program's document and then place the combined image into a second program's document for use by a third program. This "nesting" is not the ideal environment for smooth work flow.

Studio Usage

A job may call for combining elements in a manner that can be described as "nesting." A photograph manipulated in an illustration program and ultimately placed into a page layout may cause delays in printing. This may, however, be the only way to get a precise alignment for such a placed image.

Related Topics

1 | Create the Placed Images

Create the placed images in their respective programs and assemble them into a file that will support the EPS format (the ability to Save As an EPS file). Be sure that you have (1) the original images available on your system; and (2) the placed images folded into the assembled art.

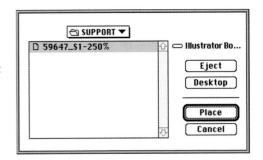

2 | Place the Nested Image into Adobe Illustrator

Save the assembled document in the EPS file format and use the Place Art command (in the File menu) to bring this file into Illustrator. You may position, layer, and treat the placed image as if it were any other object.

3 | Coloring

If you are using another drawing program to create the placed image, be sure that the file does not contain any custom colors. This could cause problems when separations are required. All custom colors must be converted to CMYK before saving an image or illustration as an EPS file.

David Barnundo

Comments

A file's resolution primarily depends on the file type. Some file types have a fixed resolution (such as Paint and Tiff), while other file types have an adjustable resolution for resizing (such as EPS graphics).

Bitmap-based files (Paint and Tiff) are limited in resolution by the original bit size; as a bitmap graphic is enlarged, the resolution goes *down*. Encapsulated PostScript (EPS) files create images through mathematical curves. Resolution of PostScript files is only limited by the resolution of the output device. The only time an EPS file becomes fixed for resizing is when it is packaged as a PostScript file for downloading to a printer.

Studio Usage

Because of the many file types used in the work environment, you should know the difference between the types when concerned about resolution, resizing, and printing. When working with PICT, PAINT, and TIFF files, resizing is limited to reduction only (unless a bitmapped special effect is the goal). Resolution of bitmapped images increases when sizes are reduced, but resolution quickly becomes distorted when the image size is increased. Placed EPS Illustrator files can be scaled before printing without losing the smooth curves of the original file size. An image's output resolution is primarily based on its original resolution; whether a 72 dpi graphic is printed on a 300 dpi laser printer or a 2400 dpi imagesetter, the printer only has 72 dpi of information to create a printed image.

Related Topics

Illustrator as a
Page Layout Program   127

1 | Setting the File Resolution

Before beginning an illustration, set the final print resolution in the Document Setup dialog box. For imagesetting, 1270 dpi is common, but you should check with the printer if you are not doing your own imagesetting. Changing the resolution only adjusts the resolution of objects drawn after setting the resolution. To change the resolution of existing objects, use the output resolution in the Attributes dialog box (⌘-Shift-A) under the Objects pull-down menu.

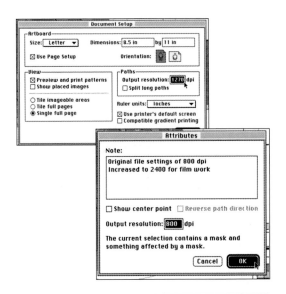

2 | Working with Imported Files

PICT files that are placed into Illustrator lose their resolution when they are enlarged. To use the files at a larger size, the file should be converted to Illustrator format with Adobe Streamline, autotraced in Illustrator, or redrawn manually. EPS files placed into Illustrator can be scaled up or down without loss of detail.

3 | Resizing Illustrator EPS Files

Scaling objects while in Illustrator causes no loss of resolution. Resolution problems result after exporting the file to a page layout application. To export the file as an EPS file, use the Save As command under the File pull-down menu. In the Formats box, scroll up to select EPS. To save as a PICT file, hold the Option key down while copying to the clipboard. Then you can place the file into the application that requires PICT files.

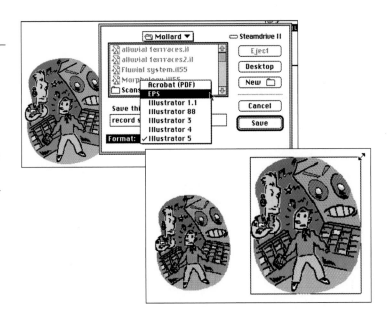

4 | Previewing Exported EPS Files

Notice that the EPS file size is much larger than the version that is saved in Illustrator. The saved version includes a version of the file for previewing in a page layout application. Without a preview, the file will appear as a block with a cross that passes through diagonal corner points. A preview can also be created for exporting to Windows in the Preview box.

Ned Shaw

Comments

PostScript® graphics are formed with lines and filled shapes to create objects. Converting a filled graphic to a silhouette by changing its line stroke and fill characteristics is a simple task. Taken a step further, the silhouette (or outline) can become a mask for multiple images, or it can be repeated over and over in the design.

Studio Usage

A silhouette is commonly used to frame a product within itself. Depending on the image, the silhouette is created by using the Duplicate command or by tracing a PICT image or template. The silhouette can be manipulated in position, scale, fills, and layering just like any graphic element.

Related Topics

1 | Creating from a Photoshop File

A selected scan, paint, or clip art file can generate an outline in Photoshop for use as a silhouette in Illustrator. Use the Pen, Lasso, or Marquee tool to trace around the object and save the trace's path. Go to the Export submenu (under the File menu) and choose Paths to Illustrator. A Save dialog box appears, allowing you to name the trace file and choose its location.

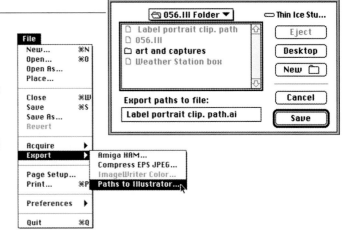

2 | Positioning and Coloring the Silhouette

The new element can be colored like any other object. If needed, move the colored object into its page and layer position. Any other necessary modifications may also be done at this time.

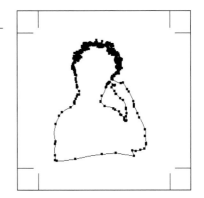

3 | Using a Silhouette as a Mask

Converting a silhouette to a mask creates a detailed mask similar in shape to the original image. First, position the mask object over the object(s) you want to mask; select all the affected elements. The mask object must be layered *above* the other objects! Choose Make Mask from the Objects menu. The topmost object becomes a mask, with all other selected objects masked out. Group the mask set (⌘-G) to avoid accidentally moving an object out-of-mask.

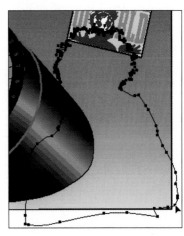

TP Design

Comments

Creating a single document using elements from many different documents (with all their different formats) can relieve many headaches in design and help speed up the production and proofing process of an illustration.

Studio Usage

Adobe Acrobat solves many problems, especially when dealing with service bureaus. You can have your fonts, images, and illustration all in one file package—compressed and ready to print. The service bureau or receiving person needs only the Acrobat Reader to open, read, and print the files in the package. Sharing and distributing documents becomes much easier because the original programs, fonts, or files are not needed to view or print the documents.

Related Topics

1 | Save the Document in EPS Format

First, retrieve the document that contains the nested EPS (Encapsulated PostScript) files. A nested EPS file is an image that was placed into another program that was then placed into a third program. Make sure that this document is saved in EPS format; Acrobat does not recognize any other formats.

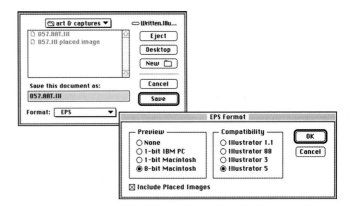

2 | Using the Acrobat Distiller

After launching Acrobat Distiller, a dialog box appears, allowing you to choose the document(s) that you want to convert. You also can set the program's working preferences (such as compression for placed images, which fonts to include, and so on). The Distiller will convert and compress the selected file(s) and save them into a PDF (Portable Document Format) document.

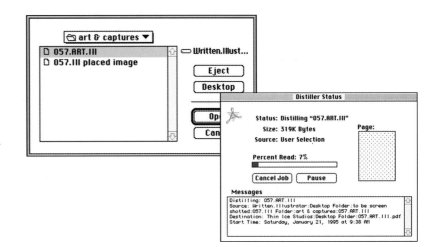

3 | Placing the PDF File into Illustrator

Nested files in PDF format are brought into Illustrator as if they were any other placed images. Select Place Art from the File menu to import a PDF file. After the dialog box appears, select the desired PDF file. If the PDF document has more than one page, another dialog box appears, allowing you to select any other page(s). After all the desired files have been placed, save your document in either EPS, PDF, or Illustrator format.

Design Smiths

Comments

Illustrator, as the name implies, is an illustration program. Having the ability to place your illustrations (via the EPS format) in a page-layout program greatly enhances the capabilities of both programs.

Studio Usage

The EPS (Encapsulated PostScript) format is the most common format used in the desktop publishing world, and it is the only format that Illustrator supports and exports. Being able to control not only the format that Illustrator exports in, but also the file size of the preview (not in dimensions, but in file size) is one of Illustrator's greatest features.

Related Topics

1 Exporting to Another Program

When you prepare artwork that will be used in another program, such as QuarkXPress or PageMaker, you will need to save the illustration in EPS (Encapsulated PostScript) format. Select the Save As command in the File menu. Choose the EPS file option under the file name and click Save. A second dialog box appears, allowing you to select the preview options. "No preview" means that no preview will appear when the EPS file is placed in another document. One-bit preview creates a black-and-white preview (similar to an old Mac's screen) into the EPS file, allowing you to see the placed image in the target application. Eight-bit preview creates a 256 color preview. One-bit IBM is for page layout programs used on PC compatibles. After you make your choices, click OK and then Save. Now any application that can place an EPS file into it will be able to use it.

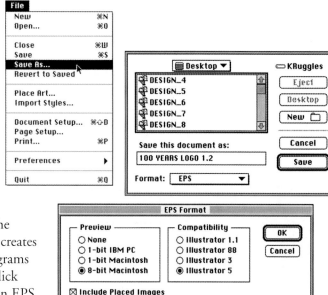

2 Importing EPS Files into Illustrator

To import an EPS file into Illustrator, select the Place Art command in the File menu. An Open dialog box appears, allowing you to select the EPS art file. The EPS art will appear on the page with whichever EPS preview attributes were selected for it. When saving the document in the EPS format, you have the option of "folding" or putting the placed image(s) into the Illustrator file by clicking the Include Placed Images check box.

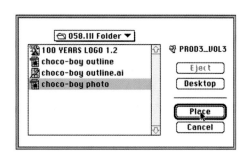

3 Tips and Tricks

Never place EPS images more than one deep in a document. (For example, don't create an image in Illustrator; place it in PageMaker; take the PageMaker document into FreeHand; and so on.) This creates major headaches for service bureaus and printers because the imagesetter must launch each program separately for each image in order to retrieve all the colors in the "folded" document. It's much better to place each image separately into one final document.

If you only need a simple black-and-white preview for the placed EPS file in a page layout program, use it! Color previews can sometimes double or even triple the illustration's file size, which yields longer print times and slower screen redraws.

Lithographic Issues *Determining a Spread or Choke*

David Bamundo

Comments

Spreads and chokes determine the way that colors bleed into each other. They also allow for more accurate printing. A trap is needed if a light colored ink comes in contact with a darker colored ink during the printing process. A spread trap is needed if a light colored object is surrounded by a darker color; a choke trap is needed if an object is surrounded by a lighter color.

Studio Usage

Spreads and chokes are a way of life in prepress shops. For designers on a budget, learning to apply these traps can result in better printing jobs and more satisfied clients.

Related Topics

1 | Examine Your Document

First, examine your document for objects that will need to be trapped. A trap is needed if a light color comes in contact with a darker color. Color on a white background and reverse type on a solid background do not need to be trapped. For all objects that need to be trapped, you can make a notation in the Attributes dialog box (⌘-Control-A). This way, you can keep track of what has been trapped and what needs to be trapped.

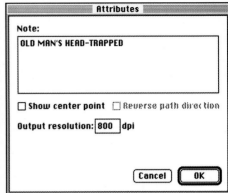

2 | Determining a Spread

A spread is necessary if a light-colored object is surrounded by a darker color. The spread will enlarge the lighter color so that it will "spread" into the darker color. To spread the color, first make sure that the Overprint box is turned off for the object. Copy the light-colored object (⌘-C) and paste the copy behind the object (⌘-B). Set the stroke weight on the object to twice the trap width that your printer recommends; only the outside half of the stroke will show. Color the stroke with the fill color (if needed, dilute the color 50%) and turn the Overprint check box on. Your spread trap is now finished.

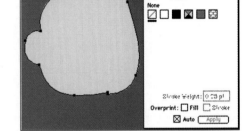

3 | Determining a Choke

A choke is needed if an object is surrounded by a lighter color. The "choke" allows the lighter color to slide under the object, eliminating any problems with gaps. To create a choke, first make sure that the Overprint box is on and copy the object (⌘-C). Paste the copy behind the object (⌘-B). Open the Paint Style palette and set the stroke to the surrounding color (if needed, dilute the color 50%), with twice the trap width that your printer recommends. (Only the inside half of the stroke is affected.) Turn the overprint for the fill off, and turn it on for the stroke. Your choke trap is now finished.

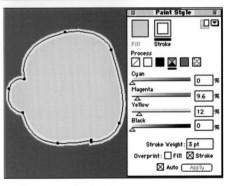

You should not perform any trapping until you are ready to print your file. For viewing purposes, the traps in the screen shots are much larger than normal.

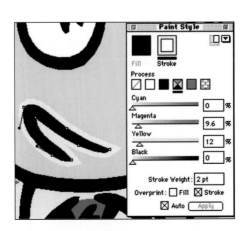

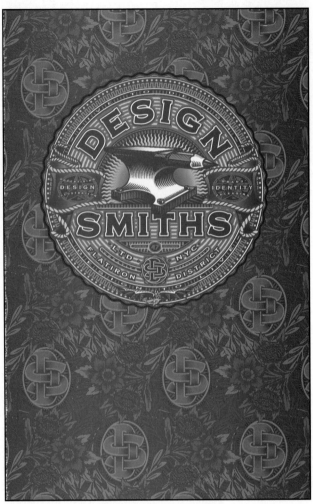

Design Smiths

Comments

Flexographic printing is a common printing technique used for packaging. This printing technique enables you to print on surfaces that would be impossible to print on with a standard offset press, and allows for greater flexibility with both product design and shapes.

Studio Usage

Mechanical preparation of artwork for flexographic printing has its own peculiarities, due to the nature of the process itself.

Related Topics

1 | What Is Flexography?

The process utilizes a rubber plate that will stretch and flex to fit onto the object being printed. The press uses a flexible planetary drum (similar to an offset press) to hold the rubber plate in place. Artwork is distorted, allowing the rubber plate to stretch in one direction (typically 3-5%), which causes the artwork to distort. Predistorting the artwork allows the work to appear corrected when printed.

2 | Distorting Your Artwork for Flexography

Select the artwork only—do not select any register or crop marks. Distort the artwork using the Scale tool dialog box. Choose the nonlinear setting and set the horizontal scale to 90–99% (different presses require different amounts of distortion—check with your printer before doing this). Do not set the vertical scale to anything other than 100%. When you have set the percentages, click OK and save the changes. The artwork should now appear somewhat compressed and should work for flexographic printing. Good communication with your prepress site is vital in this specialized process.

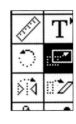

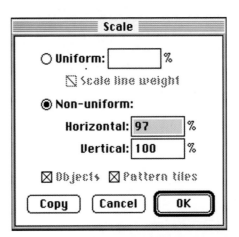

Charles Akins

Comments

Drop shadows are used to create a "3D" effect, adding a sense of depth to an illustration. Shadows help to define that depth by defining the direction of the light source.

Studio Usage

Drop shadows are used as special effects—drawing attention to an item in an illustration, advertisement, or design.

Related Topics

1 | Select the Item

Select the object where you want to create a drop shadow. For the Drop Shadow filter to work, an object must be a path. If the object is type, see Step 3.

2 | Use the Drop Shadow Filter

Select the Drop Shadow filter from the Stylize submenu located in the Filter menu. A dialog box appears, asking you to choose the direction of the drop shadow, as well as the intensity and distance. After you have made your choices, click OK. The drop shadow will appear behind the object that you originally selected, grouped with the original object.

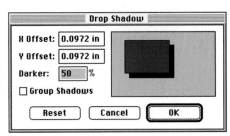

3 | An Alternate Way to Make Drop Shadows

Another way to make a drop shadow is to select the object (or type), copy it (⌘-C), and paste a copy behind the selected object (⌘-B). Then move the pasted object with the Move command (⌘-Shift-M) or with the cursor. Finally, color the object with the desired color.

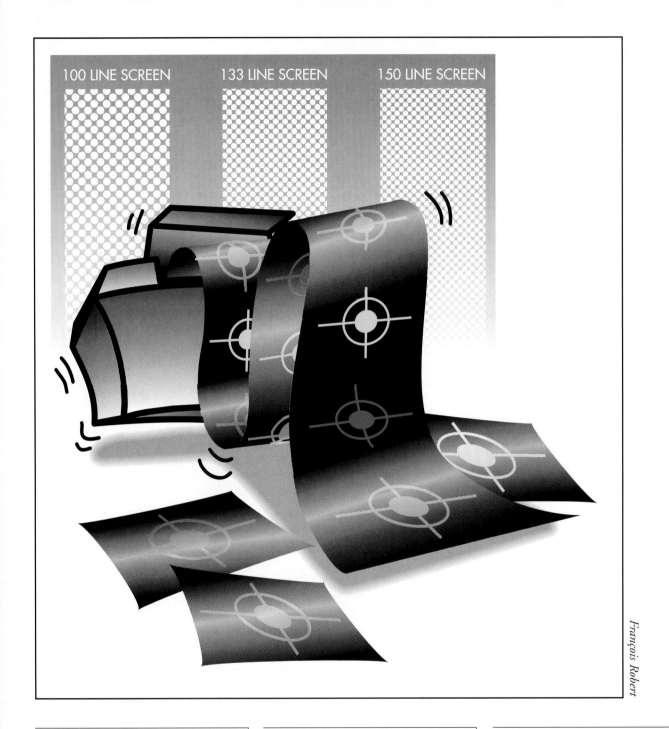

100 LINE SCREEN   133 LINE SCREEN   150 LINE SCREEN

François Robert

Comments

Changing the attributes available in a Postscript Printer Description (PPD) file causes a printer or image-setter to produce images that a normal PPD file cannot produce.

Studio Usage

This tip is especially useful in screen-printing situations that call for very low-resolution screens (typically 30-55 lpi). Being able to modify the PPD file greatly simplifies the setup of a document in Adobe Separator, a program that controls the printing of document color separations.

Related Topics

Working with Adobe Separator   65

1 | Select the PPD File to Modify

First, select the PPD (Postscript Printer Description) file that you need to modify. Make a copy of the file before modifying; it is difficult to return a file to its original state. Rename the copy with a descriptor, like "MOD," "45lpi," or symbols, so that you know the difference when you select the PPD file in Separator.

2 | Modify the PPD File

To modify the PPD file, open it in a word processing program. The file is read as text only, and it opens as a bunch of Postscript strings that make no grammatical sense. Scroll to the section that you need to modify and select it. If you want to add an extra set of separation capabilities, copy that section and paste it after the section you copied. Next, reselect the copied section. Open the word processor's search-and-replace function and type into the search area the parts that you want to change (lpi/dpi settings, page sizes, screen angles, etc.). In the replace area, type in the new values that you want to insert. Most word processors allow you to make changes to only the selected text; selecting the text beforehand keeps you from making changes to parts of the PPD that you don't need changed. After you have finished making your changes, save the document in text-only format and close the document.

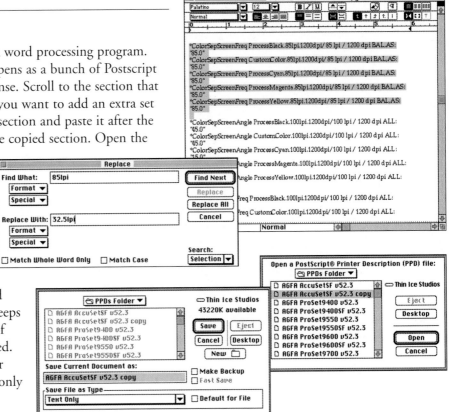

3 | Using the Modified PPD File

To use the modified PPD file with Adobe Separator, select the Open PPD button, located near the top right of the Separator window. Scroll to the modified PPD file and select it. Separator will now load the file, and your modified PPD settings will become available.

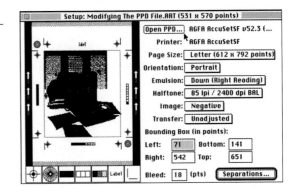

4 | If You Don't Have a Word Processing Program

If you do not own a word processing program, you can still modify the PPD file in two ways: using TeachText or opening the PPD as a text document in Adobe Illustrator. TeachText is truly the difficult alternative, as it has no search-and-replace function. Illustrator, on the other hand, has that function in its Find Text filter. Just remember to enclose the PPD text inside a text box (preferably large) before importing the file. After you have modified the file, use the Export filter to export the text file.

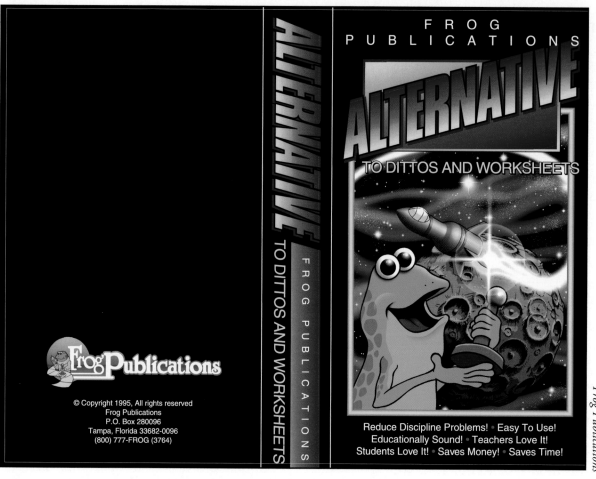

Comments

"Rich black" is black with extra color (called a "kicker" or "bump" plate); it is added to give black a richness that would otherwise be missing. Trapping against this kind of black can be tricky; you don't want the kicker showing through in the reversed areas.

Studio Usage

Rich black is used to give a lustre—a sense of quality to printed materials at no real added cost of production. Traps are needed for any reversed-out areas on the kicker printing plates, but they are not needed on the black plate (this would cause distortion of the reversed objects). You can use a Pantone® as a bump as well.

Related Topics

1 | Set the Type to White

First, set and select all the type that you need to have reversed against the background. Then open the Paint Style palette and color the type with a white fill (with no overprint). Press the Return key to set the changes.

2 | Setting the Trap

Copy the selected type (⌘-C) and paste the copy of the type behind the original (⌘-B). With the copy of the type still selected, return to the Paint Style palette and give the type a stroke. This stroke should be colored 100% black, with no cyan, magenta, or yellow present.

The stroke weight should be twice as thick as the trap that your printer recommends; strokes go both inside and outside the path, and in this case, only the outside half of the stroke will appear. Turn off the overprint on the stroke and set the stroke attributes to rounded ends and joins. This will cause the "rich" part of the black to be spread away from the reverse type, allowing for clean reproduction of the type.

3 | Colored Type against Rich Black

To trap colored type against rich black, try this variation: when pasting the copy behind the original type, set the stroke color the same as the fill color, with the overprint on. Then copy the stroked type and paste the copy behind the stroked type (⌘-B). Change the color of the stroke to 100% black and turn off the overprint. You should not perform this operation until you are ready to go to print with your illustration.

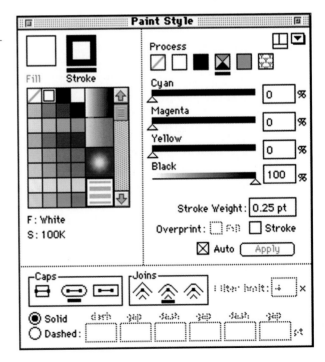

that JAZZ

TP Design

Comments

Trapping is a necessary part of the printing process. Building overlaps of color into an illustration prevents printing press color shifts (those nasty white "smileys" that you may see on color boundaries in non-trapped art).

Studio Usage

Traps usually are applied to an illustration after the project is approved for production. Colored type is more difficult to trap than regular objects because of the need to keep the integrity of the type intact. The proper kind of trap must be applied to avoid making objects look ugly and to avoid destroying type.

Related Topics

1 | Determine the Type of Trap Needed

First, you must determine whether you need a choke trap or a spread trap. You need to choke the type if its color is darker than the background. A spread is needed if the type is lighter than the background.

2 | Setting a Choke

To set a choke trap, select the type. Set the type to Overprint in the Paint Style palette. Copy the type (⌘-C) and paste it behind (⌘-B) the original type. Open the Paint Style palette and set the fill color to the type's color, with the overprint option off. Add to the type a stroke that is twice the width that your printer recommends for trapping; one half will go inside the path, the other half goes outside. Set the stroke's color to the *background* color. If the resulting color mix is too obvious (for example, blue type on a yellow background that produces a green trap line), you can reduce the tint of the stroke (30-60% reduction is a good starting point).

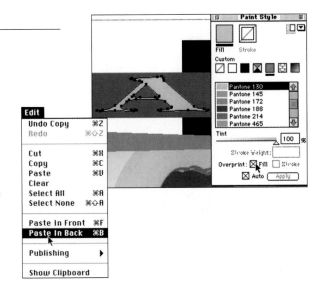

3 | Setting a Spread

To set a spread trap, select the type and open the Paint Style palette. Set the fill color (with the overprint set to off) with no stroke. Close the Paint Style palette and copy the type (⌘-C). Paste it behind (⌘-B) the original type. Again, open the Paint Style palette and add a stroke that is twice the trap width that your printer recommends. Color this stroke with the *type* color and set the overprint to "on." If the resulting color mix is too apparent, you can cut the tint of the stroke (30-60% cut is usually sufficient).

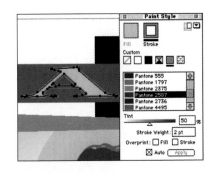

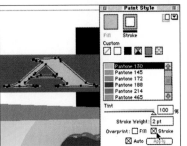

4 | Tips and Tricks

Trapping should be done after you have confirmed that no changes are to be made to the illustration. You may want to make a copy of your file before trapping; if any changes are needed, you will still have the original file.

Chris Spollen

Comments

Using Adobe Separator for separations is especially useful if you need to make special screens and adjustments that are not available in page-layout programs.

Studio Usage

Separator, which comes with the Adobe Illustrator package, is great for making sure that your work will print properly and for making adjustments that you could not make anywhere else (unless you have a Scitex in your studio!).

Related Topics

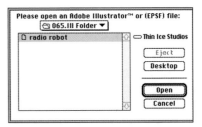

1 | Open the Document in Separator

Select the document that you want to separate with the Open command under the File menu. Adobe Separator can work with any program available, as long as the document is saved in EPS format.

2 | Choose the Printing Options

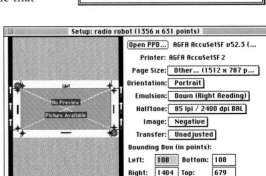

After you have selected your document, the Separator window appears. The controls for separating your document are to the right of the window. At the top is the PPD (Postscript Printer Description) file that Separator is using. To change this file, click the Select PPD button. Then select a PPD file that matches the printer that you are using. You will find a set of 6 pop-up menus that allow you to set how your page will be separated and printed. The Page Size sets the size of the page; the Orientation sets the settings as landscape or portrait. The Emulsion pop-up menu enables you to set emulsions up or down; the Halftone option gives you your halftone options. The Image option sets either a negative or positive image, and the Transfer pop-up enables you to import a custom transfer map. Use the Bounding Box fields to adjust precisely where Separator will crop the image being separated.

3 | Choosing Separations

Click the Separations button in the bottom right corner. A new window appears, listing all the process and custom colors available in the document that you are separating. To select a color to print or convert, click yes/no in the appropriate column. You can set the screen ruling and angle by clicking on either color's number in the appropriate column. A dialog box appears, allowing you to set a different screen and angle together or to separate them. After all your colors are selected, close the Separations window.

Color	Print	Convert To Process	Frequency	Angle
ProcessCyan	Yes	n/a	85.0	15.0
ProcessMagenta	Yes	n/a	85.0	75.0
ProcessYellow	Yes	n/a	85.0	0.0
ProcessBlack	Yes	n/a	85.0	45.0

4 | Printing Separations

To print all separations, use the Print command under the File menu. If you need to print only a few specific colors, use Print Selected Separations, also located under the File menu. You can print composites of the images you select in your document and then save the separations into PostScript files to be downloaded later.

5 | Tips and Tricks

Always try to do a "pre-flight" of your job on your laser printer before sending it off to the service bureau. If the job prints on your printer, it will probably print at the bureau or printer. You can spot any printing problems with the separations first and get an idea of how long it will probably take to print at the service bureau (most bureaus charge for extra running time).

Lithographic Issues *Using the Trap Filter*

Chris Spollen

Comments

Trapping is used in the printing industry to allow for plate shifting during the press run. The colors overlap, providing a "buffer," which covers for any shifting that may occur on press.

Studio Usage

Traps often are created automatically in page-layout programs such as QuarkXpress; however, these programs may not trap the placed images that reside in a layout. Therefore, illustrations must be trapped manually. The Trap filter helps to automate this process and speed up production time.

Related Topics

1 | Select the Objects to Trap

First, select the objects that need to be trapped. The Trap filter will not work with patterns, gradients, placed images, strokes, or type. You can, however, convert type to outlines; this enables you to use the Trap filter with decorative font text.

2 | Using the Trap Filter

Next, select the Trap filter. The Trap filter is located in the Pathfinder submenu under the Filter menu. Once selected, a dialog box appears, allowing you to set the amount of trap needed (you should get this information from your printer). After this information is set, you may proceed to the other options.

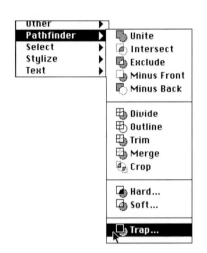

3 | Setting the Options

The Height/width field controls the ratio between horizontal and vertical trap lines, with a higher percentage number giving you thicker horizontal lines (100% makes the horizontal lines equal to vertical lines). This setting is used to compensate for paper stretching on the press. The Tint Reduction field enables you to set how much overprint color is used in the trap; 100% gives you full color in the trap. You may need to set this lower (yellow trapped on blue gives a green line for your trap) so that your trap(s) are not so obvious. The Convert Custom Colors to Process and Reverse Traps do exactly as they say; you may need to use them if you are trapping a custom color for process printing or reversing the traps if the trap filter didn't trap the color that you wanted trapped. After you have made your settings, click OK. Your trap, already set to overprint, will appear. Do not do any trapping on your illustration until you are certain that no more changes need to be made.

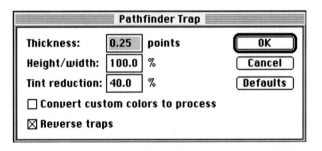

Lithographic Issues *Creating Gradients*

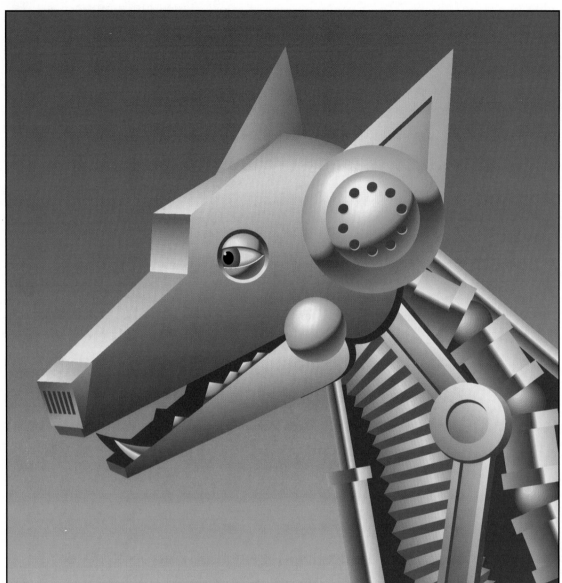

Kenneth Batelman

Comments

The vast majority of objects are not the same color from one side to another. The gradient (or "fountain color," as it is sometimes called) is designed to create realistic shading in an illustration.

Studio Usage

Gradients can speed up the creation of an illustration, as well as create smaller Illustrator file sizes. Shading, shape, and dimension are enhanced by the proper creation and usage of gradients.

Related Topics

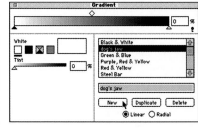

1 | Create the Gradient

Open the Gradient palette under the Window menu. Make sure that the full palette is open by clicking the flag located on the right. Then press the New button, or press Duplicate if you want to modify an existing gradient. Name the gradient and press Return to set the name. Under the name field, you can choose between a linear (straight) or radial (round) gradient by selecting the appropriate radio button.

2 | Add and Move Color Points

To add a color point to the gradient bar, click the spot where you want the point to appear. A point (triangle) will pop up at that spot. To move that point, click and drag it to the new spot. To remove a color point, select it and drag the point down, off the palette. You also can adjust the midpoints of the gradients (these are the diamonds on top of the gradient band) to affect the transition of color from one color point to another. If you need the same color to appear elsewhere on the gradient bar, select the color point and option-drag the point to its new location.

3 | Coloring the Gradient

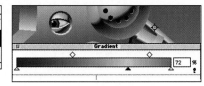

To choose a color for a selected color point, first decide on a color model that you will use for the gradient. If you are using custom colors, make sure that you do not blend across two custom colors—use the CMYK model instead. Otherwise, be consistent across the gradient (this will create a more printable gradient). After you have colored one color point, move on to the next. If you need to load in a color from the illustration (assuming that you are working in preview mode), access the Eyedropper tool from the Tool palette. With the color point selected, control-click on the color with the Eyedropper tool. The color appears at the color point.

4 | Using the Gradient

After the gradient is set, select an object that you need to paint with the gradient and apply it. If you need to change the direction, use the Gradient Vector tool on the Tool palette. Click a starting point for the gradient and drag the angle with the mouse until you have reached your end point. If the gradient's position is still not the correct angle, try dragging with the Gradient Vector tool again (until it is correct).

5 | Tips and Tricks

After an object is filled with a gradient, you can adjust it by leaving the Gradient palette open. While in Preview mode, you can move the color points displayed on the gradient color bar. Remember that all objects painted with that same gradient will be affected by any changes.

Kenneth Batelman

Comments

Illustrator maintains "anchor" points for each object. In the case of circles or squares, one anchor point is in the middle. With rules, there is one anchor point on each end. The anchor points are the control points of the line or curve on an object.

Studio Usage

One of the most important uses of anchor points is to determine blends between rules or objects. The anchor point becomes the location at which the blend(s) start and stop.

Related Topics

1 | Select the Object

Select the object to which you want to add anchor points. If you need to add anchor points to type, first convert the type to outlines.

2 | Use the Add Anchor Points Filter

Select the Add Anchor Points filter under the Create sub-menu in the Filter menu. The filter adds one anchor point between each two anchor points that already exist. This new anchor point will be dead-center between the two existing anchor points, so you can use it as a line segment centering device (in the example shown here, it was used to help center the gradient on the columns).

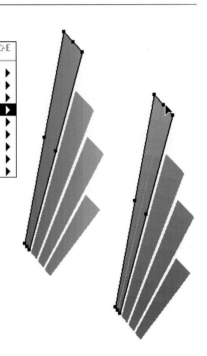

3 | Modify as Needed

After you have used the Add Anchor Points filter, you may need to either move some points (use the Hollow Arrow tool for this), or to add more anchor points. If you need to add more anchor points, use the keyboard shortcut (⌘-Shift-E).

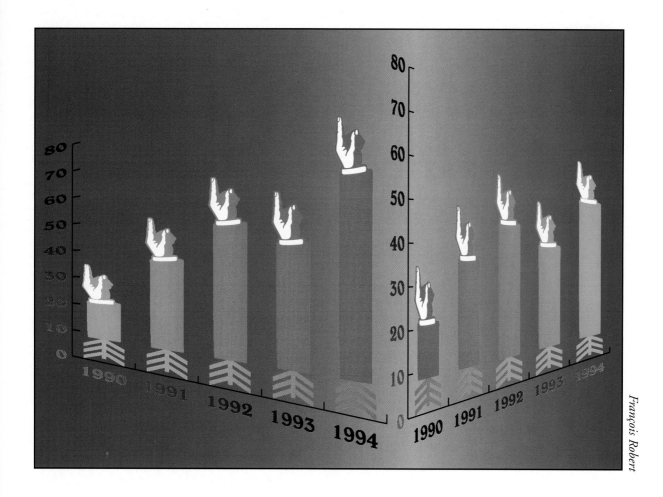

François Robert

Comments

Any graphic representation of data—such as a pie chart, bar chart, line or area chart, etc.—has much greater impact when you make it interesting by using pictures instead of shapes.

Studio Usage

For example, why not use barrels instead of boring lines in a chart for an oil company brochure? If your client is a car dealer, why not put stacks of Plymouths in a pile instead of using a plain-Jane rule?

Related Topics

1 | Set up the Graph

Start by selecting the Graph tool at the bottom of the Tool palette. Click and drag a box, or click on an illustration to open the Graph Size dialog box. Enter the desired graph size and click OK. A graph data box appears; you can either enter or import data from an external file, such as Excel or Lotus documents or data from a database program like FileMaker. Click OK and a default graph appears.

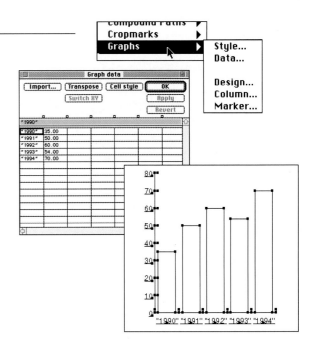

2 | Create a Custom Column

Creating a custom column is similar to creating patterns. First, create the artwork for your graph. Remember to convert *all* type within the art to outlines! Then draw a rectangle around the artwork and *move* it behind the artwork (⌘-minus). To add a sliding feature, draw a horizontal line and convert it to a guide (⌘-5). Make sure that the guide is unlocked (⌘-7). Select the artwork, the rectangle, and the guide (if needed) with the Group Selection tool. Go to the Object menu and select Design from the Graphs submenu. A dialog box appears, allowing you to save the new column design to your document.

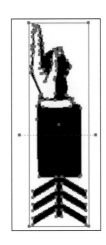

3 | Use the New Column

To use your new column design, select the graph and choose Columns under the Graphs submenu in the Objects menu. A dialog box appears, allowing you to select the column options (and the artwork that you created) for your graph. After you have make your selections, click OK. The graph updates itself to the new settings.

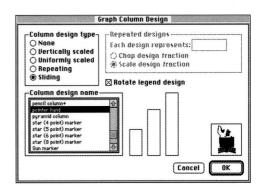

Midnight Oil Studios, Ltd.

Comments

The computer maintains the sizes of various objects by understanding (mathematically) where their centers, left and right sides, and tops and bottoms are. The process of aligning objects relies on these stored measurements to distribute space, align sides, tops, bottoms, or middles of different objects on a page.

Studio Usage

There are few mechanicals without some degree of symmetry in object placement. No matter how hard you try to visualize, your eye is never as accurate as using the Distribute filter in Illustrator.

Related Topics

1 | Select the Objects to Be Distributed

At least three objects must be selected for a Distribute filter to work. The objects can be anything—lines, shapes, or type. With open type, the filter will distribute the type from the point where the type was created. Area type or type on a path will be distributed by its defining shape.

2 | Choose the Distribute Objects Filter

There are two Distribute filters: Horizontal and Vertical. Both are located under the Objects submenu in the Filter menu and work without dialog box options.

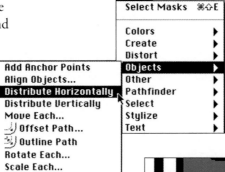

3 | Experiment with Distribution

You can use the Distribute filters many different ways. One excellent use is to repeat a group of elements and use them as placement markers for custom guides.

TP Design

Comments

Illustrator maintains a lot of information about a document and even keeps some memory and location data "set aside." One example is the views function, which enables you to zoom in (or out) for a particular view or detail of an object and to save that exact location permanently as part of the drawing.

Studio Usage

If you've been using Illustrator, you know that drawings can get pretty complicated. If you're working on a particular portion of an image, or need to call attention to a particular detail, then you should experiment with this method.

Related Topics

Using Multiple Windows   47

1 Creating the Custom View

First, make sure that the view you are about to create is the way you want it to appear. Select New View from the View menu (⌘-Control-V). A dialog box appears, asking you to name the view that you just created. A good suggestion is to name the view for the area that it shows, like "Upper Left 200% Preview" or "Full Layout Wireframe." After you have named the custom view, click OK. The custom view is saved, and it appears at the bottom of the View menu.

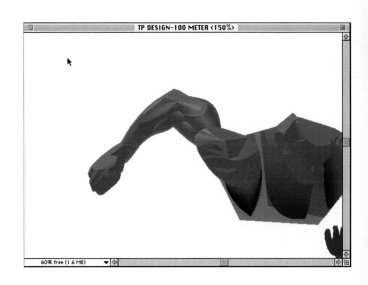

2 Using the Custom View

To use a custom view, select the view that you need from the View menu, or you can select it from the keyboard using ⌘-Control-number or letter. There can be only 25 custom views in a document at one time, so choose your views carefully.

3 Editing Custom Views

To edit the name or to delete a custom view, choose the Edit Views command from the View menu. A dialog box appears, listing all available custom views in that illustration. To rename a custom view, select the view. Its name will appear in the Name field below the list, where you can modify it as needed. To delete a view, select a view again and click Delete. The view will be removed from the list.

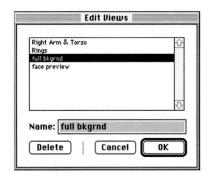

Scott MacNeill

Comments

You can make complicated drawings much easier to work with by using layers. The addition of layers may initially seem to complicate an illustration, but they actually help organize elements. Layers should contain similar elements for organization and printing purposes, not simply because they are available. Although the only limit to the number of layers an illustration can include is the amount of RAM memory on your computer, the prime limit of layers should be based on organizational purposes.

Studio Usage

The ability to lock and hide layers makes working on complicated illustrations much easier. By organizing the layers to isolate related objects, managing a complicated illustration becomes a simple task. Layers are used to isolate text, geographic, topographic, and trail information in map making. Layers also are used to lock and isolate elements. By locking these elements, the editing of other elements will be displayed much faster.

Related Topics

1 | Managing Layers

Layers should be created during the planning process of an illustration. The layers should be made to group similar objects. Layers also can be used to isolate text and layers that need to be turned on and off for printing purposes.

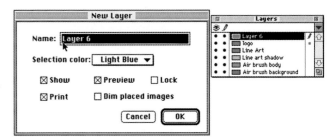

2 | Naming the Layer

The name of a layer should reflect its contents or use. Because files are often used by more than one person, it is best to use names that others working on the file will understand (rather than leaving the names at the default Layer 1, Layer 2, and so on).

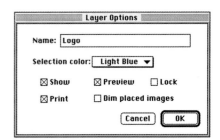

3 | Color Coding

When layers are created or changed, colors can be chosen for that layer. The color helps indicate on which layer selected objects are located (for example, when items are selected, control points highlight a color assigned to each layer). Colors can be changed by double clicking on the layer name in the Layers palette located in the Layer Options dialog box.

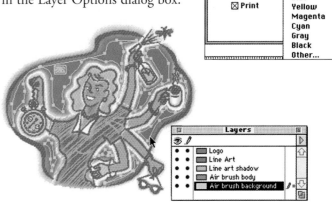

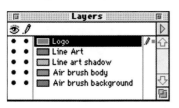

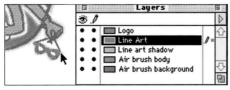

4 | Layer Management

As an illustration progresses, the properties of the layers can be changed to simplify the illustration. By moving, hiding, and locking layers, additional layers can be added or existing layers can be moved, locked, and deleted as required. Remember that all changes to the properties of layers should be made to simplify the illustration, not further complicate it.

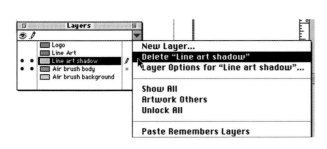

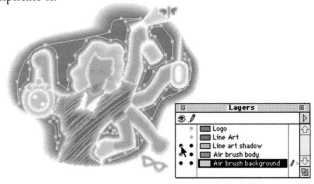

Michael J. Partington

Comments

When you select a single object to rotate, it either turns on its anchor points or at a point that you determine by clicking with the Rotation tool. If you have multiple objects to rotate simultaneously, the rotation command can produce unpredictable results.

Studio Usage

Usually, you are using rotation, alignment, and scaling in a series of steps. You should always plan your drawing early and apply techniques such as this as part of a "drawing plan."

Related Topics

1 | Select the Objects to Rotate

For the Rotate Objects filter to work properly, you need to have more than one object selected. If one object needs to be rotated, use the Rotation tool.

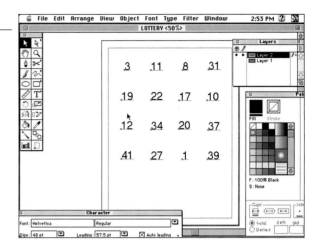

2 | Use the Rotate Objects Filter

Select the Rotate Objects filter under the Objects submenu in the Filter menu. Choose the amount of rotation desired; to choose the direction of rotation, use a plus or minus sign. (It works the same as the Rotation Tool dialog box.) If you want a random rotation effect, click the check box. With the filter set to random, objects will rotate in both directions. It is important to remember that each object will rotate on its own anchor point!

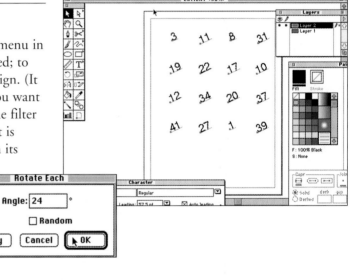

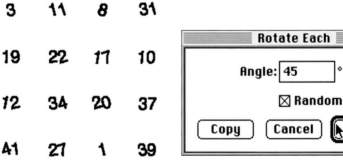

3 | Using Tools in Succession

When you work with a selection of multiple objects, you might consider grouping them before you rotate them and then ungrouping them again to apply an align filter for further multiple object manipulation.

Deborah Drummond

Comments

When you select more than one object with the Scaling or Rotation tools, the position of the objects at the time of the command can have an effect on what the tool does to them.

Studio Usage

Whenever you create multiple shapes that have to fit into or on top of each other, you should refer to this example, which addresses the issues that affect this process.

Related Topics

Rotating Multiple Objects   73

1 | Select the Objects

Select the objects that you want to scale with the filter. This filter works well with all objects, therefore type does not need to be converted to outlines.

2 | Choose the Scale Objects Filter

Select the Scale Each filter from the Objects submenu in the Filter menu. In the dialog box that pops up, you can alter the scaling both horizontally and vertically. You can also invoke a random scale factor by checking the box below the scaling fields; this will create a random scale of your object.

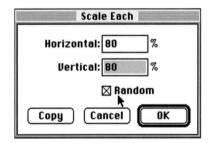

3 | The Random Factor

When you select the Random check box in the Scale Each dialog box, the percentage settings in the Vertical and Horizontal scaling fields serve as the maximum percentages that the Random scale filter is allowed to use.

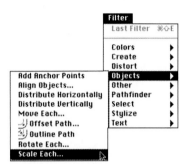

4 | The Filter is Different from the Scale Tool

When you click OK, the filter will execute your settings, scaling each object from its own center without moving it. This is different from the Scale tool where you can have multiple origin points with the filter, but only one origin point with the Scale tool.

Managing Objects *Using Layers*

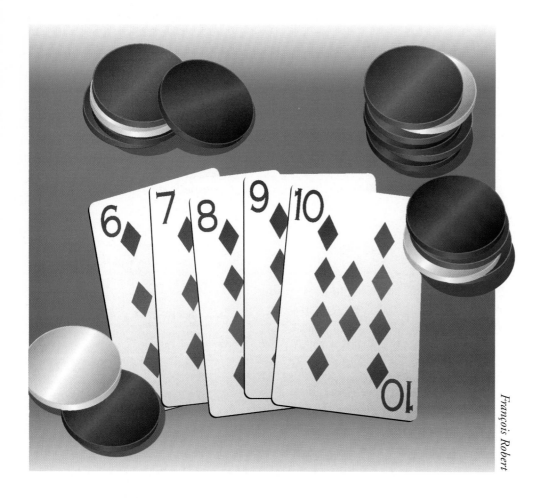

François Robert

Comments

Layering allows you to place specific, related elements in a "work area" without grouping them together. Then these elements may be separated from the other components of a drawing to make the assembly of the drawing simpler.

Studio Usage

Almost any drawing can benefit from the use of layers. Guides, for example (a vital component in any structured illustration), can really get in the way when you're trying to grab an object. Putting them on a layer lets you work without ever touching them. Locking alone won't work because you might want to lock and unlock elements other than guides as you're developing the illustration. Forms, backgrounds, page borders, and any other object that may get in the way or that you may want to hide should be placed on its own layer.

Related Topics

1 | The Layers Palette Controls

To use the Layers palette, first open it by using the Show Layers command under the Windows menu (⌘-Control-L). You'll see several icons on the palette. The eye icon controls the view; clicking the eye will hide all the layers not selected. The pencil icon handles your ability to write on layers; clicking it locks all layers that are not selected. A column to the far right in the Layers palette shows whether an object has been selected on that layer and whether you can draw there.

2 | Creating and Naming a Layer

At the top right of the Layers palette is an arrow that reveals a pop-up menu. Options on this menu include: making and deleting layers, controlling layer options, controlling layer previews with other layers in artwork mode, and using Paste Remembers Layers, which keeps the layer structure of pasted objects intact. When you select a new layer, the Layer Options dialog box appears, allowing you to name and set the attributes for that layer (color, name, previews, and so on). After these attributes are set, click OK. The new layer will appear on the Layers palette.

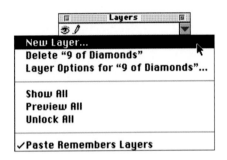

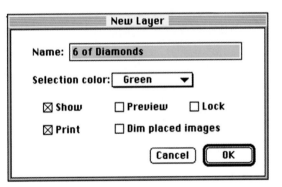

3 | Shuffling around Layers and Objects

To move a layer up or down, select the layer in question in the Layers palette and drag it up or down in the Palette window to the position that you need. To move an object from layer to layer, first select the object on the page. A small box appears in the Layers palette, next to the layer that the object is on. Drag this box in the Layers palette to another layer where you want the object to move, and then the object appears on that layer.

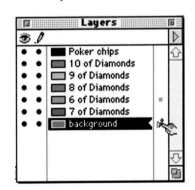

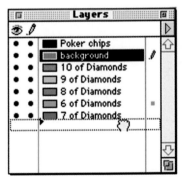

Paths and Lines *Arrowheads*

Bill Morse

Comments

Arrowheads are an important element in illustrations, and they can take a considerable amount of time to produce manually. Adobe Illustrator's Create filter will generate dozens of different styles automatically.

Studio Usage

If you own this book, you've already had to create arrowheads for things like callouts, technical illustrations, and diagrams. This useful filter provides a way to generate some really great arrowheads with a simple mouse click.

Related Topics

The Pen Tool   45

1 | Select an Open Path

Select an open path where you want to place the arrowheads. The path must be open (a line, not a square or circle) and cannot be a type path.

2 | Choose the Arrowheads Filter

Select the Add Arrowheads filter located in the Stylize submenu under the Filter menu. A pop-up dialog box shows your options. The Size field sets the size of the arrowhead; the Start, End, and Start & End buttons place the arrowheads in a location. Using the Style window, you can select 27 different styles of arrowheads, both arrows and feathers. The specified arrowheads will appear centered on the endpoint of your line.

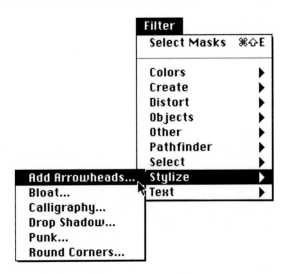

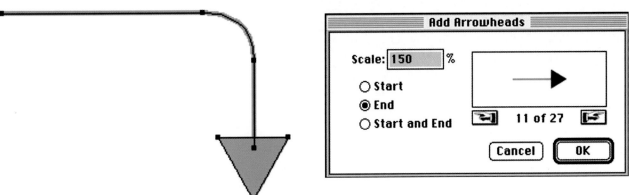

3 | Tips and Tricks

Arrowheads act like normal paths; they can be colored, altered, and mutated like any other path. If you need to apply the same arrowhead to several different lines (as on a map), use ⌘-Shift-E to repeat the arrowhead as you select each line in succession.

Charles Akins

Comments

Illustrator gives you the option to define lines in terms of strokes that can be altered into different patterns. A line pattern creates effects that are difficult to achieve in any other manner.

Studio Usage

Lines do not have to be solid. Dashed and dotted lines often are used for design elements such as coupon borders, leader dots, and strings of lights. You can create many simple objects with a line pattern quickly and without taking up a great deal of memory.

Related Topics

1 | Select the Path to be Stroked

Select a path to be stroked. If you want to apply a stroke to type, convert the type to outlines first. (It will print just fine, but it cannot be previewed onscreen.)

2 | Open the Paint Style Palette

Open the Paint Style palette (⌘-I) and select the stroke width and color that you want to apply to the path. You can have a fill in this same path, but separate objects for fills and strokes may be a better option.

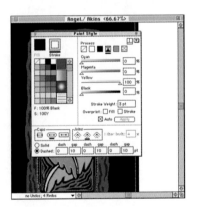

3 | Apply the Stroke Options

The bottom of the Paint Style palette must be open; this is where all the stroke options are located. Click the Dashed radio button to create a dash effect. A series of boxes will become active, allowing you to set the length of the dash (the first, third, and fifth boxes) and the space between dashes (the second, fourth, and sixth boxes). To create a dot effect, set the Caps and Joins to Rounded and set the dash to zero. Set your desired gap, and your dots should appear.

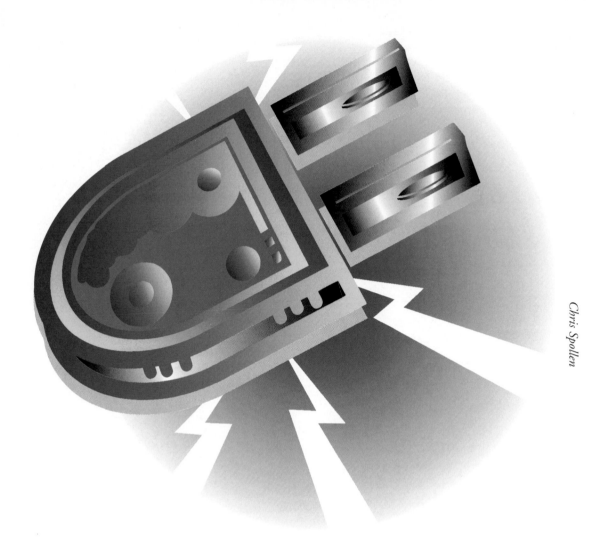

Chris Spollen

Comments

You can use the Intersect filter to cut the shape of one object out of another object.

Studio Usage

It is often necessary to create a shape that is actually part of another shape. For example, you can cut out the edge of a complex shape and use it as a highlight or reflection on another object.

Related Topics

1 | Select the Objects to Intersect

First, select the objects that you want to intersect. The Intersect filter prefers that the objects be closed paths, but open paths will work as long as the end points are located outside of the intersection. If you need to make an intersection with the original paths, make copies of the paths and apply the Intersect filter to the copies.

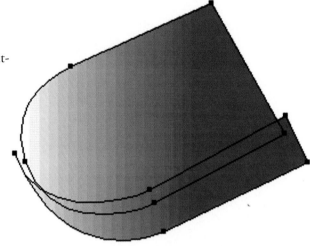

2 | Use the Intersect Filter

Then select the Intersect filter in the Pathfinder submenu under the Filter menu. After the filter has completed its work, only the intersection of the original paths is left as a new object.

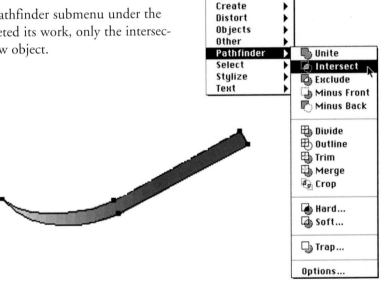

3 | When Another Filter May Be Better

You may want to use the Divide, Crop, or Subtract (Front or Back) filters instead of the Intersect filter to create a different object with other elements left in place. You also may want to work with copies of the paths that you intend to intersect; this provides you with the option of trying several filters and previewing the results.

Galloway

Tim Dove

Comments

Excluding the outline of one shape from another creates a third shape. This is another in a series of filters called "Pathfinders," which come with Illustrator. In this example, the shape of one object is excluded from the shape of another.

Studio Usage

Complex geometric shapes can be very difficult to draw freehand or even assembled from separate geometric shapes. The Exclude filter makes this task simple and creative.

Related Topics

1 | Create the Objects to Intersect

First, create the objects needed for your illustration. Make sure that any type is converted to outlines and that you are not working with guides.

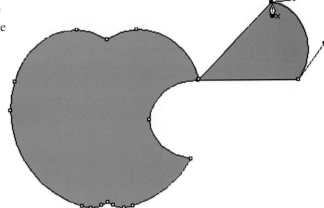

2 | Select the Objects that Intersect

Select the objects where you want to remove the intersection. The Exclude filter prefers to work with closed paths, such as circles, polygons, and so on, but it will work with an open path. Make sure that the paths are overlapping (intersecting) each other. The filter does not work if no overlapping exists.

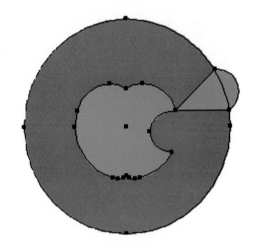

3 | Use the Exclude Filter

Choose the Exclude filter in the Pathfinder submenu under the Filter menu. This filter produces an object that looks the same in Artwork mode, but it appears to have a chunk missing in Preview mode. If one object is completely inside another object, the effect is similar to compounding paths (Compound Paths from the Object pull-down menu).

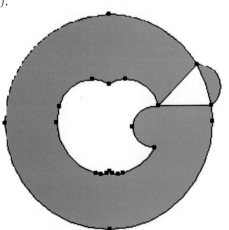

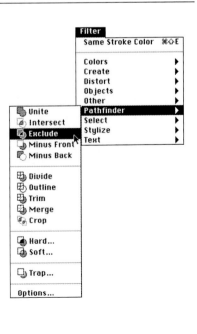

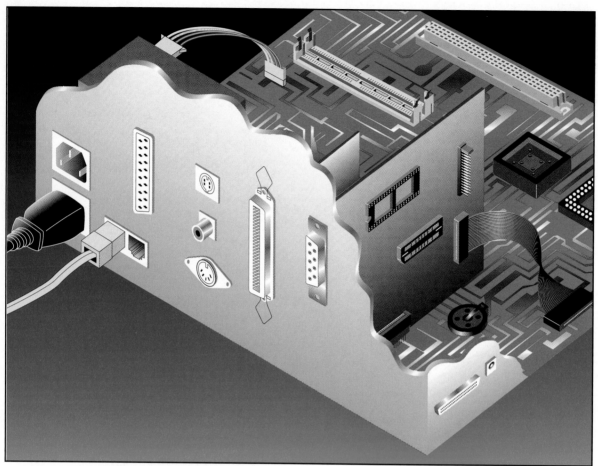

Bill Morse

Comments

The appearance of a single filled line is created by combining two lines to make them appear as one. The background stroke, being wider, works as the outline and the foreground stroke acts as a fill or hollow portion.

Studio Usage

This method of creating hollow lines uses less memory (in terms of control points) than the hollow paths created by the Stroke Path filter. Hollow lines are often used on maps to designate different road types, flight paths, and rail routes. The effect is also an alternate way to create special borders for ad layouts.

Related Topics

1 | Drawing the First Path

Create a single path that follows the complete path route. Adjust the path's color characteristics to match the outside or stroke portion of the final line. If round end points are required, select Round End Points in the Paint dialog box.

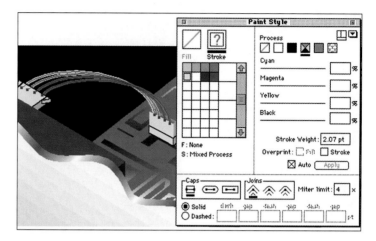

2 | Copying and Pasting the Second Path

With the first path still selected, Copy it (⌘-C) and then Paste in Front (⌘-F). With the path selected, change the line weight and color characteristics to represent the inside—or hollow—portion of the path. Select both paths and Group them (⌘-G).

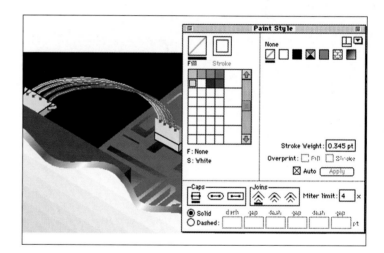

3 | Creating a Railway Track

An accurate railway track map symbol can be created by adjusting the paths. Set the first path as a half-point line, and then give the path that is pasted in front a weight of four points and a dashed line pattern, creating very thin dashes. More dashed line fills can be created using dashed path patterns over solid paths.

David Bamundo

Comments

Many illustrations and effects require that you create an outline (or "offset" to set away) around or outside of an existing object.

Studio Usage

The Offset Path filter allows you to automatically create outlines around objects. It creates masks, halos, cutouts, or shapes that require outlines.

Related Topics

1 | Select the Object to Offset

Select an object to be surrounded by a new offset path. If an object is type, it must first be converted to outlines.

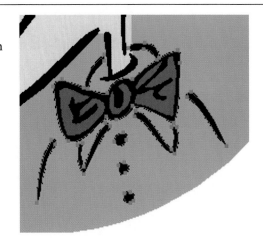

2 | Select the Offset Path Filter

Select the Offset Path filter from the Objects sub-menu in the Filter menu. A dialog box appears. Enter the necessary settings in the dialog box. Click OK, and the offset path appears.

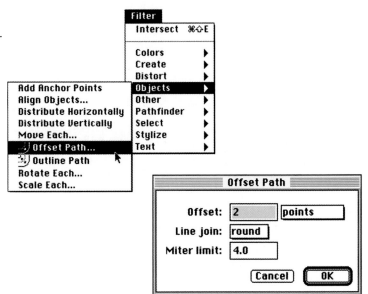

3 | Cleaning up the Effects

The Offset Path filter often creates overlapping paths with extra points. When this happens, use the Unite filter to help clean up the united paths.

Paths and Lines *Outlining Paths*

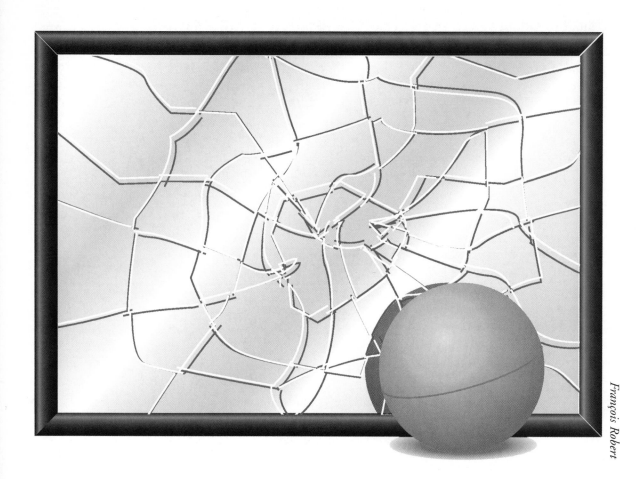

François Robert

Comments

Outlining paths can be used to convert a stroked path into a fill. For example, you can do this if you want to paint a stroke with a gradient.

Studio Usage

The Outline filter is great for creating neon effects, as well as a whole bevy of manipulative tricks, such as distortion, roughening, and so on.

Related Topics

1 | Select the Objects

Select the objects that you need to have outlined. For this filter to work, you need to select two or more overlapping paths (either open or closed paths work fine), and any type must be converted to outlines. (The filter doesn't recognize type as having a path.) This means that you should always work on a copy of an important element before you apply the process to your entire document. It's always a good idea to copy original files containing actual typefaces before you convert them to outlines.

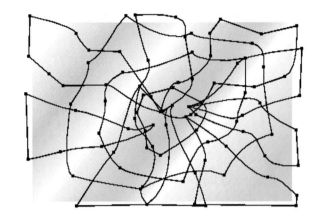

2 | Use the Outline Filter

Select the Outline filter located in the Pathfinder submenu under the Filter menu. When the filter's work is done, you will find that all the paths are split into their component lines (no closed paths) and that everything is painted with a one-point black stroke. This function is a very powerful one, and can be used in many different ways. As is often the case with filter technology, it pays to spend some time applying filters and carefully analyzing the results. You never know when you might get a brilliant idea just looking at what a filter does to objects.

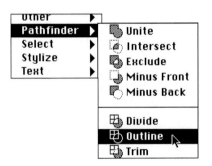

3 | Cleaning Up Your Lines

The filter may result in some "junk" being left around, such as extra points, weird little shapes, and unneccessary lines. You should consider checking and cleaning up any artwork processed through this filter. Again, do your work on a copy, just in case you sneeze and hit the Save key while running this (or any other) filter.

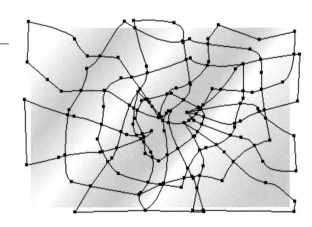

Ned Shaw

Comments

Many situations call for the creation of multiple copies of a single (or grouped) element. Illustrator provides very accurate methods of duplicating objects a fixed number of times.

The pins that adorn the dancing chips in the above illustration are one example of stepping and repeating an element within the context of a drawing.

Lines, circles, or repeating groups of individual elements in any drawing can benefit from this solution.

Studio Usage

Many drawings contain elements that are repeated in some manner; these drawings can benefit from duplication tricks that speed up the process. When preparing files for print output, stepping and repeating entire designs on larger "paper" takes advantage of the extra paper area and the increased cost in the output's size. If you need a logo printed for proofing, just blend using ten steps for extra copies. Better yet, step blend two different sized logos to get a quick "size check" proof.

Related Topics

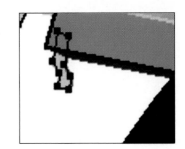

1 | Select the Object to Repeat

First, select the object that you need to repeat. The object can be a path or type. If you know how many steps you need and the distance that you need to cover, go to Step 2. If you need to make each step a set distance apart, go to Step 3.

2 | The Blending Method

To create a set number of steps, drag a copy (use the Selection tool with the Option key held down) of your object to the desired position. Select the original object and its copy. Next, group them (⌘-G). Choose the Blend Tool from the Tool palette and click the original, then the copy. Make sure to click the same control point in each object! After you click on the second object, the Blend dialog box appears, allowing you to select the number of steps that you need. Enter the number of steps and click OK, and the stepped objects will appear.

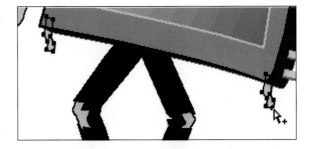

Blend

Steps: 12
First: 7.69 %
Last: 92.31 %

Cancel   OK

3 | The Moving Method

With the object(s) selected, use the Move command (⌘-Shift-M) to make a copy a set distance apart from the original. When the Move dialog box appears, enter the Distance and Angle needed to make your stepped copies and click the Copy button in the dialog box. Use the Move command again to make the stepped copy the same distance apart from the previous one. To make multiple stepped copies, use the Duplicate command (⌘-D) as many times as you need.

Move

Horizontal: 0.1098 in
Vertical: -0.0247 in

Distance: 0.1125 in
Angle: -12.684 °

☒ Objects ☒ Pattern tiles
Copy   Cancel   OK

Arrange | View | Object
Repeat Transform   ⌘D

Move...   ⌘⇧M
Bring To Front   ⌘=

Arrange | View | Object
Repeat Transform   ⌘D

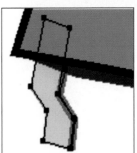

Frog Publications

Comments

The tools used to draw shapes are very accurate, but sometimes you may miss connecting the end nodes of a curve, or maybe you simply want to make one path from or shape from a combination of two or more objects.

Studio Usage

The Unite filter is another creation filter that enables you to join two or more paths or objects into a single shape. It also can be used to clean up rough sketches.

Related Topics

1 | Select the Objects to Unite

Select the objects that you want to join together. These objects can be open or closed paths, or a mixture of the two. It is very important that the paths overlap each other; both ends of an open path must be contained inside another object.

2 | Select the Unite Filter

Select the Unite filter from the Pathfinder submenu under the Filter menu. After the filter completes its work, the paths are joined together.

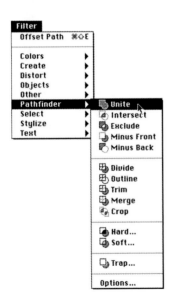

3 | Unite Filter Tips

The Unite filter compounds (combines) one object with another object if the two objects are not touching when united. This may be useful when you need to compound the letter "O," when type is converted to outlines. When the letter "O" is not compounded (united), there is no hole in the middle of it.

Paths and Lines *Using Trims*

François Robert

Comments

Trimming is another "cookie-cutter" filter method that can be used to cut one shape from another. This filter doesn't just mask the objects to make them looked trimmed, it changes the size and shape (trims) of the objects without changing the appearance of the artwork.

Studio Usage

The Pathfinder filters are extremely useful in controlling the boundary edges of complex images where many objects overlap and are not seen. In the earlier versions of Illustrator, before this filter existed, a lot of time was spent turning objects into guides and then manually cutting and fitting the shapes out of backgrounds.

Related Topics

1 | Select the Objects

Choose the objects that you need to trim. These objects can be open or closed paths, but the topmost object (the "cutter") must be a closed path. Also, make sure that the paths selected overlap each other; the filter won't work if there is no intersection of paths.

2 | Use the Trim Filter

Next, select the Trim filter located in the Pathfinder submenu under the Filter menu. Any object that has a part of it underneath the top object (the "cutter") will get "trimmed." The Merge filter acts in the same way, but the Merge filter joins together any matching fill colors. After the filter is selected, the results will appear onscreen. The filter can be "undone" by pressing ⌘-2.

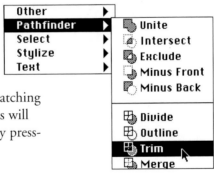

3 | Why Use the Trim Filter?

The Trim filter is useful when you need to simplify several objects and have no need to have the covered parts of the lower objects in the artwork. This allows you to save memory in order to preview the illustration more quickly.

Planning a Drawing *Controlling the Illustrator Environment*

Javier Romero

Comments

You can create a file called *Adobe Illustrator Startup* that will automatically set a wide range of defaults—before you start working. These settings aren't available through the standard preferences tools. By creating a set of objects in this file (containing your favorite colors, patterns, and blends), you can predetermine the state of your working environment.

Studio Usage

Artists have their favorite colors, patterns, fonts, page size, and working conditions. Usually, the first five or ten minutes of the day are spent setting things like screen view, tool locations, and other settings that are outside the normal preferences attributes. This solution eliminates the need to continuously set up your "environment."

Related Topics

1 | Choosing Your Favorite Colors

Start a *new* document. One of the first things to consider is your Color palette. First, go to Custom Colors and delete any colors that are already there. Because a standard set of spot and process colors is being used, open the appropriate "color books" that came with Illustrator. Create a color chart (a grid of boxes) and assign colors to a box in the grid. Continue until you have all the standard colors in place.

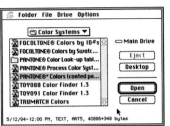

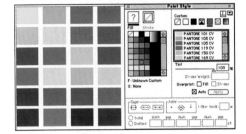

2 | Determining Standard Blends

Create (or import) your favorite blends. They will remain permanently available to you from this point forward.

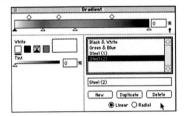

3 | Setting Patterns and Default Fonts

Standard pattern libraries can also be stored in your startup document, along with gradient libraries, color libraries, and default fonts.

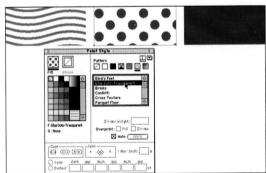
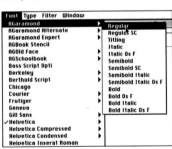

4 | Saving the Startup Document

There is a folder called "Plug-ins" within your Illustrator folder. Save this document in that folder, being sure to name it Adobe Illustrator Startup. Replace the one that is already there. This document should continually evolve as you adjust your startup defaults.

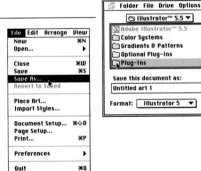

Planning a Drawing *Calibrating Critical Colors*

James Delapine

Comments

What you see on your monitor isn't always what you're going to get from the press. This entire book could be dedicated to the concepts of color management and calibration. The next few years will see major improvement in the tools that we use in relation to managing colors across different devices. For now, there is a very simple way to work with your vendors to ensure that colors critical to a specific illustration reproduce exactly as you expect.

Studio Usage

Sometimes, colors can be "close enough." Other times, though, you have to make darned sure that the colors you expect to appear are the ones that do, in fact, show up on press. This simple process will let you create a "color chart" which you can output at your vendor's location *before* you run the final job. It uses colors found in the original illustration to build a reference sheet. Remember, the press is the ultimate barometer of color accuracy, and for truly critical projects you should (for now, at least) work *backwards* from the press to your final design.

Related Topics

1 | Simplify the Colors in the Artwork

As you develop an illustration, you often find yourself with more colors than you can use. This is obvious in the number of colors you find when opening the Custom Colors dialog box. Click the Select All Unused and delete the selected colors to simplify the document and to find out how many colors are actually in use. In this illustration, the number turned out to be eight.

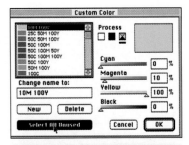
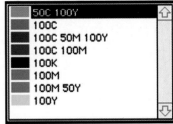
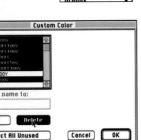
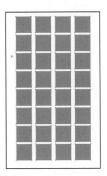

2 | Create an Array of Custom Colors

While the original artwork is open, create a new document. In that document, create a grid of squares as high as the number of custom colors in the original artwork. The width of the grid should be four squares; as shown in Step 3.

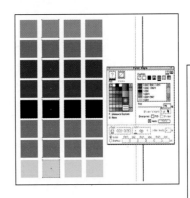

3 | Setting the Colors

Set one entire grid row at a time (all four across) and set each row to one of the eight colors.

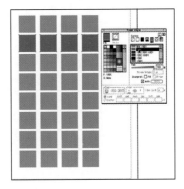
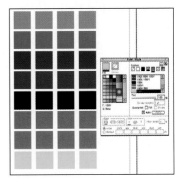

4 | Creating a Density Ramp

Because this illustration contains many blends and tints, it is a good idea to create a "ramp" of different tints (densities) to use as a reference in addition to the hues, or actual colors. To create a color ramp, use the vertical columns; set the second to 75%, the third to 50%, and the fourth one to 25%. Create the appropriate labels and output the file to film. Have a high-quality color proof printed and compare the color results to what you see on your monitor. You will then need to adjust your onscreen colors to match the proof.

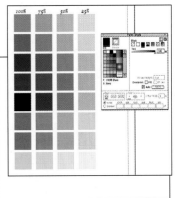

Ned Shaw

Comments

Lines are the basic building blocks of all vector artwork in Adobe Illustrator. Each line rule has specific attributes that affect how it interacts with other rules and objects in the artwork. Sometimes, computers create a look that is too precise— almost technical, as opposed to hand-drawn. Illustrator's filter technology can simulate hand-rendered art.

Studio Usage

At the end of each line is an anchor point. The location of the anchor point and the shape of the rule's end point have an effect on joining elements and creating objects of every kind.

Related Topics

1 | Lines End Somewhere

As you can see from the sample illustration, the mouse cord connects to the mouse in a realistic manner. If you turn off the Preview and look at only the artwork, you can see that the line seems to just "hang" there. What makes the preview accurate is the artist's choice of a specific end point attribute.

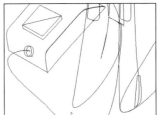

2 | The Attributes of an End Point

You can control the attributes of an end point from the Paint Style palette. It is accessed from the Window menu. In the upper right-hand corner is a pop-up icon that enables you to hide or display various paint-related settings, including line end points. You can see that the first setting (with the end point situated directly at the ending of the rule) has been selected for the example's mouse cord.

3 | How Attributes Affect Lines

Besides the obvious attributes of line weight and color, end points and joins (how two lines "act" at a corner) have a dramatic effect on how art appears.

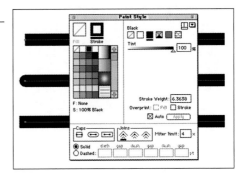

4 | Planning the Use of End Points and Joins

Some artwork, such as the example of a Celtic "knot," depend heavily on how you plan your joins and end points in your illustration. If you have a corner or join that doesn't look quite right, make sure to check the corner and join attributes.

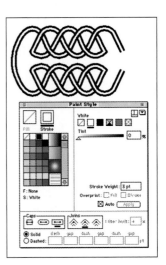

Planning a Drawing *Creating a Color Chart*

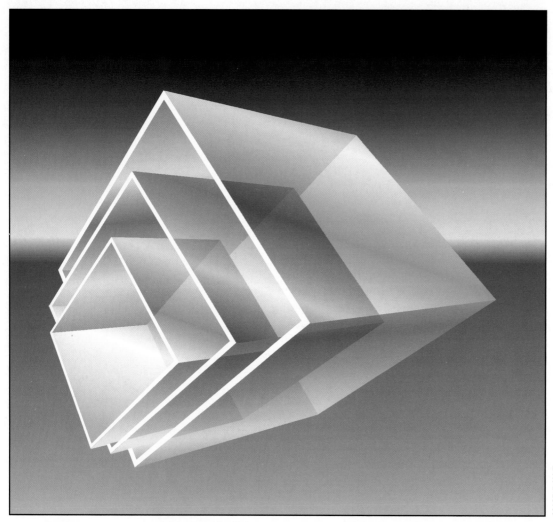

Bill Morse

Comments

Consistent color throughout the entire production process is critical; what good is it to spec a color, only to have a shift occur because the imagesetter wasn't calibrated to the printing press? The color chart is the method used for this calibration; it sets the adjustments needed throughout the production process.

Studio Usage

Color charts are used to help calibrate and coordinate monitors, output devices, proofing, and printing. The use of color charts will ensure that the PMS 186 that is printed in the final piece will look the same as the PMS 186 that you saw on your monitor.

Related Topics

Adjusting Colors   1

Managing the Color Palette   15

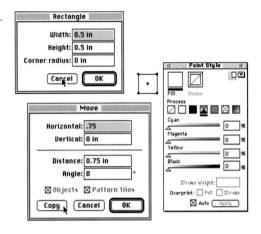

1 | Creating the Color Chart

Start by opening a new document in Illustrator and naming it Color Chart (or any other appropriate name). Create a box about ½-inch square, and duplicate this square 9 times, moving the square 1½ times its own size (this movement can be horizontal or vertical, but not diagonal). Select the first square and color it 10% of a color (CMYK model). Select the last box created and color it 100% of that same color. Finally, select all the boxes and choose Blend (Vertically or Horizontally) from the Colors section of the Filter menu. The colors should now be blended in 10% increments; it is a good idea to annotate each value above the box, for reference.

2 | Creating a Color Mix Chart

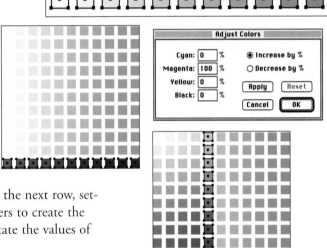

It is often necessary to see a mix of colors to determine the interaction of the inks. To see this, take the color chart that you created above and duplicate the series of squares ten times in the direction perpendicular to the original boxes. With the last row of boxes selected, choose the Adjust Colors filter, located in the Colors section of the Filter menu. A dialog box appears, allowing you to add 100% of a second color. Click OK and the new color mixes will appear in that row of squares.

At this point, you can either (a) repeat the same filter on the next row, setting the adjustment down 10%, or (b) use the Blend filters to create the color mixes required. Again, after you are finished, annotate the values of the new color for reference.

3 | Printing the Color Chart

Before printing your color chart, consult with your service bureau and/or printer to find out the amount of dot gain expected on-press; this affects the colors immensely and needs to be planned for in the prepress stage. You can set up curves in Adobe Separator, using the transfer function available at the bottom right-hand side. In this transfer table, enter the dot-gain characteristics that you need for any specific press; this table also can be saved for future reference. After the film for the color chart is output, check your color key (or matchprint, Iris proof, and so on) against your monitor. Assuming the proof is accurate, adjust your monitor or transfer table as needed. Finally, check the printed piece against the proof and your monitor. Again, adjust the monitor and/or the Adobe Separator transfer table and output the final film again, if necessary.

4 | Consistency Is the Key

It is very important that you establish a good relationship with your regular printer so that the results are consistent. Changing printers just to save a few pennies here and there is not always worth it. You will have to recalibrate your entire system just to adjust to the new printer's presses and techniques (lots of time wasted here) and run a new set of matchprints, proofs, and so on, which can cost more than the money you saved by switching printers in the first place.

TP Design

Comments

The "image area" (the area that actually contains text or graphics) of a document often lies in the middle of the "trim area" (the portion of the document that remains after the printer cuts off any extraneous material). Crop marks show where trims are to be made during final production.

Studio Usage

There are many reasons to use crop marks. They are required on any job that is designed in the middle of the paper. Crop marks also are invaluable if you want to place two or more mechanicals on a larger page. Printing multiple mechanicals on a larger page will save the printer time and it will save you money.

Related Topics

1 | The Difference between Crop Marks and Trim Marks

Crop marks in Illustrator are different from crop marks in other programs. In Illustrator, crop marks are used to define the bounding box for Adobe Separator; they do not print from within Illustrator. This type of crop mark is appropriate for most printing applications because it appears in all separations.

2 | Creating Crop Marks

To create crop marks, draw a rectangle around your artwork. With the rectangle selected, choose the Make Cropmarks command under the Object menu. The rectangle disappears, and a set of crop marks appears in its place. These crop marks do not move; they can only be removed with the Release Cropmarks command.

3 | Using Trim Marks

The Trim Marks filter can be used if you need more than one set of crop marks or if you need to set the crop marks in a different position than the Cropmarks command allows.

Planning a Drawing *Custom Grids*

Mike Dowdy

Comments

Grid sheets are used to reproduce regular jobs with a specific set of page layout dimensions. Editors and designers use layouts to build a custom grid to match the layout specs for copy and graphics. With Illustrator's ability to create guides, custom grids can be created to use over and over again.

Studio Usage

Any project employing a standard format can use grids. Newsletter and newspaper layouts, catalogs, yearbooks, and clip art libraries all can be created with the help of custom grid sheets.

Related Topics

1 | Create the Grid

Determine the image area for the layout and set the rows and columns with the Rows & Columns filter—a Text option under the Filter pull-down menu. When using the filter, be sure to set it to Preview.

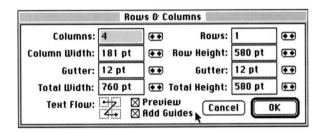

2 | Save the Grid

Convert the resulting boxes into text areas if they are required for layout—otherwise delete them. Save the file as a grid file in a grid library—if one exists—and then lock the file on the Finder desktop using the Get Info Finder command (⌘-I). This will save the file as a template and protect it from being overwritten.

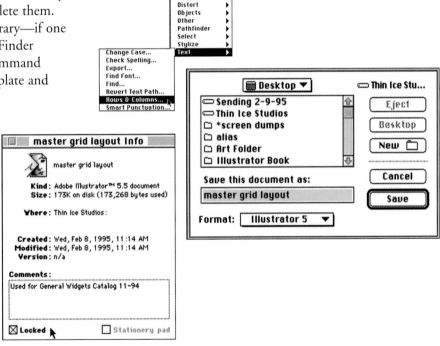

3 | Proceed with Layout

Reopen the file and save it (Save As) using an appropriate name and location. Following the guides, add the artwork and copy to the file. Guides will speed up the layout process and help achieve a standard reproducible style and format.

Bill Morse

Comments

As each grid is created it should be saved in a grid library. Building grids is a time-consuming part of design, but using premade grid files saves time and eases work. With a bit of careful management, a useful library of grid files can soon be created.

Studio Usage

Jobs that repeatedly use the same style and layout should have grid files saved and archived for future use. Service bureaus that do big business in newsletters often have huge libraries of grid files used to reproduce individual newsletter layouts quickly. The initial time spent building a grid file pays off every time the file is used in the future.

Related Topics

1 | Locking the Files

Before files are archived, they should be checked to be sure they are locked. It's important to lock a file if you use it as a template. That way, you can use the template repeatedly without worrying about losing it or making changes accidentally. The locked file can be opened but not changed — the only way to save changes to the file is with the Save As command. Select the file in the Finder and then choose Get Info from the File pull-down menu. Check the box in the lower left corner of the Info window to lock the file. This also protects the file from being accidentally erased.

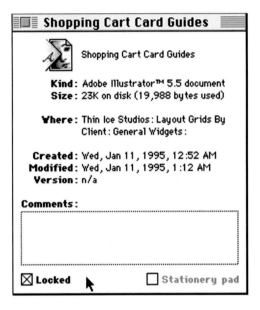

2 | Archiving Logic

To make the grid files work efficiently, they should be organized by group. You can group them in several ways: by client, by application, by style, or by a combination of these or other identifying characteristics. The method you choose will depend on your work methods and the variety of your work.

3 | Folders

After the grid groups are established, the files should be placed in appropriate folders in a location where they can be accessed quickly.

Stephen Bornstein

Comments

Each time Illustrator opens, it calls upon a special startup file to rebuild itself. This file can be customized to open with custom color palettes and specified fonts. Custom startup files can be created to match client specs when opening a particular program. You'll save time choosing fonts and reduce the risk of using the wrong fonts or colors in a job.

Studio Usage

The different preferences from the Preferences selection under the File pull-down menu are your way of customizing the feel of Illustrator to your needs, style, and so on. Setting and choosing your own preferences is a matter of personal taste; however, these preferences can and will affect the way you work.

Related Topics

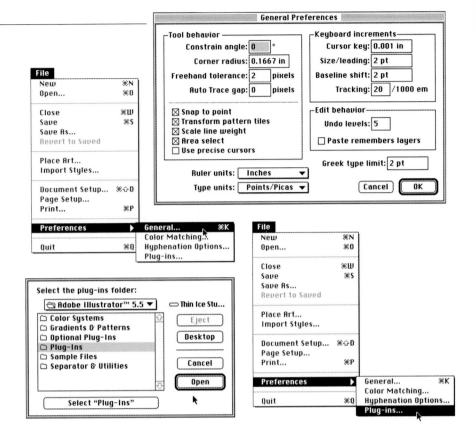

1 | Main Preferences File

You can modify Illustrator's operations through the application's General Preferences dialog box (⌘-K). Common changes made to the Preferences are Ruler units, Freehand tolerance, Trace Gap distance, number of Undos, and Snap to point. Using Illustrator without setting the Plug-Ins folder from the Preferences pop-up menu will slow down its operation as well as disabling the program's Plug-Ins.

2 | Custom Startup Files

Create a new Startup file that includes custom specifications used by an individual client. You can include such things as fonts, colors and blends, and page size. If the customer adds anything later, you should add that information to the file as well. The information included in the file will become the default setting when it is used as the Startup file.

3 | Saving a New Startup File

Save the new file as Adobe Illustrator Startup and place the file in the application folder where you want it to be used. Startup files can be created for different clients and stored until you need them later. If a user is experienced in writing PostScript Information Riders files, they can also be used to customize specific program actions such as screen frequencies.

Steve Sullivan

Comments

As designers, we must concern ourselves primarily with design. Despite this, there remains the potential for considerable dollar savings if the final design is "stepped and repeated" to take advantage of the imagesetter's large printing area.

The figures here show a die-cut project being manually imposed to eliminate manual stripping later on.

Studio Usage

There are many types of projects for which this "step and repeat" may apply; Illustrator is often used as a stand-alone page layout program, eliminating the need to export artwork into a page layout program. On single-form projects such as die-cut designs, business cards, flyers, inserts, and similar projects, maximizing the space available on a large-format output device will eliminate manual stripping prior to producing a printing plate. You must closely communicate with your printer if you want this technique to work!

Related Topics

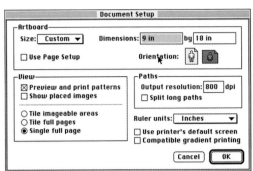

1 | Making the Page Larger

Document Setup controls the size of the "paper" on which the artwork resides. When we opened this file, the document size was 9" × 18". The vertical measure of the paper is doubled by setting the height to 18".

2 | Measure the Artwork

Often, artwork contains invisible items (boundaries, masks, and so on). In the example, lines are drawn to act as "markers" so that the visible portion of the artwork can be measured. You should make sure that the Measurements palette is open. Then use the ruler to measure the distance between the two rules. In this case, you should be concerned about the vertical distance (top to bottom of the visible artwork). The measurement is shown as 7.2431 inches.

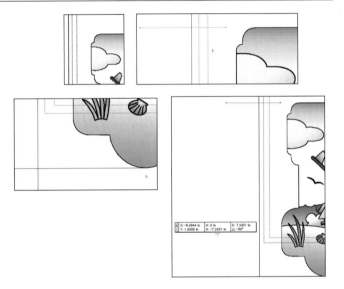

3 | Step and Repeat

Once you've arrived at the distance you need to step, measure the height of the visual elements, option-click the Arrow tool to move (step) and clone (repeat) the artwork using exact measurements.

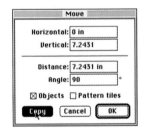

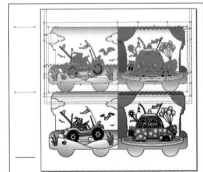

4 | Determining Imposition

In this example, we're using a method called "work and turn," which has one image rotated against the other. To accomplish this, double-click the Rotation tool and "flip" the duplicated image first. Make sure to check the "Pattern tiles" box if your artwork contains any patterns (otherwise, they won't "turn" with the rest of the artwork). Check with your printer for the placement of any cut or trim marks.

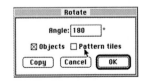

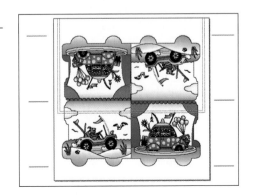

Into the New...

BOSTON
CITY
HOSPITAL

Enrico Design

move day 1994

Comments

A perspective grid is a helpful aid in three-dimensional drawing. This grid defines a vanishing point and the angle element to use while approaching that point. The number of key elements in the illustration determines how many grids are needed at the vanishing point. Custom vanishing point grids can be created for each drawing.

Studio Usage

With the increased demand for three-dimensional drawing comes a need for the use of perspective grids. Successful three-dimensional drawings place the viewer into the drawing by using vanishing point perspectives. Vanishing points help create the illusion of 3D within the two-dimensional limits of a video monitor or paper medium.

Related Topics

1 | Placing the Horizon Point

The horizon and vanishing points are determined based on the positioning of the illustration's key elements and their relationships to each other. One key element and one vanishing point are shown in the example.

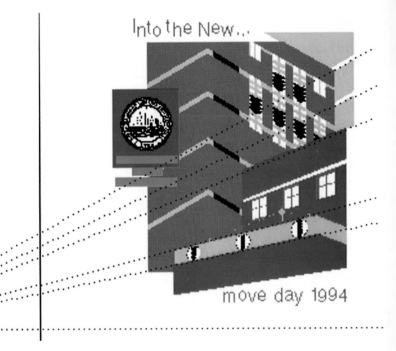

2 | Scale and Blend

Smooth perspective grids can be built with the Blend tool. Create a rectangle around the main object in the foreground; create a second rectangle reduced to an appropriate size based on the horizon location. Select both rectangles and then use the Blend tool on a common corner point. Enter the number of steps required in the grid.

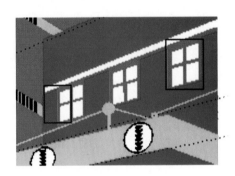

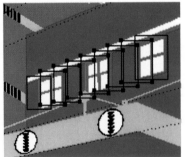

3 | Creating the Guides

Select the paths to be used in the grid and convert the paths to Guide Lines (⌘-5). Delete unnecessary paths. If the perspective grid is needed for more than one job, the file should be saved and locked. Use the Get Info command to convert the file to a template by locking the file.

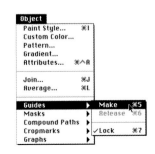

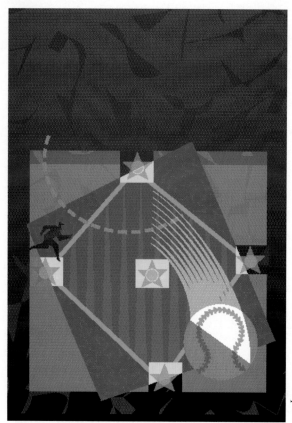

Bill Frampton

Comments

Moving the zero point creates a custom guide to handle simple measurement and placement tasks. Setting the zero point enables you to use the vertical and horizontal rules as a measuring device. As the zero point is moved, so are the horizontal and vertical ruler units, enabling you to align elements in more complex arrangements than guides or grids allow. The zero point can be moved innumerable times as required for each job. The new zero point position is only saved for the current document, not for future ones.

Studio Usage

The positioning of the zero point is often used to check measurement and placement relationships in a design. Beyond use as a guide and measurement tool, the zero point position affects where tiles in patterns begin tiling (pattern tiles top left corner match the zero point) and where the bounding box in Adobe Separator appears (the Adobe Separator crop begins at the zero point position in the Illustrator File and centers the file in the remaining area of the page size set in Adobe Separator).

Related Topics

1 | Determining Element Location

With the rulers turned on, move the pointer to the lower right-hand corner where the vertical and horizontal rulers meet.

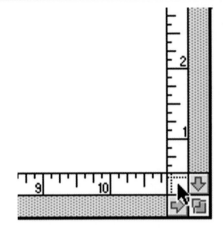

2 | Moving Cross Hairs into Position

Click and drag the dotted cross hairs in this corner onto the drawing board area and drag them into the position where the new zero point will be located. While setting the new zero point, the cross hairs show both the vertical and horizontal ruler guides to assist you in positioning the zero point. When you release the mouse button, the cross hairs vanish, but the zero point remains. The cross hairs can be used to measure the new position because the previous zero point does not change until the new zero point position is set.

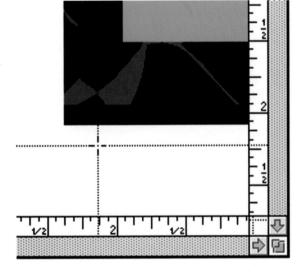

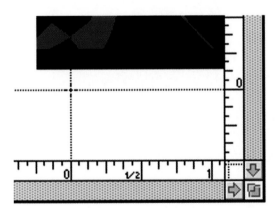

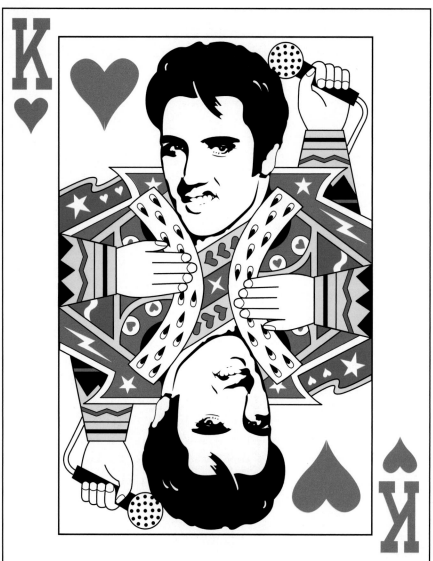

Steve Sullivan

Comments

Quick access to file information benefits both in-house and out-of-house work. In-house, file information is used for archiving purposes and to know quickly what is included in a file for reproduction. Out-of-house, file information gives service bureaus quick information for requirements needed to print the file.

Studio Usage

When a file is being prepared for printing or saved for export, the file tracking information is needed. The Document Information filter creates a list of important file statistics. In simple files the information is not as critical, but complicated files that include Pantone® colors, many fonts, and placed images should have a record made of their contents.

Related Topics

1 | Checking the File

Any time a document is opened, the document information can be checked. The check can also be made in mid-job; for example, to check whether fonts used in the file are installed on the current system.

2 | Document Info

Select Document Info from the Other option under the Filter pull-down menu. The filter creates a list of important file tracking information. The dialog box displays a brief list of the main topics and information. More detailed information on the tracking topics is available by selecting the Options box.

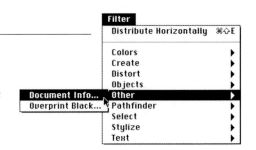

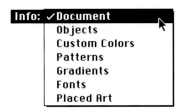

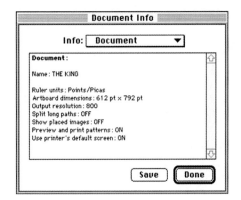

3 | Saving the Information

If the information is needed only for a working check on the file, the dialog box can be closed afterward. If the work is completed and the file is being saved to storage or sent for printing, the document tracking information should be saved with it. The document information is saved as a TeachText file and should be included on disk and in printed form when sent to a service bureau or printer.

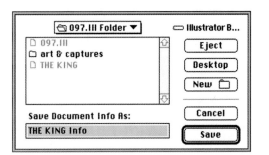

Planning a Drawing *Trim Marks*

Ned Shaw

Comments

When printing a job, trim marks determine where the finished piece begins and ends. These marks denote the "live area" in a job and also help the printer by saying "cut here!"

Studio Usage

Trim marks are used almost everywhere in the printing industry; how else would one know where to cut the paper on a job? The Trim Marks command differs from the Crop Marks command in that you can have multiple sets of trim marks, but only one set of crop marks. Trim marks also are discrete objects. Unlike crop marks, they can be moved, rotated, resized, colored, and so on.

Related Topics

1 | Select the Object(s) that Need Trim Marks

Select the object or objects that require trim marks. You can choose any object—type, open or closed paths, placed images—in your document. If you are not sure where you need trim marks, you may want to draw a shape around your art.

2 | Use the Trim Marks Filter

With the object selected, choose the Trim Marks filter, located in the Create section of the Filter menu. The trim marks will appear at 90° angles around your illustration; the original art will remain untouched.

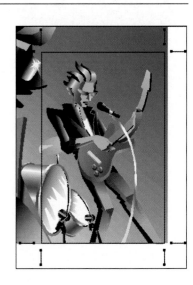

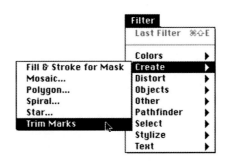

3 | Coloring the Trim Marks

Determine the purpose of the trim marks. In four-color printing, it is often desirable to have the trim marks appear on all plates. If this is what you need, select the trim marks and open the Paint Style palette (⌘-I). Change the color of the stroke to 100% CMYK (all colors) so that trim marks appear on all plates. If a custom color is needed as well, click the overprint box and Copy (⌘-C) and Paste In Back (⌘-B) the trim marks. With the Paint Style palette open, color the trim marks with the custom color (leave the overprint on, if you have more than one custom color). Repeat this step until you have marked all custom colors in your job.

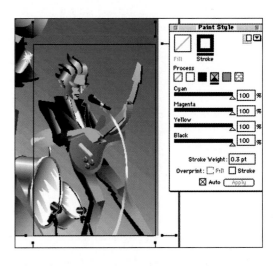

Planning a Drawing *Using Auto Trace*

James Delapine

Comments

The Auto Trace tool uses selected borders in imported bitmapped files to create Bézier curve information.

The tool traces outlines of the bitmapped files as templates, creating silhouetted parts of the completed image. The more simplified the bitmapped template graphic, the smoother the finished trace will be.

The trace tool always creates a closed path around the bitmapped template. To create partial traces the tool is dragged across the template from the desired beginning position to the end position. The trace is completed clockwise around the template.

Studio Usage

Tracing is a time-honored tradition in the illustration business; Illustrator continues this tradition with the Auto Trace tool. This tool works great when you need to convert a scan into an Illustrator file to make adjustments to the image.

Related Topics

1 │ Selecting the Trace Tool

Open a template with the Open command in the File pull-down menu. Select the Trace tool by clicking and holding the mouse button down on the Freehand tool and sliding the mouse to the right.

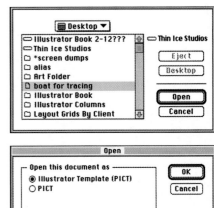

2 │ Setting the Auto Trace Gap

Before tracing, the graphic should be analyzed as to how smooth the template is—the smoother the template, the less need there is to set the Auto Trace gap. Auto Trace gap sets how many pixels the Trace tool will cross over before including an area in the trace. The Trace gap can be changed for different traces in each illustration. Setting the freehand tolerance in the preferences also affects the accuracy of the auto trace—this should be set depending on the quality of the template and the desired quality of the final trace.

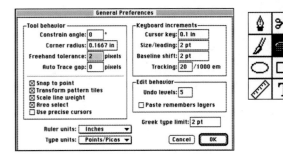

3 │ Beginning to Trace

Working on complicated templates is easier if you change the view to Artwork Only. The Trace tool can be used to trace inside template areas as well as around templates. To trace inside template areas, click inside white areas in the template. To trace around the exterior of the template, click on the outside of the template.

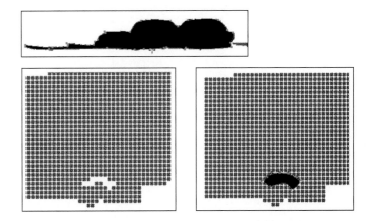

4 │ Clean-up and Coloring

Even with the smoothest of templates, detailed areas should be checked at a magnified view. At the higher magnification the trace is easier to adjust to match the template better. Setting color attributes and arranging the elements' layering positions also needs to be done at this stage. Resetting the view to Preview shows the final artwork. To view without the template, select Hide Template under the View pull-down menu.

Planning a Drawing *Using Document Setup*

Mike Doudy

Comments

The Document Setup dialog box is used mainly to set the size of the program's art board—the drawing area available for use. This variable art board size allows graphic artists and designers to work on projects in the final size rather than limiting the program to work only with common page sizes. Document Setup also controls document attributes that can be set to meet users' work habits—to make working much easier for all levels of a project from the artist's conception to the press room.

Studio Usage

Whether setting up the art board to match the design or to match the printer size, the more precise the Document Setup is, the smoother the job flow will be. Settings chosen in the Document Setup are also dependent on the final production of the job.

The visible page boundary makes the setting of printed tiles very easy by displaying what is printed based on the specifications set in the Document Setup and Page Setup dialog boxes. By watching the page boundary, you can greatly simplify stripping of printed tiles to save time, paper, and film.

Related Topics

1 | Setting the Page Size

Choose the Document Setup dialog box from the File menu. The art board size is set in the Artboard area by selecting standard page sizes in the Size box or by entering specific sizes in the Dimensions box. The page Orientation is easily switched by selecting the appropriate icon. Selecting Page Setup automatically matches the art board to the size selected in the Page Setup dialog box.

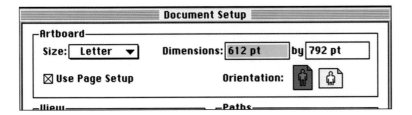

2 | Setting Tile Options

The View options can be set to match specific job needs and work habits. Tiling attributes become important when you print files that are different than those printed by the selected printer. The Single full page selection (the default) displays a single printable page boundary on the selected art board. The Tile full pages selection displays page boundaries for full pages that fit on the selected art board. The Tile imageable areas displays all tiles that fit on the selected art board.

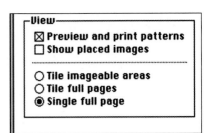

3 | Ruler Units

The Points/Picas system is a good choice because it is a standard that is used worldwide in the printing industry. The Points/Picas unit gives finer control in small movements and detailed drawing.

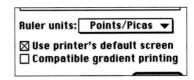

4 | Further Job Customization

The Documents Setup's path controls affect the printing characteristics of paths. The default resolution of 800 dpi is set to match most general printing jobs. The output resolution formula is "Flatness equals Printing Device Resolution divided by Output Resolution Setting." Changes in output resolution only affect objects drawn after they are made. The Split Long Paths option allows files with complicated lines to be printed by printers that could not otherwise handle them—if a file refuses to print, try this option after saving a copy of the original file before splitting the paths.

Planning a Drawing *Using the Move/Copy Command in Grid Design*

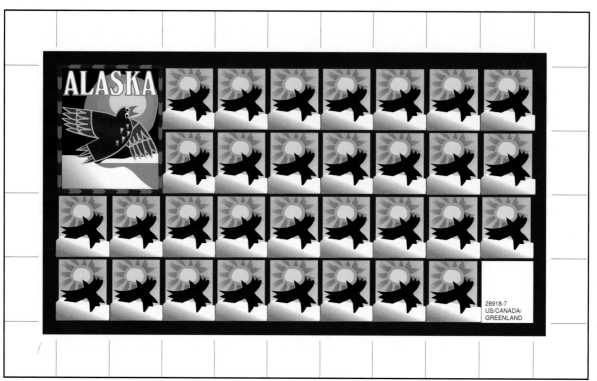

28918-7
US/CANADA/
GREENLAND

Antler & Baldwin

Comments

Because basic grids are made of uniformly spaced guides, a grid page can be built using a step-and-repeat combination. After the grid unit and sizes are known, creating custom grids becomes an easy task. When the grid lines are in place, they are converted to locked, nonprinting guide lines.

Studio Usage

Projects that require even spacing between elements benefit from the use of grids. The grids allow alignment of many objects along a common plane. Grid pages are commonly used in page layouts, catalogue work, and form design.

Related Topics

1 | Set the First Grid Line

Draw the path or element on which the grid will be based. The element should be at an end margin of the grid, not the middle.

2 | Duplicating the Grid Line

With the path selected, activate the Move palette (⌘-Shift-M). Set the vertical and horizontal distances, and then select Copy. Directly after the move/copy, select Repeat Transformation Function (⌘-D) and repeat until the required grid is built. Repeat the same process for other grids needed for the job.

3 | Converting the Grid

When all grid lines are completed, select all (⌘-A), convert the objects and paths to guides (⌘-5), and save this Illustrator file.

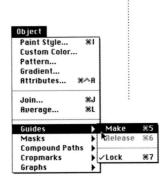

4 | Locking the File

To ensure that the grid sheet is not overwritten, lock the grid file on the desktop. Switch to the Finder, click on the new grid template file, select Get Info from the Finder's File pull-down menu (⌘-I), and then select the Locked option in the dialog box. This forces the file to work as a template. The file will open but changes cannot be saved to it. All changes must be saved by using Save As under the File pull-down menu. Another option is to create all your guides on their own layers.

Stephen Bornstein

Comments

Guides are useful as alignment and reproduction tools—any shape's position can be locked and the shape converted into a guide object or guide line. This element is left on the art board as a nonprinting element and may be discarded later. Before digital guide lines became available, graphic artists used non-repro blue guide sheets and pencils to align work on their paste-ups. Too often today, guide lines are forgotten and not used as a strong design tool.

Studio Usage

Any project can benefit from the use of guides. They are used to align graphics and text in all layouts. When copied and reproduced, guides also are used to reproduce curves and corner points in the illustration's development and font building design stage.

Related Topics

1 | Snap to Point

The Snap to Point feature increases the effectiveness of guides. When dragged within two pixels of a guide, the object being moved will attach itself to the guide. Snap to Point is turned on in the General Preferences dialog box (⌘-K) from the File pull-down menu. If the object being moved is selected by clicking an anchor point, the object will align to the guide on that anchor point. If the object being moved is selected on a path, the object will align to the guide on that path.

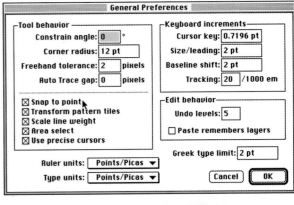

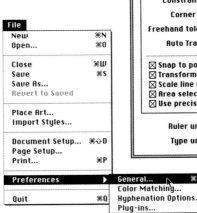

2 | Creating Guide Objects

Any object can be converted to a guide. When the object is in position for converting to a guide, leave the object selected and choose Make (⌘-5) from the Guides options under the Object pull-down menu. The object can be converted back to a path later by selecting Release from the same Guide options menu area.

3 | Moving and Copying Guides

Once guides are created, they are locked. But they still can be moved and copied for more guides. Choose the Selection tool. Press the Control key and then the Shift key after the tool is a V-shape. The Selection tool can then select guides without converting them back to paths. Pressing the Option key while dragging a guide for a move leaves the original guide in place and creates a duplicate guide.

Preparing a Drawing for Export *Using Acrobat to Send Files*

James Braun

Comment

Sending complex PostScript files to different people in order to gain client approval is very problematic. You have to make sure that everyone in the loop has a system large enough to handle the file—not to mention the same fonts. This example provides a simple way to simplify documents so that they can print anywhere and anytime.

Studio Usage

Currently, Acrobat isn't suitable for moving high-resolution color images around so this solution is really only good (at this point) for design approval (although color does reproduce pretty accurately). In the future, this trick will evolve into the standard method of transferring files from the creator site to producer environments.

Related Topics

Using Adobe Acrobat for Nested EPS Files   57

1 | Using Acrobat Writer

There are two important components that you need in order to utilize this trick. The first is built into Adobe Illustrator—it's called the PDF Writer. You can access the writer by Saving As PDF format. PDF stands for Portable Document Format.

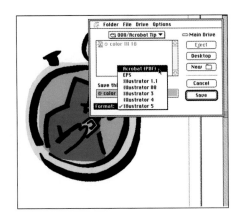

2 | Acrobat Reader

The second component is an application called Acrobat™ Reader 2.0, which is available free of charge from Adobe Systems. (You can find it on America Online in the Software/Illustrator section or you can call Adobe directly and they'll tell you how to get it.)

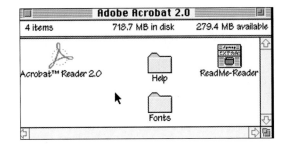

3 | Sending the File to Another Site

You can freely distribute Acrobat Reader to the person responsible for the approval of the design. Just double-click the file and view it—no matter which machine or system configuration you use. The file will display perfectly. The control strip at the top of the page allows you to add notes, insert other PDF files, and turn pages (if the document has more than one).

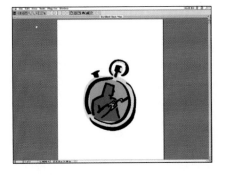

4 | Adding Other File Types to the Package

If you have files created in other applications that you want to send along with your designs, you can use a program called Acrobat™ PDFWriter; it acts like a printer. Go to Chooser and select it as if it were a laser printer. After making your selection, the print dialog box in any other application will change to reflect the Acrobat options.

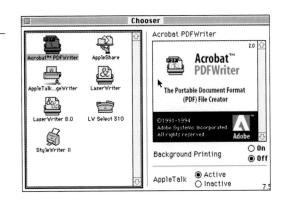

Preparing a Drawing for Export *Communicating with Vendors*

Ned Shaw

Comments

By working with service bureaus and printers you can calibrate your equipment with theirs to create final jobs with expected results. The time and expense of setting up calibration between departments and business is saved by reducing the costly image-setting and press changes.

Studio Usage

It is a sign of professionalism when an artist calibrates files with a service bureau. Any large-scale, color print job should not be run without calibrating the different phases of production.

Related Topics

1 | Creating a Calibration Page

The target calibration page should include shades of black and common colors used in the job. Blends, traps, color mixes, and font samples should also be included. In fact, common elements in the job should be included on the target page sheet.

2 | Sending the File

The target page should be sent to film from the application that is used for final output. Because each application varies slightly in how PostScript information is sent, sending from the final application removes unwanted variables. The goal in calibrating is to use a standard file for calibration. If the entire job is being created in Illustrator, send the file from Illustrator. If the final output is created in another application such as Photoshop, the target page should include all elements, Illustrator files, Photoshop files, and font samples used in the job.

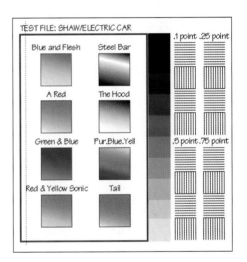

TEST FILE: SHAW/ELECTRIC CAR

Blue and Flesh · Steel Bar · A Red · The Hood · Green & Blue · Pur.Blue.Yell · Red & Yellow Sonic · Tail · .1 point · .25 point · .5 point · .75 point

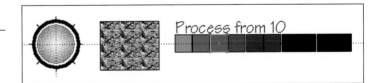

Process from 10

3 | Making Adjustments

Service bureaus appreciate clean files that include the required illustration files and font information. After a calibration print is made, the print is assessed for possible adjustments. Other than halftone screen frequencies and color models, most changes and calibrations will be made at the service bureau or press room. Once a calibration has been made and approved, keeping future work consistent is important. When changes are made—for example, new scanners, color changes, or software upgrades—new calibrations should follow.

Preparing a Drawing for Export *Exporting to Photoshop*

Chris Spollen

Comments

There are many times when it makes sense to export an illustration to Photoshop in order to achieve effects that you can't accomplish with drawing tools alone. The two programs work very well together, and being able to export an illustration in a form readable by Photoshop is a very important skill.

Studio Usage

Anytime your creative vision calls for "painting" (or "painterly," as it's sometimes called) effects, you might consider saving the drawing and importing it into Photoshop to complete. Examples include finer airbrush techniques, random scattering of very small objects (like confetti, for example), fills that aren't defined by a rule (look at a modern comic book), and other features simply cannot be accomplished in a vector program.

Related Topics

1 | Save the Illustration in the Proper Format

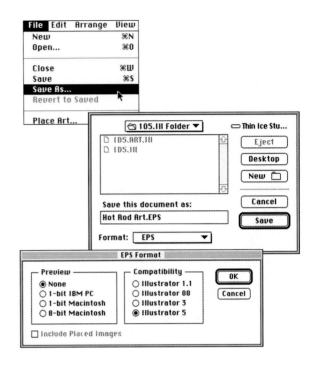

Before you export your illustration to Adobe Photoshop, make sure that your illustration is saved in an EPS format. To make sure that your document is saved properly, select the Save As command under the File menu. Once selected, choose the EPS file format option with the pop-up menu under the file name field. Click the Save button and a second dialog box appears, allowing you to select the preview options (none, 1-bit, or 8-bit). If you are just exporting the illustration to Photoshop, choose the None option. This will save file space, and Photoshop will have less information to wade through as it converts your illustration to a bitmap image.

2 | Exporting to Photoshop

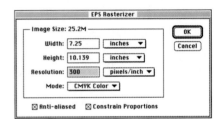

If you want to start a Photoshop document with your Illustrator file, open it in Photoshop with the Open command (under the File menu) or just drag the file's icon onto the Photoshop program icon (or its alias). After this, a dialog box appears, allowing you to set the size, resolution, and the color model (grayscale, RGB, or CMYK modes) of the illustration. After a model is selected, your illustration will appear in a new window and you can edit it like any other Photoshop image.

3 | Tips and Tricks

Before exporting to Photoshop, always remember to delete all ruler guides. Photoshop sees these as objects and will include them when converting the illustration to Photoshop.

To export gradients to Photoshop 2.5 and later, first convert the Illustrator document to version 3 and then export to Photoshop. Older versions of Photoshop do not understand the color gradients' mathematical descriptors and will color the areas black. As an alternate method, take a screen shot of the gradient in preview mode and pull the screen shot into Photoshop. The result is a low-resolution image (72dpi), which works great for backgrounds being projected onto a screen or displayed on a monitor.

If you want to keep the original Illustrator document, remember to save your Photoshop document with a different name from the original Illustrator document.

Preparing a Drawing for Export *Using Photoshop For Trapping*

Charles Akins

Comments

Trapping is a technique that allows for shifting on-press without destroying the registration of artwork. Using Photoshop to do your trapping can save lots of time, but only if you have a powerful enough machine to handle the processing chores (forget about using that old SE for this type of work!).

Studio Usage

Photoshop is sometimes used as a trapping program; when you export an illustration to Photoshop, all trapping issues of the exported artwork are taken care of automatically. This is especially important if your illustration contains "floating traps," where an object appears on a background that goes from light to dark.

Related Topics

1 | When to Use Photoshop for Trapping

Examine your Illustrator document and determine whether there are any "floating" traps. A floating trap occurs when an object appears partially on backgrounds both lighter and darker than itself. Making a trap for this kind of object can be difficult in Illustrator, so it makes sense to use Photoshop to manage this type of trapping. Another reason to use Photoshop is that it is currently impossible to trap gradients in Illustrator (unless you like black lines around everything). Note that patterns will not trap unless you created traps in them when they were designed.

2 | Setting Up for Photoshop

When you have completed your artwork in Illustrator, save the document in EPS format (you can choose Preview, but No Preview would be best in this case) at the size that you need for final output. Make sure that you set no traps in Illustrator if you are going to do the trapping in Photoshop.

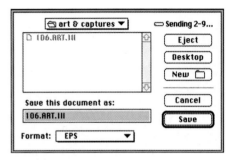

3 | Importing into Photoshop

After the illustration is all set, open the illustration in Photoshop as CMYK with the dpi set at twice the line ruling (halftone dot) that will be used. Make any necessary adjustments or modifications, and save the document under a different name (so that you won't lose the original Illustrator file) in the appropriate format.

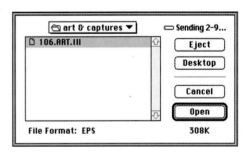

Gary Poyssick

Comments

Photographs often can make a powerful visual statement when simplified or "posterized." Blended colors are broken into a smaller number of nonblended color areas. Objects within a given tonal range are converted into colored shapes, much like creating an image from cut construction paper.

Studio Usage

Although Adobe Streamline really can't be covered in detail in the format of this book, it is a very powerful addition to the Illustrator program. This example is one of our favorite tricks, and we often use it for T-shirt illustrations, such as the "Sail Clearwater" image shown here.

Related Topics

1 | **Select the Image**

Open the image that you need in Adobe Photoshop. Using the Posterize command, convert it into an 8-color image. This eliminates most of the tones and reduces the image to a group of common colored shapes.

2 | **Save the Image**

Save the image as a TIFF file with the Save As command from the File menu. You can use a wide variety of file formats for Streamline, but TIFF works very well for this solution.

3 | **Open the Image and Choose the Correct Settings**

There are a number of predetermined conversion settings built into Streamline. The one called Eight Color Posterized Image was used in this example.

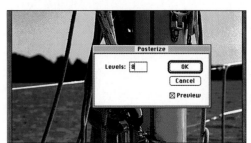

4 | **Convert the Image**

Click the Convert button to see the program go through each of the eight steps. The number of colors that you want is determined by the conversion settings. After a short while, the program will beep, indicating that it has completed the conversion of the bitmap image into a vector illustration. Using Streamline can create some memory-hungry files when printed, so loosen the tightness settings if you encounter a printing problem.

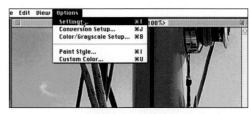

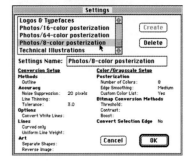

Antler & Baldwin

Comments

Some fonts look too modern for their intended use, although otherwise their design may be perfect. The antiquing technique described here can make a font look like one produced in the 17th century instead of the 21st.

Studio Usage

Sometimes you need to create a different look than normal, and this look may suit your purposes. This technique can also be applied to objects; but care must be taken not to overdo it.

Related Topics

1 | Select and Convert the Type

Select the type to convert. You must convert the type into outlines for this technique to work. Remember that after the type is converted to outlines, you cannot make changes in size, kerning, and so on.

2 | Select the Roughen Filter

Select the Roughen filter from the Distort section under the Filter menu. A dialog box will appear where you can set the amount of roughening needed to create the antique effect. Click OK and the filter transforms your artwork.

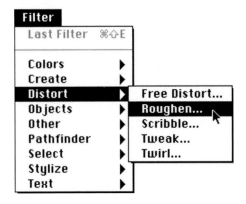

3 | Suggested Settings

Analyze some examples of old typesetting. You should see that most type is not very rough. Setting the amount of offset down to the 3–5% range should provide enough movement to create the right effect. Also the number of segments per inch should be around 10–15 for a capital or ascending letter (for a 36-point letter the Segments field should be set to about 30 segments per inch). For a true antiquing effect, make sure that you use an authentic old serif font (Caslon, Times, Century Old Style, etc.). There were no sans serif fonts before the 19th century, and an "antique" one would be obviously phony!

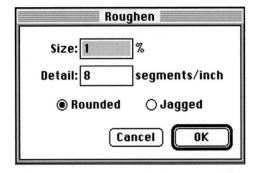

Steven Soshea

Comments

Elegant writing is mimicked by the Illustrator filter. The Calligraphy filter applies a calligraphic style to filled and stroked, closed, and open paths. The filter combines the effects of three commands: Convert Open Paths to Closed Paths, Tweak, and Combine Path. With practice, the filter can give a hand-drawn effect to objects created with the Freehand, Pen, and Geometric Object tools.

Studio Usage

The filter gives a fast, customized, pen-drawn effect to text and objects. Existing art can be converted to a hand-drawn style with this filter. In traditional calligraphic lettering, the pen angle changes as strokes are laid down. The filter uses only one angle, so an averaged angle is selected. A similar effect is created with the Brush tool set to calligraphic pen angles when drawing artwork. The filter can be used to create custom fonts, stylized artwork, and posters.

Related Topics

1 | Selecting the Path

Select the paths to be converted. Converted text should first be made into a compound path to keep open letter shapes hollow after the filter is applied. The current fill color is used in the object after conversion, and the stroke is converted to None.

2 | Converting the Path

Choose Calligraphy from the Stylize options under the Filter pull-down menu. The values entered in the Pen Width and Pen Angle boxes greatly affect the filter's results. The settings in these boxes can alter the style mood much as font selection can change a message's mood.

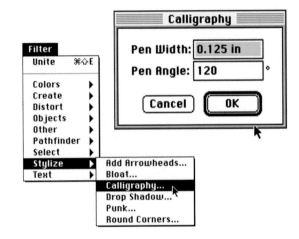

3 | Setting Pen Size and Angle

Variations of pen angle and size create the design characteristics of letters. The thicker the stroke, the heavier the resulting letter—an effect similar to bold-face type. For roman-style faces, use a low pen angle to create thin horizontal strokes. For script faces, use a higher stroke angle to thin the vertical strokes. A zero pen angle is across the horizontal axis. Try an angle; view the effect; and then repeat until the correct angle is found for the intended style.

4 | Editing

After the filter is applied, the element can be further manipulated to meet the design needs. The Scale and Shear tools were used after the filter in the sample artwork.

Tim Dove

Comments

Outlining an object involves placing color completely around its outside. This retains the integrity of the object, while helping (via the outline) to distinguish the object from other objects around it.

Studio Usage

Outlines on type are used to draw attention, to help the object "break out" of the surrounding background, to create a 3D effect (although somewhat primitive), or to fatten up reverse type so that the type maintains readability after the printer's ink dot gain is factored in.

Related Topics

1 | Select the Object or Type to Be Outlined

Select the object to be outlined. If you are outlining type, it is best to convert the type to outlines before you begin this procedure. Illustrator has a hard time drawing outlined type onscreen (it scatters into four different directions); however, the type will print correctly. Make sure that your objects are colored with a fill and a fattening stroke, if needed.

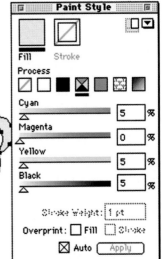

2 | Copy and Paste

Use the Copy command (⌘-C) and then the Paste In Back command (⌘-B). Next, select the Paint Style palette and apply a stroke to the (already selected) copy that is placed behind the original object. Adjust the stroke width as needed to get your desired look.

3 | Stroke Widths

Remember to double the stroke weight of the outline of the object in back. One half will go inside the path (which is covered by the fill on top); the other half will go on the outside (which is the only part of the line that is visible).

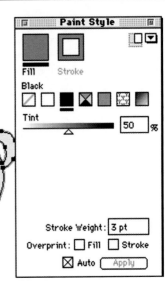

Stephen Bornstein

Comments

Styles are applied to letter shapes for a particular effect. To learn how these effects are created one must understand the components of letterforms. Each different rendering of the alphabet characters is called a typeface, and each variation of that typeface is called a font.

Studio Usage

A specific typeface is chosen for a certain reason—to help convey the feeling of the message. Whether the designer can explain why the typeface has a certain feel to it or not is less important than whether it has the intended influence on the design. Some influenced feelings come from repetitive use of certain fonts for certain messages, and some typeface feelings arise purely from design factors.

Related Topics

1 │ Common Characteristics

All typefaces have common characteristics, which are used to help distinguish typefaces from one another. Characteristics such as upper-case, lowercase, and serifs are commonly known. Characteristics such as x-height, cap-height, descenders, ascenders, and baseline are less known outside of the typesetting studio. The baseline—an imaginary rule upon which all text rests—is the point where the aforementioned characteristics relate to each other.

UPPER CASE
lower case
Serif Type

CAP-HEIGHT
x-Height
ppp ddd

Baseline dg

2 │ Categories of Type

Typefaces can be roughly divided into three groups—serif, sans-serif, and decorative. Serif type has serifs (the extra decorative line caps and tails on a character); sans-serif (from the French "sans," meaning "without") does not. Decorative type is specialized and used mostly in large sizes and for short messages—such as headlines—since they are usually difficult to read at length and at small sizes.
Subgroups of these main categories include Roman—upright type; Italic—slanted type; Weight—the thickness of the type stems; and Extended and Condensed—which refer to character width and spacing.

Serif Style Type
San-Serif Type
Decorative Type

Roman Type
Italic Type

Book Weight
Bold Weight

Extended
Regular
Condensed

3 │ Measuring and Identifying Type

A traditional tool used to measure type size is the E-scale—the capital letter 'E' was defined as the standard height. The E-scale measures type from the baseline to cap height; it is best used on roman fonts rather than italic fonts. Type is measured with a unit called point. There are 72 points in an inch and 12 points in a pica. Type size is measured from the top of the ascender to the bottom of the descender on any given typeface. The cap height of a typeface generally measures about $\frac{2}{3}$ to $\frac{3}{4}$ of the type size.

4 │ Uses of Type

Type has two main uses: display and body text. Display typeface sizes are 14-point and larger; they are often used in headlines and posters. Body type is generally below 14 points; it is used for longer bodies of text, from short advertisements to encyclopedias. Using and designing type (typography) is an art that is always changing.

Midnight Oil Studios, Ltd.

Comments

Designing letterforms to develop a custom typeface can be very time consuming. Using Illustrator as your "canvas" can be an efficient way to compose your creative typographical ideas.

Studio Usage

Your font library may not satisfy your creative needs for a particular project. Illustrators' various tools offer extensive capability for custom font design.

Related Topics

1 | Draw the Typeface

When creating your own typeface, you may want to start with traditional media (pencil sketches or ink on paper, etc.) to establish the style of the typeface before putting it into the computer. If this is the preferred method, you can scan a document and trace it with the Auto Trace tool, or use Adobe Streamline to make guides (or even finished art) for creating your font in Illustrator.

2 | Using Guides

When you reach the electronic drawing stage (after tracing), open a new Illustrator document. Create separate layers for guides and letterforms. Next, set guides for the baseline, x-height, ascender, and descender of the font, using the ruler guides. If you have Streamlined letterforms, you can now place these onto your guides for sizing and orientation. If you want to redraw the letterforms, convert the letters to guides (⌘-5) and place them on the guide layer.

3 | Using the Pen Tool

If you are drawing or redrawing your letterforms, use the Pen tool or the Freehand tool to draw the outlines; draw through the shape and use the Unite filter as needed. You also can use the Rectangle tool (excellent for sans serifs), the Oval tool, or the Brush tool to create letterforms.

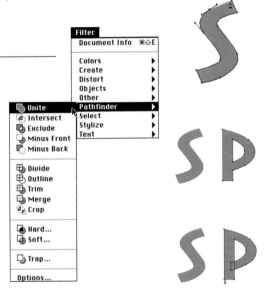

4 | Cleaning Up the Letterforms

You will need to clean up the letterforms to use them in your illustration. Color all the letterforms black; use the Unite filter to eliminate any overlaps; use the Compound command (⌘-8) to make letters like "B" print properly. When you have finished designing your alphabet, save the document.

5 | Choices to Make

If you want to use the typeface as an occasional headline font, you can leave it in Illustrator format and use it like electronic press-type. If you want to use the font for typesetting (a Type 1 font), you will need to get a type creation program, such as Fontographer.

Tim Dove

Comments

Strokes on type are defined by their position in regard to the edges of the letterforms. An inline goes on the inside, or fill, of the letterform, while the outline surrounds the letter.

Studio Usage

In order for the inlines to show properly, the inlining of type is a technique that is really just a creative use of masking. When done correctly, inline type can create quite an effect.

Related Topics

1 | Create the Type

First, set the type for the inline. Make sure that you have it kerned properly and that there are no spelling errors. Then convert the type to outlines by using the Create Outlines command in the Type menu. Now choose Release Compound Paths (⌘-9) from the Object menu. Finally, with all the type objects selected, re-compound them as one unit (⌘-8). You may have to fix any problems with compounding by reversing the path direction (on the Objects Attributes dialog box) on the affected paths.

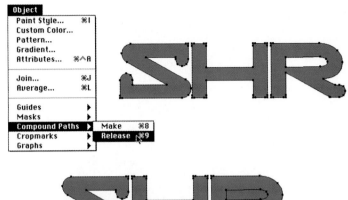

2 | Copy the Type Outlines

Copy the type outlines (⌘-C) and paste the new outlines behind the original ones, using the Paste In Back command (⌘-B). Color the bottom outline (as needed) with a fill and double the stroke that you need in the final lettering.

3 | Apply the Mask

Select both the top outline and the one just colored, and apply the Masks command. The top lettering outline acts as a mask, and the bottom outline appears with the inside half of the stroke showing (the outside half is masked off).

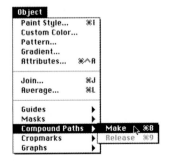

Midnight Oil Studios, Ltd.

Comments

Kerning is the amount of space between individual characters; it is a basic part of typography and font design. The fact that there is visually less space between a letter 'e' and an 'i' [ei] than between an 'e' and a 'w' [ew] is an example of kerning. Font kerning information is not always adequate for all situations. Electronic composition allows a vast array of alterations to fonts. Font kerning information is often pushed far beyond its limits; this is when letter kerning adjustments come into play.

Studio Usage

When fonts are used in situations that they were not designed for, such as headlines, display sizes, or when type follows a curved path, kerning adjustments are often necessary. Illustrator allows you to increase or decrease kerning as required. Kerning is usually required with type sizes above 24 points.

Related Topics

1 | Type Gazing

The only way to spot kerning infractions is with the eye. Some kerning infractions are obvious—letters crashing into each other—while others are more difficult to notice. A quick trick for catching extra kerning is to squint while looking at the page. This distracts the eye from recognizing letters and allows it to see the contrasts in letter spacing instead.

2 | Auto Kerning

The Auto kerning option in the Character dialog box uses the kerning information designed into the type's digital file. Auto kerning does a better job, for example, than leaving the kerning calculation up to the program. The program uses more general kerning information, while Auto kerning uses the specific kerning information that is included with each font's design.

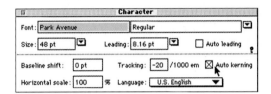

3 | Increasing and Decreasing Kerning

Kerning is increased with positive numbers in the Kerning option box in the Character dialog box. Insert negative values in the box to reduce kerning. Kerning also can be adjusted in preset increments by depressing the Option key and the appropriate direction arrow key—each click representing one increment. The amount of kerning for each key click is set in the Preferences dialog box (⌘-K). The Option-and-Command key combination boosts each click to 10 increments. The left arrow direction key reduces kerning, and the right arrow direction key increases it.

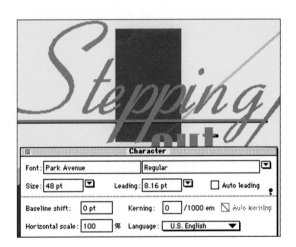

4 | Monitoring Kerning

Both kerning and tracking are monitored in the Information dialog box. To find out how much kerning is applied to a kerned pair of characters, select the space between the two letters with the Type tool. The measurement will appear in the Information dialog box.

Typography *Letter Spacing*

Charles Akins

Comments

Spacing between characters is set by the original font designer or typographer. However, this space information can be adjusted between any two characters, groups of characters in words, and between all the characters in sentences and paragraphs. Adjustment of spacing between individual characters is called kerning; adjusting spacing between multiple characters is called tracking. Tracking does not adjust character shape—as horizontal scale does—it adjusts only spacing.

Studio Usage

The character spacing information cannot include all the necessary information for all the variables you may adjust when working with type in Illustrator. The need to adjust character spacing usually results when a font is used at a large size, such as in headlines. Character spacing also is adjusted to emphasize a font's mood. Reducing the character space adds a sense of urgency, while increasing the space makes the characters appear more formal.

Related Topics

1 | Adjusting Kerning

The amount of kerning required is generally set by eye. Most digital fonts have the kerning information built into their files; to use this prebuilt information select Auto kerning in the Character palette. To adjust kerning further, use manual kerning. Manual kerning can be applied by entering values in the Character palette or by using keystrokes. With the text cursor positioned in a paragraph, press the Option key in combination with the left arrow key to tighten kerning, and press the Option key with the right arrow key to loosen kerning. Adding the Command key to the previous keystrokes increases the kerning value by five times. The amount by which keystroke kerning moves letters is set in the General Preferences dialog box.

2 | Adjusting Tracking

Tracking is spacing between more than one character. It does not alter character shape as horizontal scaling adjustment does. A negative value placed in the Tracking box on the Character palette tightens tracking; a positive value loosens the tracking.

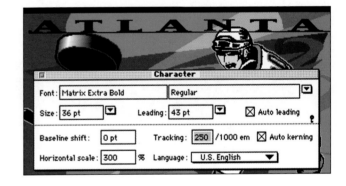

3 | Using Ligatures

Ligatures are single characters that represent more than one letter, like æ, fi, or Œ. Ligatures work only if the selected font includes ligature characters. The Smart Punctuation filter activates ligatures from the Text selections under the Filter pull-down menu. The Smart Punctuation filter also eliminates the need to remember specific key combinations for the ligatures.

François Robert

Comments

In many designs, adding dimension to type adds "height" to the page elements and introduces an additional cognitive response from the viewer. Adding dimension can make images "jump" off the page.

Studio Usage

Although the issue here is type, this sequence can be used to add dimension to other objects. The use of dimensional type is particularly popular in silk screening and sports designs.

Related Topics

1 | Controlling the "Viewing Point"

Looking closely at the letter "B" in the sports logo, you can see that the letters display depth by means of the sides of the object slightly offset to the bottom and right of the actual letters. The placement of an object's sides is determined by the "viewpoint" of the audience. If you're looking from above and left, the sides of the object are below and to the right of the letter being "raised." Experiment with the positioning in your own artwork.

2 | Creating the Object

In the example, the original object is isolated and magnified to show its fill and stroke attributes. You can see that it has a one-point white stroke and is filled with a custom gradient. The new element creates a dimensional colored object by using the Copy and the Paste In Back commands; this creates a clone.

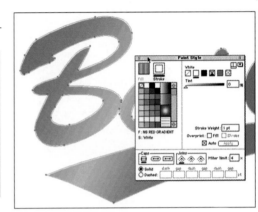

3 | Fatten the Object

Remember that at this point (immediately following the Paste In Back command) the rear clone is still selected. Color and fatten the stroke by changing the appropriate attributes. The apparent "height" of the object is determined by the extent to which you fatten and offset.

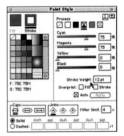

4 | Create the Offset

The fattened letterforms shift down and to the right of the original (blended, white stroke) art element. This produces the illusion of depth, shadow, or height and establishes the viewing position of the audience. You also can select the Move/Copy dialog box to offset the fattened object by holding the Option key and clicking on the solid arrow tool.

Typography *Managing Type Elements by Layer*

FIGURE 5-1   The European Community

Bill Seabright

Comments

The purpose of layers is to isolate illustration elements. (There often is a need to isolate text.) Creating an additional layer to place text allows more control of text through the Layer Control palette. The layer controls make selecting text easier by locking access to other non-text layers. The text layer also can be hidden when editing the illustration portion of the project.

Studio Usage

Illustration files that contain text tend to become cluttered, making individual element selection difficult. A layer for text can be useful in any project that deals with text; often, a separate layer for text will be found in files that are used with text—such as maps, technical illustrations, and files for multimedia use. Printing a separate text-only layer also makes proofreading and text editing easier.

Related Topics

1 | Creating a Layer

To create a new layer, activate the Layers palette (⌘-Option-L). Click and drag the triangle in the top right corner of the palette to access the pull-down menu and select New Layer. Assign the layer an unused selection color and name the layer "type."

2 | Adding Text

When adding text to the file, select and highlight the "type" layer in the Layers palette. Now all new text will be placed on that layer. Move existing text to the "type" layer by selecting the text and then viewing the Layers palette. A colored circle should appear to the right of the appropriate layer's title. Click the small circle and drag it to the "type" layer.

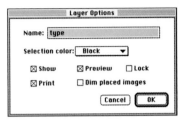

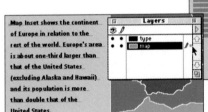

3 | Viewing and Printing Text

When layers are created, they must be active for drawing and viewing. To make viewing and printing changes to the text layer, use the palette buttons below the eye and pencil icons on the Layers palette. The layer marked by the bullet button is active for viewing and/or editing. The eye allows a layer to be viewed; the pencil enables editing to be done in that layer. To print only the "type" layer, the print option for all the other layers must be turned off. Double-click the layer's name in the Layers palette and select the box next to Print so that the 'X' is gone. Although a layer may be turned off for viewing, it will still print unless the Print option is unchecked in the Layer Options dialog box.

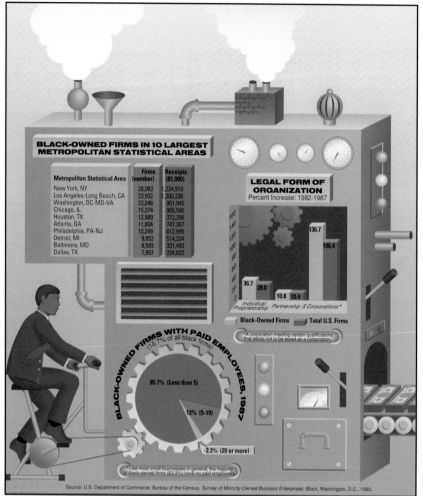

Kenneth Batelman

Comments

A grid is designed by using the selected leading as an element common to all page elements; then you must decide on the page depth, picture box size, pull-quote depth, and paragraph spacing. With all page elements sharing a common divisibility based on a common grid, uneven column depth is eliminated. This is also called "ranging."

Studio Usage

The concept of baseline grids is familiar to designers with a typesetting background from the pre-electronic era. With electronic publishing applications, the concept of mathematics and design are often forgotten—often with the result of sloppy typesetting.

Related Topics

1 | Leading and Column Depth

Set either the leading in the Character dialog box (⌘-T) or the column depth as a priority, and then select other size and depth characteristics. If the leading is set first, then the column depth is made a multiple of the leading. If the column depth is set first, the leading should be a division of the leading. The grid is then based on the selected leading—text with 12-point leading has a 12-point baseline grid.

Metropolitan Statistical Area	Firms (number)	Receipts ($1,000)
New York, NY	28,063	1,234,910
Los Angeles-Long Beach, CA	23,932	1,300,336
Washington, DC-MD-VA	23,046	951,945
Chicago, IL	15,374	908,500
Houston, TX	12,989	372,256
Atlanta, GA	11,804	747,367
Philadelphia, PA-NJ	10,249	612,995
Detroit, MI	9,852	514,324
Baltimore, MD	8,593	331,493
Dallas, TX	7,857	234,823

2 | Picture Box and Quote Box Depth

After the leading and column depth are set, the sizes for picture boxes and pull quotes are decided. Again the size, in depth, should be a multiple of the leading so that it fits the baseline grid. After the sizes are set, picture boxes can be added to columns as puzzle pieces with the total always ending up in the same location. Picture captions must also be considered when placing pictures into the grid formula.

3 | Type Styles and Paragraph Spacing

Spacing before and after paragraphs must also fit the baseline grid by being a multiple of the leading. Changes in type and leading sizes for headings, subheadings, and captions must also fit the grid by being a multiple of the leading. Extra points of leading may sometimes be required to make all columns consistent. When placing the extra leading, use paragraphs with final lines that are full or nearly full; this way, any additional white space is not so obvious. Try to do the opposite for paragraphs that need to be compressed.

Paragraph

Alignment

Indentation
Left: 0 pt
Right: 0 pt
First line: 0 pt

Leading before ¶: 16 pt

☐ Hang punctuation
☐ Auto hyphenate

Midnight Oil Studios, Ltd.

Comments

Typesetting is often completed by designers and writers. In the past, the conventional typesetters' work included more than typing. Part of the job was typesetting punctuation. Some of the most common typesetting punctuation marks are typesetter's quotation marks, em spaces, and em dashes.

Studio Usage

The importance of typeset punctuation is aesthetic. Newspaper editorial copy and ads are good examples of typesetting punctuation in action.

Related Topics

Readability   120

Using Special Characters   123

1 | Spacing

Letterspacing works differently in Illustrator than on a typewriter. Double spaces should never be used after periods. Kerning information for capital letters and periods includes extra space. In fact, double spaces have no place anywhere in typeset text. Designers should learn to use tabs rather than spacing with the space bar. Tabs, rather than spaces, should also follow numbered headings to create hanging indents.

2 | Em Spacing

The advantage of em spacing is that it changes relative to type size. An em space is equal to the same number of points as the set type size. For example, in 12-point type an em space is 12 points. An en space is half of an em space, and a thin space is one-quarter of an em space.

3 | Typesetters' Quote Marks and Apostrophes

"What is it now?"

To insert curly—or typesetters'—quote marks, key combinations must be used instead of the keyboard's quote/apostrophe key. Opening quote marks are made with the Option-Left Bracket key combination; closing quote marks are made with the Option-Shift-Left Bracket keys. Opening single quote marks use the Option-Right Bracket keys, and closing single quotes are made with the Option-Shift-Right Bracket keys. Many applications make these substitutions automatically with settings for "smart quotes."

4 | Periods and Commas with Quotation Marks

"Which door?"

Typesetters' curly quotes are a big step toward professionalism.
Another convention of American typography is that periods and commas *always go inside* the closing quotation mark. Computer programs and certain very academic papers deviate from this, but it's an ironclad rule for general text.

5 | Dashes and Hyphens

The hyphen [-] is made with the Hyphen key alone. It is used to connect compound words, to break words at the end of lines, and to connect *noncontinuous* numbers, like telephone or social security numbers: 212-555-1212 or 111-22-3333.

The en dash [–] is made with the Option-Hyphen key combination, and is slightly longer than the hyphen. It is used to connect *continuous* number ranges: "the years 1485–1512" or "pages 195–337"; in compound adjectives when one element is an open compound: "the Buenos Aires–London flight"; or when the elements of a compound are themselves hyphenated, as in "a semi-public–semi-private party."

The em dash [—] is made with the Option-Shift-Hyphen combination. It is the longest of the three marks, about the width of a capital M in the working font. The em dash indicates a break in thought—or a change of pace—and is the punctuation mark usually called a dash. Never use two hyphens for an em dash. Typewriters had to, but typesetters use the real thing.

Comments

Readability refers to more than the use of proper English. The language is important, but before taking the time to digest a body of text, the reader must be lured into the message by the design. Good design compels the reader to take time to read the message. The two should work together, not overwhelm one another. With Illustrator's ease of adding type and graphic embellishments to a design, it is easy to design for readability. As soon as a written message is part of a project, readability becomes a major factor of design.

Studio Usage

Readability is important in any project with text. In advertising, where readers are interrupted from their planned reading to take time for a self-sponsored message, designing for readability is highly important.

Much time is spent in choosing font, weight, leading, letter spacing, column width, tracking, and kerning in commercial ad design.

Related Topics

1 | Font Selection

Your choice of font should be based on readability, design, and the audience. The first decision in font selection should be between serif and sans serif type. Generally, serif type is used in large bodies of text because it is easier to read. Sans serif type is used in short messages and headlines because in small text blocks it is distinct and legible at a glance.

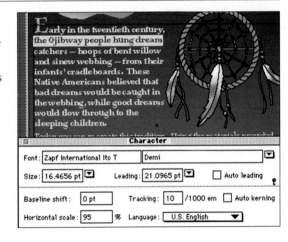

2 | Alignment

Alignment is also very important in bodies of text. The basic choices include flush left, flush right, justified, and centered. Hyphenation can be used to smooth any of these alignments. All of these alignments read well with good word spacing and letter-spacing, combined with good use of hyphenation. For reading ease, it is generally felt that well-hyphenated and well-kerned flush left text is best.

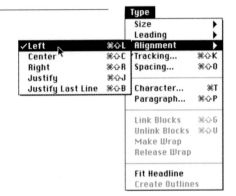

3 | Paragraph Controls

After font and alignment are selected, paragraph controls should be applied. The controls include characteristics such as leading, to control white space; first line indents, to mark paragraph separation; paragraph spacing, to add white space; and line length. Readers tend to prefer short lines of text, which require less eye movement.

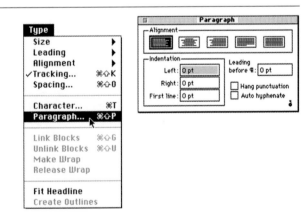

4 | Tracking and Kerning

After all design decisions are made, the document should be read, line by line, for tracking and kerning adjustments. For consistency, tracking should be set once for the entire body of text, and then checked for individual kerning adjustments. Kerning needs adjustments in more than just head-lines. Fonts aren't built for all situations, and letterspacing should be checked throughout a document.

Typography *Tracking*

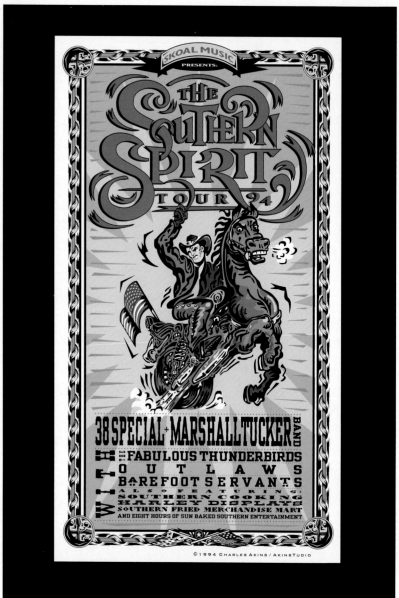

Charles Akins

Comments

When character spacing affects a word or a line of text, it is referred to as tracking. For example, condensed type is tightly tracked, while extended fonts use loose tracking. Tracking is adjusted in Illustrator when letter spacing between more than one character needs to be adjusted. Tracking acts differently than horizontal scaling because tracking only affects spacing, while horizontal scaling affects spacing and letter shape.

Studio Usage

Tracking is used to create tighter or looser lines of type without distorting the type face. It may be used to condense type to fit on one page or to extend a shorter line of type to fill more space. Wide-tracked type portrays a bold, modern look and is frequently used in today's print and television advertisements.

Related Topics

1 | Selecting the Type to Be Tracked

Select the text to be tracked with the Text tool or use
the Direct selection tool.

2 | Setting the Tracking

Any values entered in the Tracking and Kerning box will override the Auto-
Kerning value. The tracking value entered (either positive or negative) will be
the value between all characters selected. If there is kerning in the tracked type,
it is not deleted. Both tracking and kerning are monitored in the Information
dialog box.

3 | Tracking Options

Tracking can be set in the Character palette (⌘-T or ⌘-Shift-K) or by using combinations
of the direction arrow keys and the Command and Option Keys. The left arrow reduces
kerning, and the right arrow adds kerning. Holding down the Option key while selecting an
arrow key changes tracking in one-point increments; by holding the Option and Command
keys tracking is changed in 10-point increments.

Typography *Resolving Font Issues with Acrobat Distiller*

Javier Romero

Comments

Fonts can often cause major headaches when you attempt to output a project somewhere other than where the design was executed. Besides being able to save as an Acrobat file, you also can use the stand-alone Distiller software from Adobe (part of Acrobat Pro) to encode fonts directly into your illustrations—eliminating the need to send them along with the job.

Studio Usage

Eventually, you'll be able to "distill" any file—even ones with high-resolution color images—before you send them to a service bureau (or around the world for approval cycles). This is best reserved for proof cycles or for projects that don't contain any high-resolution images, such as spot colors, grayscale halftones, type, illustrations, anything but high-res. That includes an awful lot of projects. This process "distills" the PostScript and *dramatically* simplifies output (assuming the site owns Acrobat).

Related Topics

1 | Saving As...

You can save directly into an Acrobat (PDF) format from within Illustrator. This creates a clean PDF file, but it doesn't normally encode the fonts directly into the file. The printing site may still need the fonts that you used.

2 | Saving for Use with Acrobat Distiller

Another option would be to save the file as EPS; this will write the information in a form readable by Adobe Acrobat Distiller.

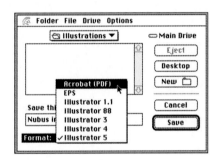

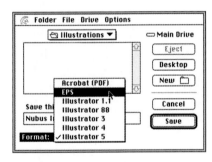

3 | Using Distiller

Under Font Embedding, select any fonts that you always send and move them to the Always Embed dialog box. You can eliminate any fonts that you know reside at the output site (this will make the file smaller). You can choose to always embed any font within any document (this is best if you don't have three million fonts on your system and you're not sure where the file might be output).

Typography *Using Special Characters*

FROM: Frog Publications

Lillypad Elementary School
#7 Magical Way
Happytown, USA 12345

Frog Publications

Comments

A standard keyboard cannot accommodate all the symbols and characters used in typesetting. Modifier keys allow access to these frequently used symbols and greatly increase the quality of the type being produced. (This way it doesn't look like something out of an obsolete typewriter.)

Studio Usage

Special characters and dingbats are used everyday: @, %, $, ®, ©,†, ™,•. Using the special symbols that are built into the font saves time and improves appearance. (The font designer designs these specifically to be used with the font in question.)

Related Topics

1 | Finding Symbols

You can search for a symbol by hitting various key combinations (the frustrating way) or by using Key Caps or some other utility that displays all characters available in the font. (The Key Caps program is used for this demonstration.) Holding down the Shift key and the Option key simultaneously reveals the available characters.

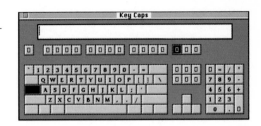

2 | Using the Symbol

After you have found the required symbol, you can memorize or write down the key combination. Use that combination in your artwork. You should memorize frequently used symbols, such as ®, ©, and • because they pop up very often (seemingly, when you least expect)! Key combina-

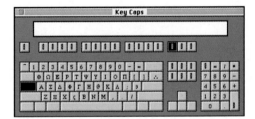

tions for symbols that you use once in a while (like foreign language letters) should be written down and kept close to your computer. (This prevents you from running Key Caps every time you need one of them.) You may be better off using Key Caps for symbols that you use only once in a great while.

3 | Creating Accents

All common foreign character symbols are available on the Macintosh (these tricks apply to other programs, too). To create an accent gauche (grave) or accent droit (aigu), the French [è] and [é], first hit the key that creates the mark (Circumflex [ê] for accent gauche and Option-e for accent droit). Then hit the letter to be placed under it. Note that the accent will not appear until you have hit the second key. (The font will not know which letter to insert until you have told it with the second keystroke.) If you find that you need to use certain letters regularly (especially for German, French, and Scandinavian alphabets), you should consider switching to a keyboard layout designed especially for that purpose. (These layouts have more accessible symbol keys.)

4 | The Symbol Font

You use the Symbol font exactly the same way that you use any other dingbat font; however, the Symbol font is even more important. Many other fonts (including most of the common ones—Times, Helvetica, and so on) make a call to the Symbol font to place the character in question. For this reason, *don't* throw away the Symbol font! Some characters (especially money symbols) are drawn only one way, and it makes no sense to type designers to redraw the same symbol over and over again. (It's like reinventing the wheel.) In all other aspects, the Symbol font behaves like any other font.

LILIACEAE

With more than 3,000 different species worldwide, the Liliaceae is one of the largest families of angiosperms, or flowering plants. The majority of family members have been cultivated primarily for horticultural display for over 5,000 years.

Lily plants are monocotyledons. Monocots are the most evolved group of flowering plants–containing fewer flower parts, their structure is simple and efficient. And, as typical in plants with parallel-veined leaves, the flowerparts of the lily are in threes or multiples of this number. It appears that the flower has six petals, but actually more often than not it has three petals and three sepals of the same color, both growing in circles around the center. There is one pistil (female), composed of a style supporting a three-parted stigma and surrounded by a ring of six stamen (male). At the end of each stamen is an anther covered in pollen; many of the Liliaceae are insect pollinated.

stigma — anther
style — filament
ovary — sepal
— ovule

Cross-section anatomy of a flower

Lillian Koponen Meldola

Comments

Setting type in full-justified columns presents many challenges to the designer. Type isn't really designed to be forced into lines that end in exactly the same place. Because the effect is achieved by forcing space between the words found in the copy, it often results in "rivers" of white space—highly unsightly!

Studio Usage

"Readability" is a vague concept: what's "readable" and what's not? The concept basically applies to eye strain. Always carefully check the spacing in justified type, adjusting individual lines manually, one at a time, whenever you are setting type fully justified. Word spacing can also be applied to left-, right-, or center-justified copy in order to fine-tune its appearance.

Related Topics

1 | Adjusting Word Spacing

Word space is calculated as a percentage of the type size selected at the time the adjustment is made. Entering a number greater than 100% results in expansion of the spaces; when a lesser number is entered, the space compresses.

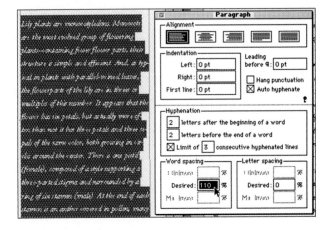

2 | Justified Copy

As we mentioned in the Studio Usage section, you should *always* check each line in justified text; there's a good chance that unwanted white space has been unintentionally added. The Paragraph dialog box allows you to determine the values for Minimum, Desired, or Maximum values.

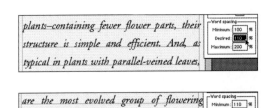

3 | Checking the Results

It often helps to zoom out from the page and put your eyes slightly out of focus. White "rivers" will almost jump out at you. Go back into a high magnification and adjust each line and paragraph as needed. Tightening spaces between words often results in lines "pulling up" as space decreases, so be careful of your line endings and avoid widows.

Typography *Blends in Type*

CAROLINA OFFICE SUPPLY

Office Products for the Twenty-first Century

Ned Shaw

Comments

A blend cannot be applied as a fill to type until the type is converted to outlines. Because type is actually PostScript code, the code information is limited, while still retaining its font information. The information takes into consideration a single fill color and screens of a single color, but it cannot accommodate graduated fills. After the text is converted to an outlined object, the fill can consist of either blends or patterns.

Studio Usage

Blends in type create eye-catching headlines in advertisements and in magazine and newspaper stories. The blended fill can be adjusted to create three-dimensional or textured type effects. Type effects created with blends also are used in film, video, and multimedia presentations.

Related Topics

1 | Converting the Type

After the blend is completed, convert the text to an object by selecting Create Outlines under the Type pull-down menu. Word and letter spacing (tracking and kerning) can be adjusted before or after converting the text.

2 | Applying the Blend

With the converted text still selected, choose Fill to activate the Paint Style palette (⌘-I). Select Gradient to apply the desired fill.

3 | Blend Directions

The fill angle on the Paint Style palette adjusts the direction of the fill. The Gradient Fill tool also can be used to adjust the fill angle and the start and finish points. The gradient fill is applied uniformly to all letters by default. With all letters selected, click and drag the Gradient Fill tool across the entire text in the direction and angle that you want the color changes to flow. An exact angle of the blend's direction can be typed in the Angle box of the Paint Style palette.

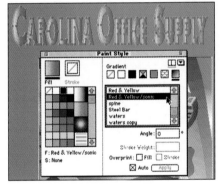

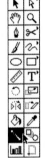

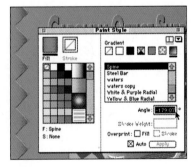

4 | Customizing a Blend

Activate the Gradient palette by selecting it under the Object pull-down menu or by double-clicking on a gradient in the Paint Style palette. Existing gradients can be edited and new gradients can be created by selecting New or Duplicate. The gradients are determined by moving, adding, and deleting the triangles below the gradient color bar. Color attributes of the triangles are adjusted when the triangles are selected. The diamond shape above the gradient bar adjusts the halfway point of the blend. To save a new blend, name it and then close the palette.

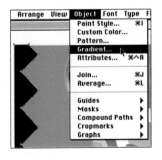

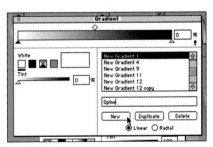

Midnight Oil Studios, Ltd.

Comments

There is more to creating an effective paragraph than hitting the Return key. Using paragraph controls, text readability can be increased. Adjustments in text alignment, indention, and spacing help provide a rhythmic flow of text for the reader.

Studio Usage

Magazines use good paragraph design to lead readers through articles by creating a logical and easy flow of information on the page. Simple adjustments to spacing and indention can make a paragraph stand out without obvious changes to font or letter weights. Paragraph controls are used to create better reading in magazines and in textbook typesetting.

Related Topics

1 | Indention

Most people don't write longhand paragraphs without First Line Indents, but paragraphs without indents are commonly found in typeset copy. This is sometimes done for style reasons, but it is often the result of poor typesetting habits. The most common error is the confusion between First Line Indent and Left Indent. The First Line Indent is just that: an indent applied to the first line only. The position of that indent is measured from the left margin. The Left Indent is the distance of the whole paragraph from the left margin. The Right Indent is the distance of the selected paragraphs from the right margin and where the selected text will stop. Usually, the Right Indent is the right margin, but it can be pulled in to isolate a paragraph, like a quotation.

> BENJAMIN KING, IN THE PESSIMIST, WROTE "NOTHING TO DO BUT WORK. NOTHING TO EAT BUT FOOD. NOTHING TO WEAR BUT CLOTHES." HE DIED AT 37 YEARS OF AGE, WITH ANY LUCK FROM HUNGER OR EXPOSURE. SURLY SOD!

2 | Hyphenation

Hyphenation can be used for all paragraph alignments: flush left, flush right, justified, and centered. Justified alignment without hyphenation can produce ugly and hard-to-read text. One hyphenation rule is to limit the number of consecutive hyphenated rows of text. Three is a common limit, but it changes depending on each job's design style. Too much hyphenation makes for hard reading and amateurish appearance. Hyphenation can be reduced by using tracking, kerning, and discretionary hyphens.

> OBVERSELY, JEROME JEROME NOTED, "I LIKE WORK. IT FASCINATES ME. I COULD STARE AT IT FOR HOURS." WHAT COULD YOU EXPECT FROM THE OFFSPRING OF PARENTS OBVIOUSLY TOO LAZY TO THINK UP A CHRISTIAN NAME.

3 | Spacing

Paragraph spacing helps distinguish between paragraphs and makes reading easier. With justified text, the page can become very "gray." Adding space between paragraphs subtly increases the white space of the page. Paragraph space should be added with the Paragraph control palette, not by using paragraph returns. Whether the space is placed before or after the selected paragraph depends on how extra space is being added to adjacent paragraphs and where the space is located in the document.

Paragraph

Alignment

Indentation
Left: 0 pt
Right: 0 pt
First line: 0 pt

Leading
before ¶: 0 pt

☐ Hang punctuation
☐ Auto hyphenate

Workflow Issues *Illustrator as a Page Layout Program*

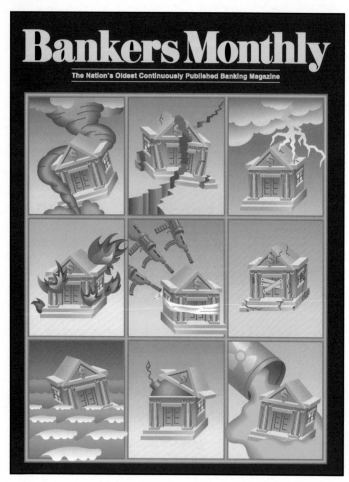

Kenneth Batelman

1 | Set Page Parameters

After the page size is set in the Document Setup dialog box, set the text columns, gutters, and margins with the Rows and Columns filter from the Filter pull-down menu under Text.

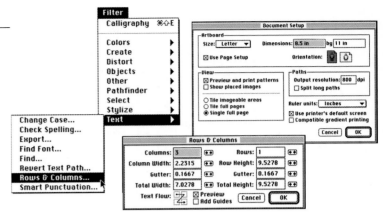

2 | Create Text Blocks

Before deselecting the newly created column and row boxes, convert to text-area boxes with Link Blocks (⌘-Shift-G) under the Type pull-down menu.

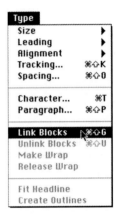

3 | Import Text

Text can be typed into the blocks or imported from another program. In the sample the text was imported as an ASCII file from a word processing program—ASCII (American Standard Code for Information Interchange) is a standard text language used by all major programs.

4 | Apply Typesetting Skills

Text flow can be changed by the text blocks' layer positions—text flows from the back to the front. After the text flow is set, text is ready for formatting to the job specifications. In the sample, the layout work used paragraph alignment, the Find filter, Find Font filter, Smart Punctuation filter, Check Spelling filter, the Tab palette, masks, imported illustrations, text wraps, and the Overprint Black filter. Because page layout is the final step before printing, the task can use nearly every feature available in the program.

Workflow Issues *Image Databases*

Scott MacNeill

Comments

Using libraries for common artwork helps to make the production process simpler and easier. Everyone who needs access to these database files will have it, without creating unnecessary duplicates of the artwork.

Studio Usage

This is where computer networking really shines! Having everything you need stored in one place can save you countless hours of work, not to mention hard disk space (with the added benefit of keeping your artwork consistent). This is especially important for logos. Why keep 50 versions of the same logo when just one in a library will do?

Related Topics

1 | Creating a Library

To create a library, first choose a place on your network where everyone who needs access to the artwork can retrieve it. Using a file server on your network is the most obvious solution. If this is not available, designating different workstations to hold certain artwork libraries is your best solution.

2 | Organizing Your Libraries

You should organize your libraries so that all the artwork within it is related—by client, style, type of artwork, and so on. When a new piece of artwork is added, make sure that the artwork doesn't exist elsewhere in the library, or in another library. Also, publish and update a list of artwork in the library(ies) to eliminate extensive searches for any needed artwork.

3 | Alternate Ways to Make Libraries

Another way to make a simple, portable artwork library is to store everything on floppy disks, SyQuests, Bernoullis, opticals, or other media. Once set up, make sure that everyone uses a sign-out sheet to obtain a library disk. This solution, of course, works best in a small office setting (under 10 workstations). Larger installations usually have a network file server and a system administrator who handles system issues and the filing of artwork

Workflow Issues *Simplifying Final Documents*

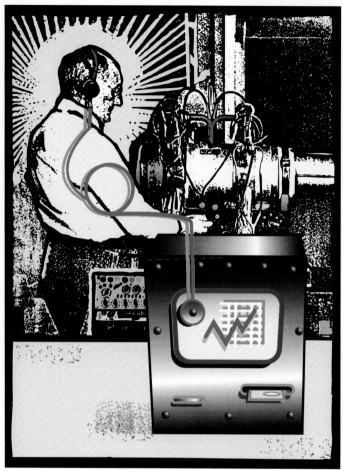

Chris Spollen

Comments

The question to keep in mind as you are finishing your illustration is, "Is there a simpler way to do this?" Many times, there is! Simplifying certain sections of your work can save you endless hassles, reduce memory requirements, and help avoid that dreaded "Cannot Print File" dialog box.

Studio Usage

The simpler an illustration is, the better and faster it will print, especially on today's high-tech equipment. Making something simpler also can save you money at your output service bureau because they often charge jobs according to the printing time, not by the page count.

Related Topics

1 | Objects and Masks

Try not to use too many masks in your illustration. Masks make image-setting equipment calculate each masked object twice (once without the mask, once with it), which slows printing. If you can, use the Crop filter instead of a mask.

2 | Colors and Gradients

If you are printing CMYK colors, make sure that all the colors and gradients in your illustration are CMYK-based. Don't forget to convert any custom colors to process colors! If you are printing only with custom colors, then stick with the same custom color model (Pantone®, Trumatch™, etc.) throughout the illustration and avoid all CMYK colors. Gradients, of course, should be built with the same custom color model; they should not be blended with other custom colors.

3 | Splitting Paths

Long paths with lots of control points can slow down an image-setting device—sometimes halting it. To split any long object paths in your illustration, open the Document Setup dialog box, under the File menu (⌘-Shift-D). Click the Split long paths check box; the paths will be split according to the output resolution set for your illustration. This will occur the next time you save your document; it is irreversible, so make sure that this is one of the last steps you take in preparing your illustration for printing. When saving this file, save it with a different name, so that the text in the original illustration can be edited later, if need be.

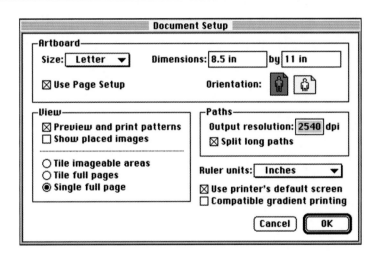

4 | Type

If you are not sure where your illustration will be sent for imaging, you may want to convert all the type in it to outlines. This will ensure that the final illustration will appear exactly as you see it onscreen; it's also a good idea if you have put a stroke on the type (to thicken it up, for example). Otherwise, make sure that the person or company receiving the illustration has the same font. You can check the font's ID and version number of the font file with the Get Info command from the File pull-down menu in the Finder. All font files are located in the Font folder of your System folder. Of course, you can always supply the service bureau with the font that's used in the illustration.

Ned Shaw

Comments

Text can be converted to outlined paths by using the PostScript® file information of Type One fonts. As a path, the text can be stroked, filled, and manipulated like a graphic element.

Studio Usage

Text must be converted to paths before it can be filled with blends. This converting feature can be used to build text-based artwork for files without the original font. Converted type also can create letter-shaped masks.

Related Topics

1 | Select Type

You must use the Selection tool, not the Text tool, to select the type to be converted. Entire text elements are converted. Individual letters on a text path must be placed as separate text elements for conversion.

2 | Convert

Tracking and kerning can be done before or after the conversion. After the conversion is complete, a guideline should be used for alignment. Select Create Outlines from the pull-down Type menu. The type is converted with the same color characteristics that it had before the conversion.

Type	
Size	▶
Leading	▶
Alignment	▶
✓Tracking...	⌘⇧K
Spacing...	⌘⇧0
Character...	⌘T
Paragraph...	⌘⇧P
Link Blocks	⌘⇧G
Unlink Blocks	⌘⇧U
Make Wrap	
Release Wrap	
Fit Headline	
Create Outlines	

3 | Transform and Manipulate

As graphic elements, the paths can be converted with one of Illustrator's transformation tools. Blended fills can be applied to the text, or the text can be set as a mask element, as in the sample.

Julie Pace

Comments

The demand for traditional copyfitting has been reduced by the ease of electronic page layout. Traditional copyfitting used font information and layout specifications from rough manuscripts to calculate type size, leading, and job lengths for final layouts. Today, copyfitting has more to do with fitting the copy into the available space by using the many paragraph controls available at the click of a button. This time-consuming function is now a visual exercise.

Studio Usage

Copyfitting principles are being used whenever you adjust type size, leading, tracking, kerning, and line length. Innumerable variables come into play when fitting copy into the available space in page layouts. Type must be copyfit to maintain balance between readability and aesthetics. Copyfitting is used heavily in book typesetting and in advertising design.

Related Topics

1 | Determining Text Areas

The first step of copyfitting is defining text areas. The area defined by dragging the Type tool determines the line length and page depth. The size of this area is based on images being used, page size, and white space needs.

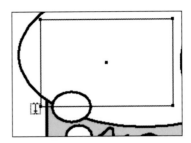

2 | Adjusting Standard Copyfitting Variables

After the copy is set by typing or by placing text, type attributes are applied. The standard copyfitting variables are adjusted in the Character dialog box (⌘-T)—including leading, indents, tabs, and space between paragraphs.

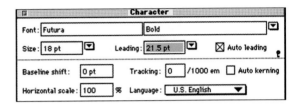

3 | Paragraph Variables

Text copy can be further adapted with paragraph characteristics. Indents, extra space between paragraphs, and hyphenation attributes are adjusted in the Paragraph palette (⌘-Shift-P).

4 | Kerning and Tracking

After the desired type and paragraph specs are applied, the text should be cleaned up manually. Tracking is very useful for repairing any word spacing problems created by justified text. Kerning of individual letters should be adjusted in headline and subhead copy.

5 | Typesetter's Copyfitting

Copy is then imported and made to fit the job specs. Before WYSIWYG ("What you see is what you get") technology, typesetters saw their work as lines of code placed intermittently in the text. Finished work was not seen until output. With any given font style, new layout sizes can be recalculated by using the known characters for pica, type size, line length, leading, page size, and the number of pages from an unformatted manuscript.

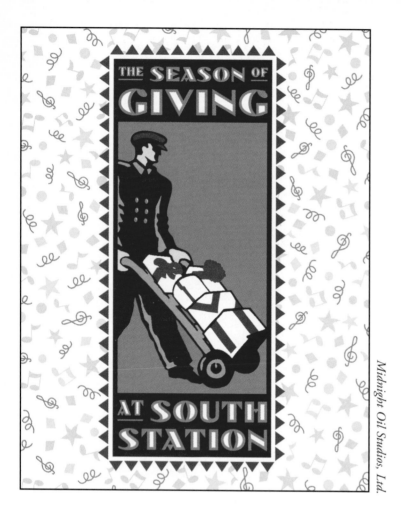

Midnight Oil Studios, Ltd.

Comments

Illustrator's word processing tools include the capability to search, find, and change fonts quickly. Assignment of a font style to a character labels the character(s) with a font code. This code communicates the font identity and style to the printer. The program uses labeling along with a search script to find and change selected fonts.

Studio Usage

In package design, type may be assigned a number of styles before a final style is chosen. The Find Font filter allows convenient switches between fonts rather than directly searching and replacing fonts with the Text tool. Another helpful use for this filter is searching for fonts that are not used in the design but are still part of the file in a space or return character. This printing problem can be avoided by searching the document before printing to find and remove unwanted fonts.

Related Topics

1 | Selecting Search Limits

Activate the Find Font filter from the Text selections under the Filter pull-down menu. The lower third of the dialog box deals with the selection. The first group—Multiple Master, Standard, Type 1, TrueType—deals with the kind of font to be searched for. Unless you know the specific type, leave all types selected. The second group—System List and Document List—determines where the fonts are sought. Highlighting Document List allows you to replace fonts only with those already in the document. Selecting System allows you to replace fonts with all those in the system that match the font types selected for inclusion in the search.

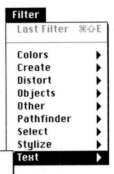

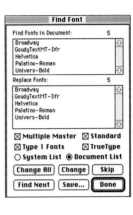

2 | Searching in the File

Once the search parameters are set, the process is very similar to using a word processing dictionary. You have the choice to search through the file selection by selection to decide upon each change or to do a single sweep with the Change All function.

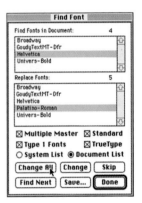

3 | Adding a New Font from the System

The filter allows fast editing of font changes. With the System list active, the font to be changed appears in the upper window. The new font appears in the lower window. If the change is universal to all appearances of the font, the Change All function should be used. If specific appearances of the font are being changed, the Find Next, Change, and Skip functions are used.

4 | Creating a File's Font List

When a file is sent to the printer or service bureau, a list of the file's fonts is usually required. The Save function creates a font usage list for the file.

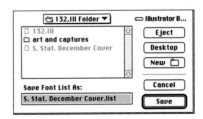

Tim Dove

Comments

When type is set in Illustrator, the program creates a baseline that the type rests upon. If you draw this baseline in Illustrator and set the type on this already created path, the type will follow the path as if it were its own baseline. Always lock down or hide other paths when selecting a path for text. This saves a lot of headaches, and it ensures more accurate selection.

Studio Usage

Type that is cast in an arch (or along a shape) is a very popular design device. Using this technique (and in combination with others), you can create attention-grabbing headlines that would otherwise be almost impossible to create.

Related Topics

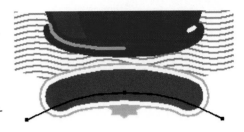

1 | Draw the Object to Place the Type Upon

First, draw the path that you need to put type on. This can be an open or closed path, drawn with the Pen tool or any of the automatic object tools—oval, rectangle, spiral, and so on. If you need to keep a copy for further modification, copy the path (⌘-C) and paste it in front of it (⌘-F).

2 | Choose the Proper Type Tool

Next, determine the proper type tool for the job. If you are putting this type on an open path (curved line for instance), you can use the regular Type tool to select the path. If you are using a closed path—rectangle, oval, polygon, and so on—you will need to use the Path-type tool to select the object. (The program assumes that you want to use type area-selection instead of type on a path.)

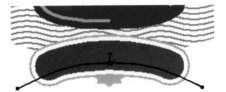

3 | Enter the Text

Once selected, a blinking cursor appears on the path; text can now be entered. All attributes that are normally available with type (except leading; there is only one line of type allowed on a path) are available here. Format the text as needed, and save your document when done.

4 | The I-Beam

When type on a path is selected with the Selection tool, an I-beam appears. This I-beam determines where your type will start or end (with flush-left or -right type, respectively) and which side of the path the type will appear on. To change the position of the I-beam, click it with the Selection tool and drag it in the desired direction. To make the type flip over to the other side, double-click the intersection of the I-beam and the path.

5 | Tips and Tricks

To make type wrap around a circle, create the circle and enter the text as normal. Select the circle with the Selection tool, copy it, and paste it in front. Lock down the first path (⌘-Option-1) and double-click on the I-beam. Enter the new text, and then select it. Open the Type dialog box (⌘-T) and enter a negative value for the baseline shift. After adjusting as needed, close the dialog box and save the illustration.

Mike Doudy

Comments

Type that is forced to fill the full line length is called justified type. Justifying type allows more type to be placed in a given space by adjusting letter and word spacing to fill the space at the ends of lines that would otherwise be lost. Justified type also may present a more formal or "businesslike" appearance than type with ragged right or left margins. Automatic justification simplifies this otherwise immense task. All the parameters that define a justified paragraph are controllable with Illustrator.

Studio Usage

Justified type is common in ad copy that must fit into blocks. Most magazines and newspapers use justified type because it gets more text into less space while leaving room for advertising. Aesthetic concerns are also reasons why justified type may be selected over other paragraph alignments, such as flush left, flush right, or centered.

Related Topics

1 | Justifying Text

Select the paragraph(s) to be aligned as justified. Because text alignment is a paragraph control, all that needs to be selected is a single space or character for the alignment to affect the entire paragraph. Select the Paragraph palette (⌘-Shift-T) and select the Justified Text box (or use the keyboard shortcut ⌘-Shift-J).

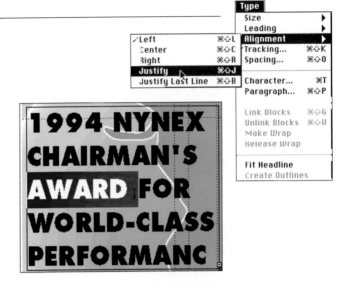

2 | General Controls

Justifying text opens the opportunity for many aesthetic problems. Many spacing problems can be cleaned up by using automatic hyphenation. Auto-hyphenation inserts hyphens at word syllable breaks to create more uniform spacing. Hyphenation controls are accessed by clicking the Display control in the bottom right of the Paragraph palette.

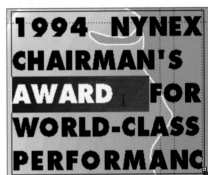

3 | Word Spacing

Word spacing affects the changes of space between words in justified text. If the justified compression or expansion between words is undesirable, adjust the percentages appropriately. The values are set as percentages away from the type size selected—100% represents no change.

4 | Letter Spacing

Letter spacing affects the changes of space between letters in justified text. If the justified compression or expansion between letters is undesirable, adjust the percentages appropriately. The values are set as percentages away from the type size selected—0% represents no change.

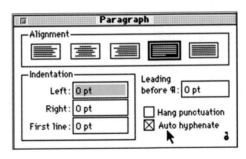

Julie Pace

Comments

Any object created with the Pen tool can be converted to a text area. After the area becomes a text area, it can be linked with other complex and regular shaped text areas.

Studio Usage

You can use complex shapes for text blocks in newsletters and especially in ad creation. Text can define the illustration through silhouetting and cropping.

Related Topics

1 | Defining the Shape

Use the Pen tool to define the required text areas shape.

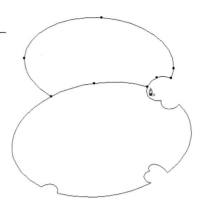

2 | Converting and Linking the Text Areas

After the text locations are defined with closed paths, convert the paths to text area by using the Area type tool. After the areas are converted, select all the paths with the Selection tool and select Link (⌘-Shift-G) under the Type pull-down menu. Text will flow from the back-most object to the foremost text area.

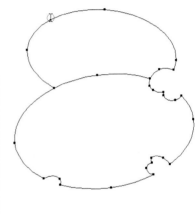

3 | Placing the Text

Enter the text with the keyboard in Illustrator or import text—using the Import Text command under the File pull-down menu—with the text I-beam active in the first text area.

4 | Adjusting Fills and Strokes

When an object is converted to a text area, its fill and stroke settings are set to none. The fill and stroke can be edited later using the Direct Selection tool. Text color attributes can be adjusted by selecting the text with the I-Beam tool.

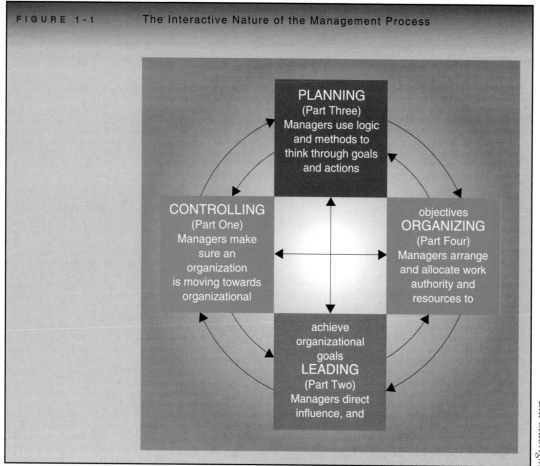

FIGURE 1-1   The Interactive Nature of the Management Process

PLANNING
(Part Three)
Managers use logic
and methods to
think through goals
and actions

CONTROLLING
(Part One)
Managers make
sure an
organization
is moving towards
organizational

objectives
ORGANIZING
(Part Four)
Managers arrange
and allocate work
authority and
resources to

achieve
organizational
goals
LEADING
(Part Two)
Managers direct
influence, and

Bill Seabright

Comments

By using Illustrator's capability to constrain text inside rectangles, you can build columns of type as in page layout programs. When type areas are linked, the selected fills are shared. Text flows from one linked rectangle to the next. The flow is controlled by drawing order, with text flowing from the backmost layers to the frontmost.

Studio Usage

This linking feature is commonly used in newsletters, newspaper and magazine ads, and in food menus— any job where a great deal of text needs to be organized for reading. Because it was not initially designed as a page layout program, Illustrator has never been used heavily for page composition. Better type controls and spell checking features, combined with the capability to build type columns, may make this an option. However, large typing tasks will still be generated in word processing applications first and then placed in Illustrator.

Related Topics

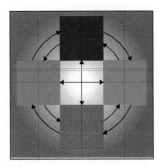

1 | Setting the Columns

Use guide lines to mark column width, depth, and gutters.
Set the page layout dimensions and select the Type tool.

2 | Drawing the Columns

Beginning with the first column, click and drag a rectangle to
represent the first column of type. If the remaining columns
are the same, Option-click and drag additional columns.
Remember that type is flowed between columns in order of
drawing sequence. Type flow can be altered by changing the
layer positions of the type rectangles—text flows from back
to front.

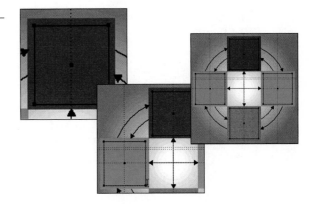

3 | Linking the Columns

Select all type rectangles and link them together using the Link Blocks command
under the Type pull-down menu. If the columns are art elements, they must be converted to type areas by selecting them with the Area-Type tool.

4 | Placing the Type

Text can be typed directly into selected type
areas, or placed from a word processing file into
Illustrator. To place a text file, use the Import
Text command in the File pull-down menu.
Select the text file to place from the dialog box,
and the text from the file will flow into the
linked text blocks.

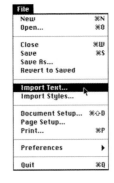

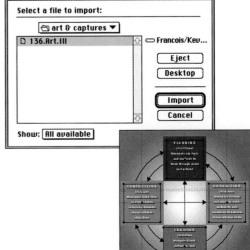

Comments

To achieve the best possible file output to print or video, the management of type in a document is important. In order to be better organized, it is useful to make a list of font files. Then fonts can be searched for and replaced as editing requires.

Studio Usage

The use of Type Management filters reduces the chance of making errors when working with fonts. One of the most common errors is forgetting to include all a file's fonts when sending a file to the printer. Having a printed font list is a fast way to know which fonts are required for a job. The Find Font filter offers a solution to printing problems by finding fonts embedded in character spaces or returns.

Related Topics

1 | Searching for Fonts

To find and change document fonts, use the Find Font filter. Open the Find Font dialog box from the Text options under the Filter pull-down menu.

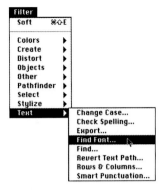

2 | Checking the System Fonts

A comparison between the two font lists—the document and system font list windows—should be made to ensure that the job's fonts are installed in the system.

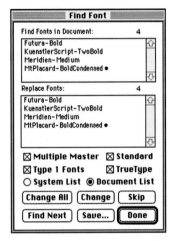

3 | Changing a Font

If you want to make changes to the font styles within a document, select Document Fonts in the second window. If more fonts will be added to the Illustrator file later, leave the System List selected in the second window. (The other options in this dialog box select which type of fonts are included in the displayed font list.) To change a font style, select it in the Document List and select the font to replace it with in the second window. Select Find Font. If the font style found is one you want exchanged, select Change followed by Find Next until you've found all fonts in the illustration. If you want to exchange all occurances of one font style, use the Change All button after the replacement for the font style is selected in the second window.

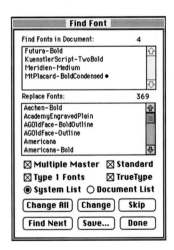

4 | Creating a Font List

A font list is useful for archival and remote printing . When all font changes are finished, select Save in the Find Font dialog box and name the file appropriately. The created file is a TeachText file that lists the fonts, document name, page size, and saved resolution. When saving the Illustrator document to a floppy disk, include this text file too. Later, when you need to print the document, the text file of the font list will be very useful.

Antler & Baldwin

Comments

Good spelling enhances communication; however, misspelled words give the impression of sloppiness, a confused message, and a misunderstanding of the subject. Don't rely solely on spell checkers—they can't replace a good editor.

Studio Usage

What good is it to do a fabulous design, only to have misspelled a word in the headline? The spell check filter helps to alleviate this problem, while allowing you to concentrate on creating your design.

Related Topics

Managing Type in a
Document   137

1 | Select the Text to Be Checked

With the Type tool, select the text you need to check for spelling. The spell checking filter will not work if the type is selected with any of the Selection tools.

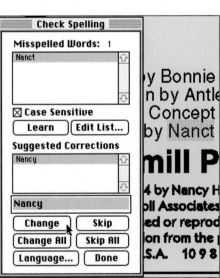

Illustrated by Bonnie Zacherle
Book Design by Antler & Baldwin, Inc.
Concept by Concept Connection, Inc.
Developed by Nanct Hall, Inc.

2 | Use the Spell Checking Filter

Select the Spell Checking Filter under the Text sub-menu in the Filter menu. The filter searches through the selected text and, if it finds any errors, calls them to your attention. The word in question appears in a field on the Spell Check palette, and as highlighted text within the document. If you feel that the word is incorrect, you can select an alternate word from the suggestions that appear below the misspelled word, or enter the new spelling. When you have selected an alternate or corrected the word, click on the Change button. If you feel that the word is spelled correctly, choose the Ignore button on the palette, and the filter continues searching. When the filter has finished searching it reports how many errors were detected, and how many words were changed. Click OK, and you will return to the illustration.

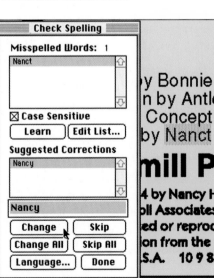

Midnight Oil Studios, Ltd.

Comments

Using the Wrap Text command, text can be forced to wrap around any shape. When an element is wrapped by text, Illustrator will prevent letter overlapping based on the text's baseline information and the element boundary. The wrap can be further manipulated by adjusting its boundary shape with the Direct Selection tool.

Studio Usage

It is often necessary for text to wrap around graphic elements placed in text columns. Text wrap prevents text from printing over photographs or graphics. Text wrap also is used to create white space in text areas and to force text out of the way for drop caps.

Related Topics

1 | Create a Wrap Boundary

Place the graphic element in the layout and create a closed path around it. You will use the path as a wrapping boundary for the text wrap. Remove the fill but leave a stroke for the wrap boundary so that it is visible for editing.

2 | Layer the Objects

When all the elements are in place, check that the items to be wrapped are above the text area boxes. You can either send the text area boxes to the back or bring the graphic and wrapping boundary elements to the front. Text wrap works only with text-area boxes.

3 | Select Elements to Wrap

Click and drag or shift-select the elements included in the wrap. With a wrapping boundary box, it is not necessary to include the graphic inside the boundary because more wraps can be added to the text area later, even after one wrap is made to the same text-area boxes. Select Make Wrap from the Type pull-down Menu.

4 | Fine Tuning

After the wrap is complete, it may need editing. Use the Direct Selection tool to adjust the wrapping boundary of the text wrap. Adjust the kerning adjacent to the wrap to fine-tune its text placement. When the wrap is satisfactory, select the wrapping boundary with the Direct Selection tool and remove its stroke color.

Ned Shaw

Comments

Illustrator creates graphs from tables with the Graph tool, but the tool should be thought of as more of a subprogram. Graphs are created from database tables. The relationship of the numbers in the tables are then displayed from a choice of six graph types and variations. The graphing and charting abilities offered by the Graph tool create a great diversity of graph styles and options to those styles.

Studio Usage

When numbers are displayed by using tables, their relationships are visible. But when the same numbers are displayed using graphs, the shapes of their relationships are seen. Graphs and charts created with Illustrator are used in news-graphics, annual reports, multimedia displays, and television reports.

Related Topics

Creating Cool Graphs   69

1 | Setting the Graph Area

Before beginning a graph, set its size. This can be done by manually clicking and dragging out its area or by Option clicking the Graph tool to activate the Graph dialog box (where the graph width and height are entered).

2 | Creating the Data Table

Data is entered manually in the Graph data dialog box. If the box is not activated, select Data from the Graph option under the Object pull-down menu. Data is entered in the selected cell. When entering data be sure to leave one row and one column for graph axis titling information. Data can also be imported into the data field from spreadsheet programs that have column information separated by tabs and rows separated by returns.

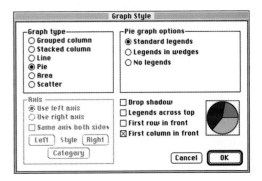

3 | Graph Types

The type of graph selected is determined by the information being compared. Bar graphs are easy to read accurately and are used for comparing information. Line graphs are used mainly for showing comparisons of technical and scientific values. Stacked bar, pie, or circle graphs are used to show proportions or the relative size of related amounts of a whole.

4 | Customizing the Graph

Graph design is done for clarity of understanding, rather than aesthetics. Aesthetics are important, but must not overwhelm the information being offered. When customizing a graph, it should not be ungrouped. After being ungrouped, graphs become an art object and lose links to the Graph data dialog box. (Changes to the data in the dialog box will no longer affect the graph.) Customization is only limited to creativity, with the goal being comprehension, after catching the reader's attention.

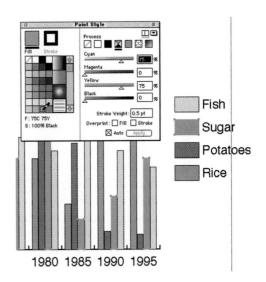

Working with Patterns *Converting Drawings to Patterns*

Lillian Koponen Meldola

Comments

Once patterns are created, they can quickly be applied to elements for dramatic effects that print fast, redraw faster onscreen, and use less memory. Patterns can give the illusion of repeating patterned tiles and the illusion of a random fill. Patterns speed up screen rebuilds and printing. By defining a fixed field as a repeating-tile fill element, complex backgrounds can be used without using a large amount of memory. Using a pattern rather than a manually drawn pattern, file size can be reduced by as much as half.

Studio Usage

Patterns are used as backgrounds in illustrations and to give textures to illustration elements. Textile designers use patterns in Illustrator to create designs for cloth, wall paper, and ceramic tile.

Related Topics

1 | Selecting a Pattern

Patterns can be found in prefabricated commercial pattern file libraries, or you can create your own. Any Illustrator pattern file library containing the pattern must also be open to add a newly created pattern to its Patterns list. The new pattern will appear in the Patterns list after the pattern has been used in the illustration and that Illustrator file has been saved. The pattern will now be part of the Patterns list.

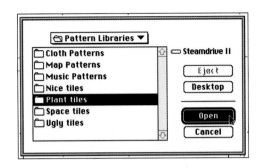

2 | Creating a Custom Pattern

Draw a pattern and the pattern area with a rectangle as the rear most object. Select the tile pattern and background. Next, select Patterns from under the Objects pull-down menu. In the Pattern palette, select New. The selected tile appears in the window. Name the file and select OK. Tiles not being used should be deleted from the Patterns list to reduce the illustration's file size (make sure to do this after the new patterns are applied).

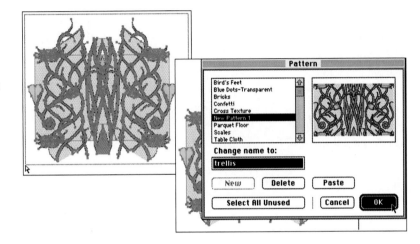

3 | Applying the Fill

Select the object that you want to apply the tile to and select the Paint Style palette (⌘-I). Select the pattern icon at the top of the palette window and then select the appropriate pattern from the Pattern fills list. The starting point of a pattern's tile is set by the location of the file's zero point and the pattern's upper left corner. By moving the zero point, the pattern shifts to the desired starting point.

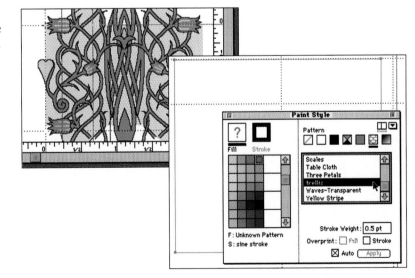

4 | Pattern Customizing

Patterns can be further customized by using the Transformation tools. In each Transformation tool dialog box there is a choice to apply the transformation to only the object, only the pattern, or both. To transform a pattern without using dialog boxes, depress the 'P' key and select the object's center-point with the Transformation tool. Original tiles can be restored by selecting Paste in the Patterns dialog box. The original tile will be placed in the open art file.

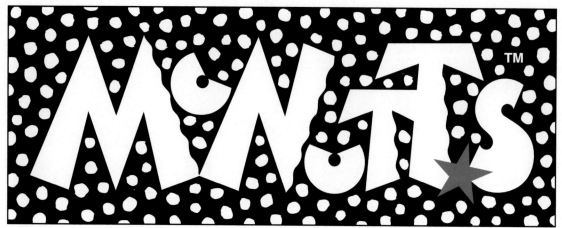

Tim Dove

Comments

Each pattern contained in a document adds to its storage size, even if it is not used in the illustration. Storing patterns in a separate library file until they are needed reduces your file size and increases the work speed in Illustrator.

Studio Usage

In a studio that uses patterns, a central storage library should be used for both custom-made and purchased pattern styles. Each time a new pattern is made it should be stored in this library for future use.

The organization of the pattern library should be designed for each studio's work habits. Any size studio can benefit from a pattern library.

Related Topics

1 | Basic Organization

When organizing a pattern library, each studio's pattern usage needs to be analyzed. Files may be stored by type, client, or dates. Studio directors will have to choose the best method for their studio. Silly names can be used for organization, but logical names work best—especially when more than one designer is using the same files. "Fruity Patterns" as a folder name may mean fruit patterns to one designer, when to another designer it may mean a defamation lawsuit against the firm. After the library format is established, its contents should be printed regularly and circulated to all the co-workers.

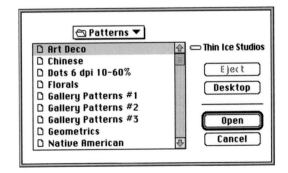

2 | Streamlining the Startup File

The default Startup File contains eleven patterns. If the patterns are not being used, they should be removed and stored in a separate file location. Patterns used often should then be added to the Paint Style palette to make them more accessible. They can be added to the paint swatch by clicking and dragging them to the swatch.

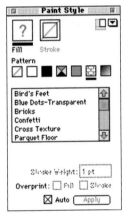

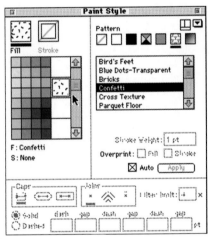

3 | Future Additions

Pattern additions to the library can be added as individual files or existing folders. When adding patterns to existing pattern folders, the file size of the new ones should be noted. Large files are slow and tend to be the first to become corrupted. A New Patterns Folder can be used if there is uncertainty about where an additional file belongs. The New Patterns folder should be a catchall for newly created patterns. A printed list of the updated pattern library should be circulated after each addition of new patterns.

Design Smiths

Comments

Patterns are sets of repeating objects used as fills. In Illustrator, creating these patterns is a simple process— designing a good pattern is something altogether different.

Studio Usage

When you need to create a large number of the same object (for a background, for example), patterns can't be beat. The thing to remember is that you need to make sure the pattern works—no obvious overlaps or gaps showing (unless you need these in your pattern).

Related Topics

1 | Creating the Object for the Pattern

Create the object(s) that you want to convert into a pattern. Make sure that the objects are not painted with gradients or other patterns. Type will work in a pattern, but if you intend to share the pattern with others, convert the type to outlines. Other users may not have the font that you used in the pattern, and the type will appear in some font they may not want.

2 | Loading the Pattern into the Pattern Palette

Once the artwork for the pattern is created, draw a rectangle to define the pattern and place it behind the artwork (⌘-minus). If you need a background, color the rectangle using the Paint Style palette. If you need a transparent background, leave the rectangle with no color. Select the artwork and the defining rectangle. After you choose Pattern from the Object menu, a dialog box will pop up. Click the New button, and your pattern will appear in a preview window on the right. If the pattern looks good, name it and click OK.

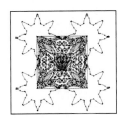

3 | Using the New Pattern

To use your new pattern, select an object to be painted, and call up the Paint Style palette. Select the fill swatch and click on the pattern icon. A box will appear where you can select your new pattern. Hit the Return key or close the palette, and your new pattern will fill the selected object in your illustration.

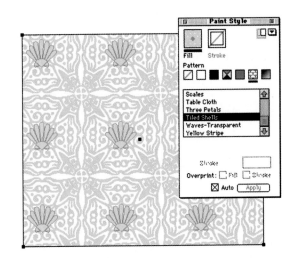

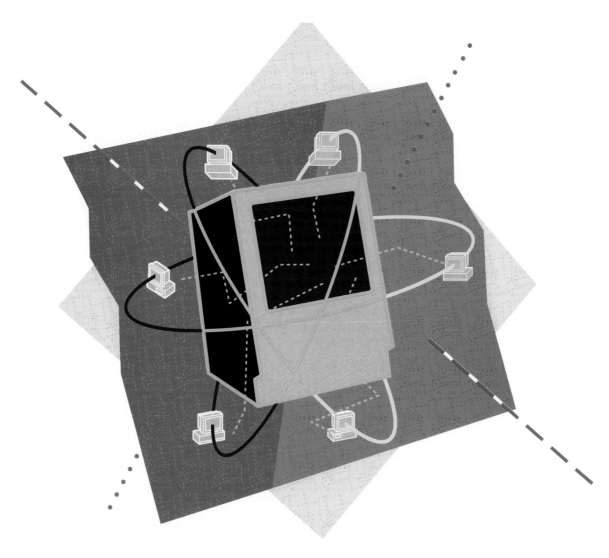

Bill Frampton

Comments	Studio Usage	Related Topics
Patterns are used when you need a repeating object or set of objects to appear in an illustration, without having to repeatedly draw those objects.	Patterns can be a real time and memory saver, but using them wisely and only when you need them will help save much consternation. Too many patterns can actually slow down printing and previewing of your illustration.	

1 | Loading Patterns into a Document

If you need to load a pattern into an illustration, select the Import Styles command located in the File menu. An Open dialog box appears, allowing you to choose a document that already has the pattern that you need. (This command also works for custom colors and gradients.) After you have applied the pattern and saved the illustration, the pattern will be saved with the illustration.

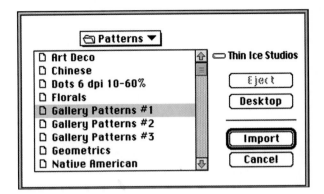

2 | Using Patterns in a Document

To use the patterns that you just loaded, go to the Paint Style palette. With the fill swatch selected, choose the patterns icon (it looks like fish scales). The list that appears contains all the available patterns. Then select the pattern that you need by either scrolling through this list or by typing the name of the pattern (if you know its name). Once selected, press Return to confirm your selection. The pattern will be saved with the document.

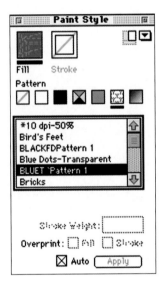

3 | Managing Patterns in a Document

If you want to speed up previews in Illustrator, you may want to turn off the Pattern Preview and Print check box, located in the Document Setup dialog box. When you go back to preview the artwork, black will appear where the patterns are placed. To turn the patterns back on, simply reselect the Preview and print patterns check box.

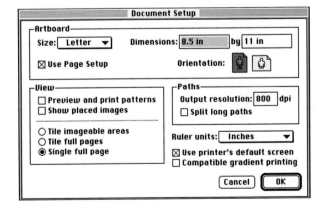

TP Design

Comments

Manual and automatic patterns offer characteristics that can benefit illustrations based on how the pattern is used. Fill selections include solid colors, shades, and patterns. Automatic patterns are created out of repeating tiles used to fill selected objects with a repeating pattern. Manual patterns are fills created of many individual objects, which are then masked to create a random pattern.

Studio Usage

Patterns are used in many illustration applications—from illustration backgrounds to textile designs used on cloth, carpets, and wallpapers. Manual patterns are used in illustrations requiring a random fill in a defined space, examples are found in medical illustrations and in advertising.

Related Topics

1 | Manual Patterns

The pattern's shapes are dispersed and overlap the border of the area being filled. They are then masked with a copy of the object to be filled. The mask hides elements outside the fill element while allowing movement of the fill elements. The advantage of manual fills is the ease with which you can adjust the tile element's randomness, rather than using the fixed repeating tiles that come with automatic patterns. Manual patterns are independent of each other, while automatic patterns begin and are linked to the Illustrator file's (0,0) coordinate point.

2 | Automatic Patterns

When uniform repeating patterns are required, automatic patterns can't be beat. By using simple geometry, custom patterns can be created. Tiles built with this method will fill objects with perfectly aligned tiles. One of the biggest advantages of automatic patterns is the creation of complex patterns that take up less memory than manually repeating elements in each tile.

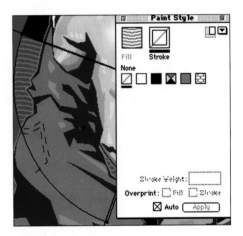

3 | Geometric Tiling

You can center the repeating element in the tile by using a square to define the tile. If a center point is not available, one can be applied by using the Attributes palette under the Object pull-down menu. Repeat the element in each corner of the square—this time centering the element that uses each corner point of the square. By positioning elements in these five spots on a square, you can create perfectly aligned tiles every time.

Mike Dowdy

Comments

Patterns are used when you need to have a large number of the same object, repeating over and over again. Using the transformation tools, you can modify an existing pattern to your needs without having to rebuild it.

Studio Usage

Why rebuild a pattern? Just resize it. The transformation tools can be set up to work only on the patterns, and this can be done with a simple, secret command. This is a big change from the previous versions of Illustrator, and a much better one.

Related Topics

1 Select the Object Containing the Pattern

Select the object painted with the pattern that you want
to transform. The object must be a path. Type should
not be painted with a pattern because Illustrator does
not like patterns applied to type.

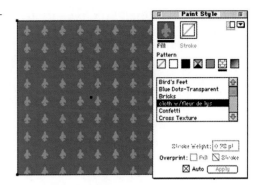

2 Use the Transformation Tools

Use the transformation tools (Scale, Reflection,
Rotation, and Shear tools) to modify the
pattern. If you prefer to modify the pattern
manually, select the tool of choice, and click
the origin point. Hold down the "P" key
while dragging the mouse. You will see a trace
onscreen, similar to transforming the object.
When you have set the desired transformation,
release the mouse button, and your transformed
pattern will appear.

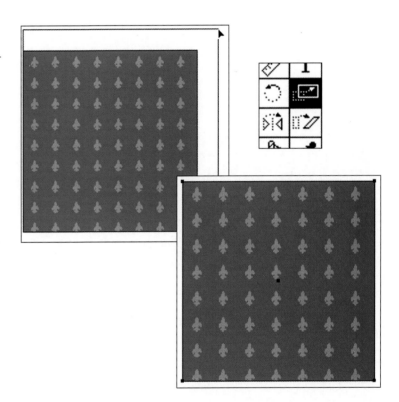

3 To Transform by a Specific Amount

If you need to transform a pattern by a set amount, hold down the
option key when using the Transformation tool on the object.
You'll see the tool's dialog box, where you can set the amount of
transformation. You can also tell the tool to work on either the
object, the pattern, or both, by clicking the check boxes under the
percentage settings.

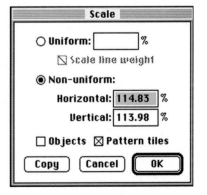

Lillian Koponen Meldola

Comments

When working with more than a single ink color, protection against press misregistration should be considered. This is done with spread and choke trapping. Press misalignment results in unprinted paper showing up between the the colors of colored artwork. By fractional overprinting of the bordering colors, a small overlap protects the printing job if the press is misaligned. The concept of color trapping applies to pattern tiles as well as regular illustrations. By building traps into custom tiled patterns, the tiles are repeated with all traps included.

Studio Usage

As soon as a second ink color is added to a job, trapping should be applied to one or both of the ink colors. Color patterns protected with trapping are used by pattern designers. Be careful when transforming a pattern! You may end up distorting the traps.

Related Topics

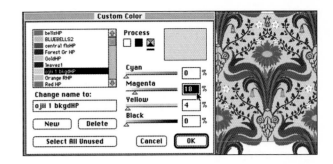

1 | Applying a Shared Color to the Background

Trapping can be avoided by sharing a common ink color between art elements and the background color. A common ink color percentage of at least 5% guarantees that ink coverage will be strong enough to cover press misregistration; 3% will work for strong ink colors, but will not show for weak ink colors, such as yellow.

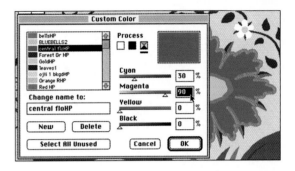

2 | Automatic Trapping

Illustrator's auto trapping works for simple art work, but it is somewhat limited for complex trapping. To use auto-trapping with complicated patterns, select bordering elements together. Next, select Trap from the Pathfinder list under the Filters pull-down menu. Illustrator then calculates an overprinting stroke with color based on the color percentage and stroke width that you set. Trap stroke width should be checked with the printer (a common width is 0.25 pt).

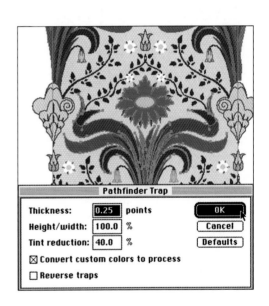

3 | Manual Trapping

Manual trapping is set by choosing whether an element from a pattern should be choked or spread depending on its bordering color and layer. It is best to overlap the lighter color into the darker at a reduced percent. Again, trapping method and stroke weight should be confirmed with the printer because trap requirements change depending on ink color, the paper, and the press used for the pattern's printing.

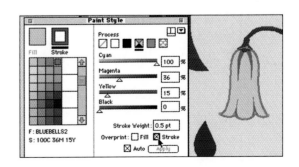

Planned Distortion *The Roughen Filter*

Ginger Reaves

Comments

Computer art can often be a little too precise. The ability to align objects, perfect kiss-fits, and other technological goodies are not always needed in an illustration. The Roughen filter allows you to "mess up" an illustration, similar to when you were a kid and messed up a classmate's hair!

Studio Usage

The Roughen filter is great for creating a "hand-drawn" look that would be difficult to do otherwise. The contrast that is created can help rev-up the sometimes sterile world of computer illustration.

Related Topics

1 | Select the Objects to Roughen

Select the objects that you want to roughen. Any type that needs to be roughened must be converted to outlines; the filter works only on objects.

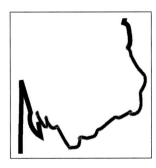

2 | Use the Roughen Filter

Next, select the Roughen filter, located under the Distort submenu in the Filter menu. Once selected, a dialog box appears, allowing you to set the displacement that the filter generates (the size), whether the roughening is rounded or jagged, and the detail. The detail field sets the number of "spikes" that the filter creates for you.

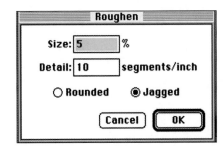

3 | Vary the Settings

Changing the settings creates a variety of effects, from the sublime to the ridiculous. A high detail number combined with a medium amount of displacement can create a "fur" effect. Low displacements can create the effect of "antiquing" or "copy of a copy." Feel free to experiment with settings; this is one filter for which experimentation is not just recommended, it's *required*.

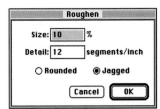

Planned Distortion *The Shear Tool*

Kenneth Batelman

Comments

Objects always appear flat with simple vertical or horizontal edges. (Look at Picasso's *Three Musicians* in the example—no true vertical or horizontal lines in sight!) Shearing objects helps achieve the same sense of depth and action in your design.

Studio Usage

A piece of art may need to be sheared (or skewed, as it is sometimes called) so that it appears with a correct perspective shape in an illustration. The Shear tool does just that—with one, or a hundred objects, selected at the same time.

Related Topics

The Scale Tool   150

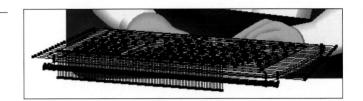

1 | Select the Objects to Shear

You can shear any object or type in Illustrator with the Shear tool. Select the object with the Selection tool (make sure that it is not locked down in a layer).

2 | Use the Shear Tool

Then select the Shear tool from the Tool palette. Click once to establish an origin point for the tool to work from; the tool icon will change from a crosshair cursor to an arrow. Next, click and drag to shear the object as needed. The tool will shear in the direction that you drag your mouse. To make a sheared copy of your object, hold down the Option key while dragging a shear.

3 | Constraining the Shear Tool

To *constrain* (that is, make it work only in one direction) the Shear tool, hold down the Shift key while dragging the mouse. This technique works great for shearing type; you can create pseudo-italic versions of your favorite non-italic fonts.

4 | Dragging

The Shear tool is far more sensitive than the other transformation tools—one slight slip and you have spaghetti on your screen! It is best to click and drag some distance away from the origin point in order to maintain better mouse-drag sensitivity when using the Shear tool.

5 | The Shear Tool Dialog Box

Like all the other transformation tools, the Shear tool has a dialog box option. To open it, select the Shear tool, and with your object selected, option-click on the object (make sure that the origin point is where you want it). The Shear dialog box appears,where you can enter the percentages needed to shear your objects more precisely (remember, positive values go right and up; negative values go left and down). Once entered, click OK and your objects will become sheared.

Mike Doudy

Comments

Scaling objects is a standard requirement in art; without it, no sense of perspective can hope to be attained within the illustration. Using scaling properly is critical in design. Without a proper balance between all the design elements, the design can look confused, boring, or just plain wrong.

Studio Usage

The Scale tool is used in almost every illustration created in Illustrator—it's that indispensable. It also is used to create distortions in objects. Starting with a perfect circle, you can easily create a flat oval by using the Scale tool.

Related Topics

1 | Select the Objects to Scale

First, select the objects that you need to scale. Any objects—open or closed paths, type, or selected guides—can be altered with the Scale tool.

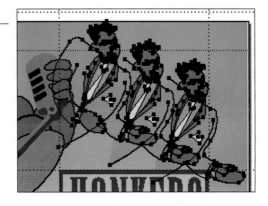

2 | Use the Scale Tool

Select the Scale tool. Click anywhere to establish the origin point from which the Scale tool will work, preferably in the center of the object(s) that you are scaling. The tool will change from the crosshairs icon to an arrow icon. Then click and drag the mouse in the direction that you need (moving away from the origin point makes the object larger, moving toward the origin point makes it smaller). If you need to scale the object proportionately, holding down the Shift key while dragging in a horizontal or vertical direction will cause the Scale tool to work in one direction only. The direction is determined by the movement of your mouse.

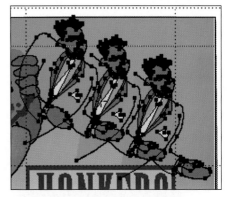

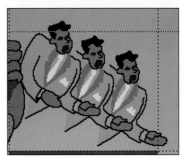

3 | Making a Copy

To make a copy of the scaled object, hold down the Option key while dragging the mouse and then release the mouse button before releasing the Option key. A copy will appear on top of the original.

4 | The Scale Tool Dialog Box

To use the Scale tool dialog box, select the tool and hold down the Option key and click the mouse button. The Scale dialog box appears, allowing you to enter the percentage that you need to scale. After these percentages are entered, click OK (or Copy) and the altered art appears.

Glossary

Additive Primary Colors. These three colors create all other colors when direct light (reflective) or transmitted light (such as on your monitor or television set) illuminates an object or scene.

Adobe Systems. The company responsible for writing the PostScript® language, Adobe Illustrator (the program this book discusses), Adobe Photoshop (an image editing program), a wide range of typefaces, the Adobe Acrobat program (a method of creating platform-independent documents), and other tools designed for the professional graphic artist and communicator.

Anchor point. In Illustrator, all objects and lines contain anchor points. They are the starting or ending points for an object or rule. The point appears as a small, solid square when an object is selected with the solid arrow tool. Otherwise, they appear as a tiny x.

Area type. Area type is type that has a boundary created by drawing a square or rectangle with the Text tool.

Artwork view. Artwork view shows any drawing or object as same-size lines, without any fill, stroke, or other attributes. This is the opposite of Preview view.

Base. The shiny side of film opposite the emulsion. This side isn't photosensitive.

Baseline. Baseline refers to the bottom of a type character, not considering any shapes that fall below this line (known as descenders) such as the hook of the letter y, the shaft of the letter p, or the bottom of a lower-case q.

Bevel Join. This term refers to how lines "act" at the points where they meet. They can be pointed, flat, or rounded.

Bézier Curve. Named after Frenchman Pierre Bézier, this term refers to curves defined by only four control points. These points are: the end points of the curve, and the angle lines (the "handles" that show at the curve-ends when a curve is selected). Illustrator is a Bézier drawing program because it makes use of this technology.

Bitmap. Any graphic that is composed of individual pixels (as opposed to curves). A Photoshop file is a bitmap; an Illustrator file isn't. TIFF and PICT are common bitmap file types.

Blend. The distribution of tones or hues that change across a given distance (linear), or within a given shape (radial). Blends can be created between open paths or between closed shapes.

Bounding box. The bounding box of an image is defined as the outside edges of a square that encloses the entire collection of objects. When you use the Crop Mark tool, you define the bounding box of objects so cropped.

But cap. Each line in Illustrator can have one of three types of endcaps. But cap describes the option that has the anchor point of the rule directly at the edge (but) of the rule.

Choke trap. The overlap of a lighter object over a darker background. This compensates for slight shifts of the paper during a press run.

Closed path. A path that has no open ends. A circle or a rectangle are examples of closed paths; any shape you draw that ends with a click on the same point at which the shape started.

CMYK. CMYK refers to the three primary subtractive printing inks, plus a fourth plate (referred to as the KEY plate; normally printed in black ink) to ensure solid blacks, shadow detail, and accurate type/line art reproduction. K doesn't stand for black (cyan, magenta, yellow, blacK) as commonly thought.

Coated stock. Any sheet that carries a gloss coating, or whose manufacturing process resulted in a "shine" or coat to the stock. The presence or lack of coating on the printing substrate (paper or sheet) produces wide variations in color reproduction and accuracy.

Compounds. This refers to two paths, where one is "cut out" or reversed from another object layered above or below the first.

Corner Point. An anchor point that joins two straight lines, a curved and straight line, or two curves that meet at a sharp corner. Points can be Averaged (⌘-L) and then Joined (⌘-J) at a corner point.

Crop marks. Marks placed on an image and used to indicate the place where the paper should be trimmed.

Custom color. A color created using premixed inks, such as those available from Pantone® or Toyo™. It also refers to colors created within an application program that isn't based on one of the standard CMYK inks. Custom colors may print separately from the four standard plates, or they may be converted to their process-color equivalents.

Custom View. Illustrator provides the ability to save a particular zoom/view setting. Simply draw a rectangle with the magnifying glass that encompasses the area that you want to return to at some later time, and save the view. All attributes of the image are saved, such as the preview mode, the layers that were visible or hidden at the time, and so on.

Dash Pattern. All dotted or dashed lines are made up of a series of on and off lines. This refers to the gap and stroke settings assigned to a specific line.

Data Series. A sequence of numbers used to plot a graph. Examples would be sales by region, percentage of financial return over a period of time, etc.

Density. The degree of opacity of an exposed film. The maximum density a specific film is capable of delivering is referred to as the film's dMax. Factors such as the type of laser used to image the film, the chemical properties of the substrate, and others determine how dense an exposed area may be.

Direction Point. The line that defines the direction in which a curve enters or leaves a specific point. The position of the direction point(s) determines the shape of a curve.

Discretionary Hyphen. A discretionary hyphen only appears in copy if the word in which it was placed falls at the end of a line.

Drag. Finding out that *Sorgon*, your crazed Black Labrador, escaped the house and ate the neighbor's prized ferret; or holding down the mouse button and moving the mouse in a specific direction (dragging an object, for example).

Emulsion. The side of film opposite the base; the photosensitive side of film that darkens (achieves density) when exposed to a light source or laser beam.

EPS. Stands for Encapsulated PostScript. A file format that describes an image in a specialized form of the PostScript language. Many applications require that you save your Illustrator files in EPS format before importing them. Most EPS files contain a bitmapped preview that can be used by such programs to display the image before you choose to place it.

Flatness. A setting that controls the complexity of curves. The flatter a curve, the less control points exist that describe the curve (and hence the "steppier" the curve).

Font. A set of characters and symbols that comprises a particular style of type.

Freehand tolerance. A value that controls the sensitivity of the freehand drawing tool as you drag it across the screen.

Gradient. A blend between densities or colors, either linear or radiating from a specific point. A gradient has a starting point (or object) and an ending point or object.

Hanging Punctuation. In classic typography, compositors made sure that any periods, commas, colons, or other punctuation characters hung outside the margin of justified paragraphs. Illustrator provides this specialized function.

Horizontal Scale. To stretch an object along the horizontal axis. This axis can be changed from 90° in the Preferences menu.

Image Area. The area of a page which is "addressable" by a specific printer; the area inside the trim; the sheet excluding any space allotted for gripper or tractor.

Insertion point. The point at which entry on the keyboard would appear on the page; the place you put the I beam of the Type tool.

Kerning. The space between two characters as defined by the original creator of the font. Examples include a predefined tightening of the space between certain characters such as T and a, P and o, and others that "fit" better if tightened. The artist may adjust these values by placing the I beam between the letters and using option-right arrow or option left-arrow.

Knockout. A colored or tinted area that is cut out by a shape that is on a higher layer. Ink coverage is eliminated in the knockout area.

Landscape. Orienting the page on the horizontal axis.

Layer. A level containing specific elements of a drawing. The artist may create many different levels to facilitate object management (i.e., putting all the guides on one layer, the type on another, and instructions to the printer on another).

Leading. Originally, this referred to a thin lead filler that was placed between lines of type in an effort to "open" the vertical spacing. Electronically, leading refers to the amount of space between lines of type.

Legend. A label placed near a graph to visually connect symbols shown on the graph with a specific data series (in an ice-cream sales chart, the blue bars may represent vanilla, the red bars, chocolate).

Marquee. The "Marching Ants" you see when you drag your pointer over a specific area of a drawing.

Masking object. An object that acts as a cookie cutter when placed over other objects. Objects that overlap the mask object do not appear in the artwork, nor will they print when output.

Moiré Pattern. An undesirable pattern that sometimes appears when mixing together process colors—especially in blend areas.

Offset. A printing technology that uses an intermediate transfer step where the image is moved onto a blanket before being transferred (offset) onto the substrate.

Open path. A path that has two open end points.

Overprint. An object that prints on top of another object, without knocking out the rear-most object (see knockout).

Path. One or more connected line segments.

Path-type. Type that has been created with a path as its baseline. Type around a curve, circle, or along a line.

Pica. One-sixth of an inch; twelve points.

Pixel. One dot on a computer display. Screen dots comprise displayed bitmaps.

Plug-in. An ancillary program that adds specific functionality to Illustrator, but it isn't part of the actual program. There is a special folder in which Illustrator looks for plug-ins.

Point. A unit of measurement equal to roughly 1/72 of an inch. 12 points make one Pica, or 1/6 of an inch.

Point-type. Type that isn't on a line; type disconnected from any object; type on a page.

Portrait. Vertical orientation of the printed page.

PostScript®. A high-level computer language developed by Adobe Systems that allows a digital image created on a computer to be output to any device equipped with the language. The output will be done at the maximum resolution specific to that particular device. Therefore, a drawing can be output accurately to a 300dpi laser printer, and, without any modification, to a 3000 dpi imagesetter (even though the two devices are outputting different size dots).

PPD file. A file that describes the particular characteristics of a specific printer. PPD files are used when outputting a file to your printer. Each printer comes with its own PPD.

Preview. A screen display of what the artwork will look like when printed. New versions of Illustrator allow the artist to work in Preview mode; older versions forced the designer to work in Artwork (lines only) mode.

Process color. See CMYK.

Progressive Color bar. A target normally found outside the live area of a four-color project that shows the press operator a range of different ink mixes. This allows the operator to adjust the densities of various inks to ensure proper reproduction.

Reflect. To mirror an object with a reversed copy of itself.

Resolution. The number of dots displayed on the screen or found within the file; the number of dots available on an output device.

RGB. Red, green, and blue. A color model (a way of describing colors). See Additive Primary Colors.

Rosette. A pattern formed when the four primary printing inks (CMYK) are printed as halftones on the same paper, but at different angles.

Scan. An image that was captured on a digitizing device such as a flatbed or drum scanner; an image captured on a digital camera.

Scanner. A hardware device capable of converting a transparent or reflective image into a series of pixels (bitmap).

Screen. A screened percentage of a solid color, measured in lines per inch. The greater the screen tint, the larger the individual dots, and the closer it is to 100% of the original color.

Segment. A specific piece of a line that resides between two points; the portion of a line that becomes selected when clicked with the hollow arrow tool.

Separation. The conversion of RGB screen data into a four-part data stream corresponding to the four primary printing inks; one of the four resultant films; a file that has been converted from RGB to CMYK but still resides in digital form.

Shear. To slant or distort an object along one or more axes.

Smooth point. An anchor point between two curves that creates a smooth connection between the curves.

Spacing. The amount of space between individual letters or numbers within a line of text.

Spot color. See Custom color.

Spread. An intentional overlap between two objects of different colors to accommodate press misregistration (see Choke).

Stroke. A line centered on a path.

Subtractive primary colors. Cyan, yellow, and magenta.

Tangent. A specific point on the edge of a circle.

Template. A bitmapped image used to define the objects in a drawing; a tracing background created in a paint program.

Tracking. The space between all the characters in a word, line, or paragraph; global kerning.

Trap. See Choke and Spread.

Zoom. To magnify or reduce your view of the image onscreen.

Listing of Artists

Charles Akins Studio
2276 Virginia Place NE
Suite C
Atlanta, GA 30305
404/231-1312

Charles Akins is a Graphic Designer, Illustrator, and Cartoonist who finds it hard to be labeled as one or the other at any given time ("Graphic Designistrator" maybe.) He enjoys the variety and challenge of creating work in many different areas, from publishing to advertising to corporate design (for clients from American Express to Georgia Pacific to Coca-Cola); and he finds inspiration in looking at graphic design as an illustrator and vice versa. He appreciates uncluttered, powerful images that communicate ideas directly but conceptually. Teaching part-time at Georgia State University School of Art & Design gives Charles the opportunity to reassess and evaluate his working approach while keeping him exposed to the ever evolving and exciting visual communications environment.

The Antler & Baldwin Design Group
7 East 47th Street
New York, NY 10017
212/751-2031

The Antler & Baldwin Design Group has been offering specialized design services to the publishing industry since 1977. A full-service graphic design studio, they offer complete electronic design and desktop publishing services from initial conceptual development to total prepress production. Antler & Baldwin design general and educational books and materials from preschool to adult level, specializing in large scale, multilevel, and continuity programs aimed at the educational market.

David Bamundo
66 Carreau Ave.
Staten Island, NY 10314
718/370-7726

David Bamundo has been illustrating on the Macintosh for three years. His humorous artwork has been commissioned by many major corporate and publishing clients. David graduated from Rutgers University in 1990. Outside of illustrating, he enjoys music, reading, and spending time with his new puppy, Fred.

Kenneth K. Batelman
407 Buckhorn Drive
Belvedere, NJ 07823
908/475-8124

Kenneth K. Batelman is the author of *Adobe Illustrator—Curves and Paths* to be published in August 1995 by John Wiley and Sons Publishing Inc. His company, Batelman Illustration, is an award winning computer graphics studio specializing in illustration, design, information and presentation graphics, packaging, charts, maps, technical and textbook illustration. Kenneth is an instructor at the School of Visual Arts in Manhattan and is available for corporate consulting and training. Clients include *Newsweek*, Simon & Schuster, Young & Rubicam, NYNEX, and Estee Lauder.

Stephen F. Bornstein
Creative Freelancers Management, Inc.
25 West 45th Street
New York, NY 10036
Contact: Marilyn Howard
800/398-9541

Stephen F. Bornstein is a graduate of the School of Visual Arts, NYC and Pratt Institute, NYC. He has worked with many design firms, United States and foreign governments (World's Fair, Smithsonian Institute, Metropolitan Museum and the Veterans Administration), in addition to many of the nation's leading companies. Some of Stephen's multinational clientele include Esso, Dow, Dupont, American Express, Pepsi, and Rohm & Haas. His firm regularly contributes illustrations for magazines including *Popular Science* and *Wordperfect*. Mr. Bornstein's familiarity with scientific, medical, financial, and engineering concepts has earned him a coveted reputation for his ability to present complex material with a simple and appropriate illustration. He is fluent in five languages and is often involved in the preparation of multilingual presentations and publications.

James Braun
FKQ Advertising
15351 Roosevelt Blvd.
Clearwater, FL 34620
813/221-0695

James Delapine
Creative Freelancers Management, Inc.
25 West 45th Street
New York, NY 10036
Contact: Marilyn Howard
800/398-9541

James Delapine works in Photoshop, Illustrator, and Painter. He is a graduate of the School of Visual Arts in New York City. Some of Jim's major clients include the *New York Times*, Campbell's Soup, Heinz Ketchup, IBM, Macy's, Seagram's, Toyota, and Tristar Pictures. Samples of Jim's work can presently be seen in Parallel Lives, an online Times serial found on America Online. For Jim, the computer is an excellent design tool, and a time-saver for reasons that include its ability for quick color changes.

Tim Dove
3948 Clayhill
Clarkston, GA 30021
404/292-8495

Will work for food...not too spicy!

Michael Dowdy
Black & White Dog Studio
3240 Henry Hudson Parkway #6H
Bronx, NY 10463
718/601-8820

I prefer a bold graphic approach that cuts through the plethora of imagery bombarding the viewer. My goal is to generate an idea that communicates simply and dramatically. I have a passionate love-hate relationship with the computer. It is hard to have a mere friendship with anything so capricious. It can make an hour seem like a second or a second pass like eternity. Ultimately, it is my most powerful tool, and it allows infinite options. My studio, Black & White Dog, handles illustration, animation, and design work.

Deborah Drummond
Art O' Fax
67 Concord Road
Sudbury, MA 01776
508/443-3160

I have been an illustrator for the past seven years working in many areas including advertising, editorial, and publishing. After buying my first Macintosh a few years ago, I began translating my water color technique onto the computer by using Adobe Illustrator. The goal was to keep the style of my other work and offer clients the convenience of electronic media. It has worked out well, and I feel only a little guilty about enjoying my work so much.

Enrico Design
Linda Enrico & Tammy Ryan
5 Hawkes Court
Harbor Office Park
Marblehead, MA 01945
617/631-2520

Enrico Design offers solutions to marketing communications problems. We take the client's message and send it through the appropriate media in a way that will most effectively speak to the target audience. We often help clients define the uniqueness of their company by clarifying and simplifying their messages—determining what visual and verbal elements best motivate their audience to receive the company's message memorably and with impact.

Bill Frampton
220 Collins Ave.
Miami Beach, Fl
305/672-3363

Bill Frampton tells the story of how he got started in computer art. "I'd sent a written invoice for $15,000 to a client of mine, and I received a call back from him and he said, 'I can't pay this. My accounting department is suspicious of written invoices for $15,000. You're going to have to buy a typewriter.' So I told my roommate that I was going to have to bite the bullet and buy a typewriter. To which he responded, 'What's a typewriter? Everyone is using word processors these days.' I replied, 'I've got a blender, but what's a word processor?' Well, the upshot of the whole venture was that I went to a computer store. Before I walked out that evening, I'd put $17,000 down and bought the whole thing without really knowing whether it would do what it could do. There I sat with this machine and said, 'I've got to make this thing fly.'"

Frog Publications
Victor Bruha
PO Box 280096
Tampa, Florida 33682
813/935-5845

Our Tampa based company writes, designs, publishes, advertises and sells educational games to elementary level schools across the United States. We also create custom designs, illustrations, and layouts for an expanding clientele looking for fresh looks in their advertising and promotions. With this much to do, high-quality and effective design is the key.

I have a philosophy with the Mac. If I don't learn something new from every job I do, I haven't worked to my potential and eventually that could ruin me as a desktop designer. What you do not know will devour you. Adobe Illustrator always gives you something new and exciting to learn.

Scott MacNeill
MacNeill & Macintosh
74 York Street
Lambertville, NJ 08580
609/397-4631

MacNeill & Macintosh is a computer studio offering illustration, Graphics and charts/diagrams to the professional market. I have twenty years experience in publishing and advertising. My clients include Pepsi, MCI, *NY Times, Newsweek, Women's Day*, and Citibank. Call for a portfolio sample package featuring my floppy Portfolio Show.

Lillian Koponen Meldola
330Sierra Vista #28
Mountainview, CA 94043
415/988-6769

My illustration work ranges from renderings of the realistic (landscapes, animals, objects), to the more stylized (pattern design), to the abstract. Currently, I am using Illustrator 5.5 and Photoshop 3.0 with a Wacom tablet on a Power Mac 7100 with 40 MB/RAM.

Midnight Oil Studios, Ltd.
51 Melcher Street
Boston, MA 02210
617/350-7970

During its ten years in operation, Midnight Oil Studios was acclaimed for its compelling design, illustration, and copyrighting. In September, 1994, the partners decided to pursue new directions and have gone on to open their own design firms. Catherine Klein now oversees After Midnight, Inc., with offices in Boston and San Francisco, while James Skiles heads up James Skiles Design Smiths, New York City. James can be reached at 212/366-9117.

Miller Brooks
Darryl Brown
11712 North Michigan Road
Zionsville, IN 46077
317/873-8100

Miller Brooks is a marketing, research, and design firm based in Zionsville, Indiana, just outside of Indianapolis. They do advertising, all types of print design (identities, packaging, brochures, etc.), multimedia, and international marketing.

Roger Morgan
211 Walnut Hill
Crawfordsville, IN 47933
317/364-6880

A graphic designer and illustrator, Morgan has worked for Macmillan Publishing for the past three years, learning 3D and animation programs, such as 3D Studio, Strata Studio Pro, and Alias Sketch! He is interested in working in multimedia and special fx for film.

Bill Morse
173 18th Avenue
San Francisco, CA 94121
415/221-6711

Bill Morse has been producing graphics since the late seventies. Before Photoshop existed, Morse designed a computer-controlled camera system, which enabled him to composite photographs and add special effects, such as glows and motion trails, textures, and air-brush simulation. Morse works primarily in Illustrator, Photoshop, and Painter. His clients include Visa, Pepsi, Disney, Nintendo, Apple, Sharper Image, Pacific Bell, and Bank of America. His work can be seen in the Creative Illustration workbook and online at the Design Link graphics BBS at 415/241-9927.

Julie Pace
678 Wellsley Drive
Lake Arrowhead, CA 92352
909/337-0731

A 1983 graduate of the Art Center of Pasadena, Julie has been a freelance illustrator for twelve years. First working in traditional mediums and now incorporating computer technology, she is represented nationally and has perfected several styles including comic book, brush expressionistic, and graphic hard line.

Michael J. Partington
Partington Design
P. O. Box 20391
Indpls., IN 46220
317/259-4415

Michael Partington is primarily a fine artist, specializing in acrylic on canvas and digital fine art. He uses various media for his digital works, including the durable Cibatrans transparency films, which are displayed in a backlighted fashion to replicate the intense color display of a computer monitor. "I don't necessarily use the computer to complete each work, but when used, even partially, my creativity seems to flow more naturally and easily," he says.

Ginger Reaves
International Shriners Hospital
2900 Rocky Point Drive
Tampa, Florida 33607
813/281-0300

Ginger is Creative Director for the Headquarters of the International Shriners Hospital for Crippled Children located in Tampa, Florida. The organization provides expert care for children with orthopedic and burn problems from birth to age 18.

François D. Robert III
3637 Blayton Street
New Port Richey, Florida 34652
813/842-3228

François has been a professional illustrator/designer for over ten years. He began working in the industry with his father, also an accomplished illustrator. Involved in the changes taking place in the graphic design community in the late 1980s, he finally made the switch to using the Macintosh in 1990. Using Adobe Illustrator, François created artwork in record time that he could only dream of before. He has since concentrated on T-Shirt design, although editorial work still appeals to him. "The shear creativity of the T-Shirt business is what attracted me to it—anything goes as long as it sells!" His work has been featured by several top screen print companies, and it continues to sell well. He is currently living in the Tampa Bay area with his wife Vicki, and his two children, Daniel and Monique.

Javier Romero Design Group
24 East 23rd. Street
New York, NY 10010
212/420-0656

Javier Romero Design Group has been in the business of communications design for nearly ten years, serving a variety of clients with creative and marketing ideas. From corporate identity and logo development to trade video, collateral, advertising and electronic media, JRDG fills a variety of needs. Working as your partner, JRDG's purpose is the development and design of effective and impactful creativity in marketing tools, no matter what the medium.

William Seabright & Associates
3330 Old Glenview Road
Suite 16
Wilmette, IL 60091
708/853-8120

William Seabright & Associates is a full-service design studio dedicated to producing high quality graphic design. Our design and production capabilities allow us to maintain rigorous attention to detail while keeping projects on schedule. We perform all aspects of design and production including copywriting, editing, printer contracts, and distribution of projects to newspapers and magazines. Our desktop publishing equipment and knowledgeable staff allow us to handle any size job, from small brochures to large projects of multi-page publications. We maintain affiliation with a service bureau that can fulfill any need for high-end outputting including repro, film, high-resolution scanning, color transfers, and photstats. Some of our clients and publishers include Douglas Dawson Gallery, Chicago International Art Exposition 1994, University of Chicago, Addison Wesley, Brown and Benchmark, and Glencoe/McGraw-Hill.

Ned Shaw
2770 N. Smith Pike
Bloomington, IN 47404
812/333-2181

Ned Shaw operates his Mighty Macintosh from deep in the woods of southern Indiana. He sketches on paper, scans then draws, and paints in Illustrator and Photoshop. He provides illustrations for national magazines, book publishers, and advertising agencies. He writes articles for artists' magazines on the state of the art and the fate of the artist. He is married to an environmentalist and has two daughters who play the harp.

Steven Soshea
673 Haight St.
San Francisco, CA 94117
415/621-4320

Steven Soshea received his BFA in general design at California College of Arts and Crafts in 1983, and he established his own office in 1986. He has worked with individuals and small businesses, as well as international corporations such as Reebok Sports Apparel, Berkeley Systems (Steven worked on AfterDark), and Macromedia. He has been published in *Print* magazine and numerous other books and periodicals.

Chris Spollen
MoonlightPress Studio
362 Cromwell Ave.
Ocean Breeze, NY
718/979-9695

MoonlightPress Studio actively participates in a wide variety of markets such as advertising, publishing, and editorial illustrations. The studio's on-going list of clients include: Asatsu America, AT&T, Bell Labs, Berkely Books, *Boy's Life*, *Byte*, Citibank, *Data Communications*, *Datamation*, *Macworld*, *Money Magazine*, Novell, *PC Magazine*, *Reader's Digest*, Rutgers, Tandem, and *Var Business*. In 1990, after taking sound advice from a respected colleague, MoonlightPress Studio's founder Chris Spollen acquired two Apple Macintosh systems and made it the company's primary tool for creating artwork. Among 1994's career highlights for MoonlightPress are some notable magazine interviews published by *Byte*, *How*, *Macworld*, *Print*, and *Step-by-Step*. The studio has produced a B/W stock Digital Illustration catalogue of archived work for the last eight years, a second catalogue is in the works, and color stocks, which will be available in 1996.

Steve Sullivan
Creative Freelancers Management, Inc.
25 West 45th Street
New York, NY 10036
Contact: Marilyn Howard
800/398-9541

Steve Sullivan is an artist who primarily works in Illustrator. He also uses Photoshop, Painter, and Freehand. He is a graduate of the Tyler School of Art and Temple University in Philadelphia, Pennsylvania. For the past twelve years, a major client of Steve's had been *Scholastic*. He has also done illustrations for a number of other educational publishers. Steve has also been involved with paintbox work in TV/Video production. He spent several years doing television graphics for Fox. Recently, Steve has been doing electronic illustration for software programs, primarily educational.

T.P. Design, Inc.
7007 Eagle Watch Court
Stone Mountain, GA 30087
404/413-8276

T.P. Design, Inc. is located in Stone Mountain, Georgia. The principals, Dorothea and Charley Palmer, are partners in design, as well as in marriage. T.P. distinguishes itself by providing a unique blend of contemporary design and creative, innovative solutions. Along with strength in design and illustration, T.P. has now entered the arena of multimedia, designing screens for clients like IBM. Our focus is not to be greater than anyone but to be different.

Index